D0914896

Westward Journeys

*Memoirs of Jesse A. Applegate and
Lavinia Honeyman Porter
Who Traveled the Overland Trail*

Emigrants Crossing the Plains
Courtesy Oregon Historical Society

The Lakeside Classics

WESTWARD JOURNEYS

*Memoirs of Jesse A. Applegate
and Lavinia Honeyman Porter
Who Traveled the Overland Trail*

EDITED BY
MARTIN RIDGE

The Lakeside Press

R. R. DONNELLEY & SONS COMPANY
CHICAGO
Christmas, 1989

PUBLISHERS' PREFACE

OUR COUNTRY has been referred to as "a nation of immigrants" because all of our families have roots in some foreign land. We can also be called "a nation of emigrants" since we have always been a highly mobile population that readily moves from state to state. An example of this mobility was quite evident in the quarter century between 1841 and 1866 when about 350,000 people used the Overland Trail to set up a new life in some part of the West.

Now, 350,000 people is a sizeable number even when compared with today's total population of 244 million, but it was a whopping part of the 25 million that was America's average population in the heyday of trail travel.

The first large company of settlers used the trail in 1843 and journeyed to what was then known as the Oregon Country by following the Platte River through what is now Nebraska and southeastern Wyoming, then almost due west to the South Pass through the Continental Divide, then along the Snake River, overland to the Columbia and on to the Willamette Valley. When gold was discovered in California, the gold seekers or argonauts used the trail through South Pass, then turned southwest through the Utah and Nevada deserts, along the Humboldt River, up and over the Sierra Nevadas, and into California.

Whatever the route, the 2,000 or more mile trip took about six months, and you had better be at your destination before winter set in. That meant that practically everyone started in the early Spring from jumping-off places like Independence and St. Joseph, Missouri and Council Bluffs, Iowa.

Make no bones about it—those were six *hard* months of riding a slow-moving wagon over a rough road or no road at all; up and down hills and mountains; crossing bridgeless rivers and streams, many of which needed to be ferried; cooking on an open fire; getting along without refrigeration, bathtubs, clothes washers and the other appliances we take for granted. It also meant surviving torrential rains, an occasional tornado, blistering heat, blinding dust and sand, swarms of insects, stampeding buffalo, a variety of diseases including scurvy and the dreaded cholera, days without water, fresh food, and forage, and the always possible attack by hostile Indians. How many of us could make such a trip today?

Surely, the trek across half a continent was the biggest event in every emigrant's life, and as one might expect, nearly everyone who made it felt called upon to relate their experiences. Those who could write kept notes or diaries. Some put their trip into narrative form. There were also the trail artists who sketched the geographical features, vistas, and people met along the way. All in all, it is estimated that between 5,000 and 10,000 accounts are in some form and about 2,500 have been printed.

This year's *Lakeside Classic* salutes the thousands of travelers who experienced the hardships of a trip on the Overland Trail. And, to let you know "what it was like," we have chosen two accounts.

The first is *Recollections of My Boyhood* by Jesse A. Applegate—a narrative by a member of the first large company of settlers who journeyed into the Oregon Country in 1843 (when the author was but eight years old) and learned how to live off the land and with the Indians.

The second—*By Ox Team to California*—is a first person account by Lavinia Honeyman Porter, a young wife and mother who traveled to Denver in 1860, but was so appalled by the people and conditions there that she persuaded her husband to continue on to California.

We believe the selections complement each other. There is little if any repetition, and the stories are quite interesting, although we have made modest changes to correct errors in spelling and grammar. Original copies were found in the Edward E. Ayer Collection at The Newberry Library in Chicago. Our special thanks go to John S. Aubrey, librarian and collection curator for his fine assistance.

Because nearly all travel on the Overland Trail occurred before the camera came into general use, nearly all illustrations from that time are simple sketches or drawings made by pioneers. Samples from the work of J. Goldsborough Bruff and Frederick Piercy (some in full color) are featured.

Bruff, who was a draftsman as well as a prolific, self-educated artist, left St. Joseph on May 10, 1849 with a company of gold seekers. After nearly six months on the trail, the party became lost in the Sierra Nevadas. Bruff's company moved ahead on foot leaving him behind to guard the property. He spent a starving winter snowed-in, but reached the gold camps in the spring with his sketchbook intact. We have chosen appropriate selections from the collection of his works at The Huntington Library, San Marino, California.

Piercy, an Englishman and professional artist, made his sketches during an 1853 trip from Liverpool to the Great Salt Lake Valley. His art, which was converted into steel engravings and woodcuts, was featured in a series of fifteen Mormon recruiting pieces that were eventually published in book form in 1860. Examples of his work were found in the Missouri Historical Society, St. Louis.

It is important to note that a specially developed map can serve as a reference for both the Applegate and Porter crossings. One will note that the boundaries of the Oregon Country are shown as they were when the Applegate party made their crossing in 1843. The other political boundaries are as of 1860 when the Porters went to California.

To edit our "two-stories-in-one" book we have again looked to Dr. Martin Ridge, Senior Research Fellow at The Huntington Library and Professor of History at The California Institute of Technology.

Dr. Ridge had just completed the job of editing our 1988 *Lakeside Classic* when we asked him to take on the 1989 selection. He is a recognized authority on western American history through his writings, and, particularly his co-editorship with Dr. Ray Allen Billington (a former *Lakeside Classic* editor) of *America's Frontier Story: A Documentary History of Westward Expansion*, New York, 1969, and as the former editor of the *Journal of American History*.

Dr. Ridge's Historical Introduction provides excellent backgrounding for the personal as well as the political benefits of migrations to Oregon and California. He also dug deeply to uncover specific information about the Applegate and Porter families which form the Editor's Comments for each story. We thank him for his contributions.

This is the eighty-seventh volume in the *Lakeside Classic* series. Like all the others, it reaffirms the objective set forth by Mr. T. E. Donnelley who, as President of the Company in 1903, wanted an example "of a book which in taste and workmanship met the exacting requirements of the book lover, but which was printed and bound on machines built primarily for the reduction of cost." Today, the original concept continues. Type is electronically set using high-speed character generation that is a mainstay of our Technical Documentation Services facility in Chicago. The various kinds of illustrations are electronically scanned; printing done on computer-controlled, four-color, narrow web offset presses; and binding and cartoning completed on high-speed lines in our Crawfordsville (Indiana) Manufacturing Division. The map was researched and compiled by our Cartographic Services unit in Lancaster, Pennsylvania.

All in all, this book represents the efforts of a team of Donnelley employees who are trained to effectively handle every segment of manufacture. This is typical of the same dedication given to all Donnelley work whether it be in the form of books, catalogs, magazines, directories, financial literature, list management, or business services.

As we have done in every Publishers' Preface since the series started, let us informally review the more important aspects of the year just ending, considered to be the Company's 125th anniversary.

We are happy to report new highs in sales and profits which represent a sustained record for thirty-one years, except for one year when an accounting change affected the latter. Dividends were again increased for the seventeenth year, and shareholders' equity along with funds for modernization and expansion also grew.

While notice is often taken of the fact that R. R. Donnelley & Sons Company is the largest printing firm in the world, it is perhaps worthwhile to examine the factors responsible. Of the tens of thousands of different printers, we are aware of many strong competitors for the kind of products we are able to produce. Keeping ahead of competition has always played an important role in our constant striving for improvement in all aspects of our enterprise. In-depth knowledge of the marketplace guides the efforts of our large, dedicated, and able sales force. It also plays a role in research and development of processes, equipment, and materials. The individual sales representative is the link to our customers and he or she must truly represent each side of the relationship which we consider a partnership. Special insights concerning needs and opportunities on the one hand are balanced by capabilities existing or potential on the other. Vital support is derived from the combination of over twenty-five thousand trained employees using modern technology. All are aware that individual security and opportunity depend in large measure on their contribution to our customers' health and success.

For the past decade or so, we have continued to restructure our organization to recognize changing conditions in the various markets we have long served. We have also expanded our capabilities to reach markets that can now be served through new technology. Our Group system has brought about decentralization which, in turn, offers better management, quick response and more specialization.

The Catalog Group, our largest, is led by Barron W. Schoder, Group President. Sustained activity and continued growth in both sales and earnings highlighted the year. Press and binding equipment were added at Spartanburg, South Carolina and planned for Warsaw, Indiana in order to meet increased demand. Targeted mailings which use our unique Selectronic® capabilities along with cooperative mailings and publication size changes helped our customers offset higher postage and paper costs.

Each of the Manufacturing Divisions in our Magazine Group participated in expansion. There has been renewed interest in our Selectronic® gathering and imaging capabilities which enables a publisher to tailor an individual magazine for individual subscribers. Nearly a decade ago we pioneered this computer-controlled technology for stitched publications, and in 1988 introduced it for squareback binding. Also, through sophisticated planning and careful follow-through, we have been able to combine shipments of different publications to reduce or hold in check rising distribution costs.

Expansion in equipment and space characterized the Book Group in its efforts to take advantage of new technology in the manufacture of trade and college books and computer documentation manuals. Recently we announced the ground breaking for a book plant in Reynosa, Mexico that will allow us to compete better with offshore facilities in the production of juvenile and professional-type books. At Crawfordsville, Indiana, a state-of-the-art preliminary facility was added. We have also entered into a joint project with McGraw-Hill and Eastman Kodak to develop a publishing/printing system that will allow educators to print by electronics customized textbook supplements. At a special facility near our Harrisonburg, Virginia plant, we will store and operate McGraw-Hill's database using an adaptation of Kodak's hardware.

The Telecommunications Group which produces a wide range of telephone and business directories had strong growth in all product lines. In spite of dire predictions decades ago that computers would adversely affect directory printing, this has become one of our most dynamic lines of business. Four-color printing in telephone directories continues to become quite popular, requiring more press capacity. The Lancaster Division expanded its plant facilities to accommodate two new presses for directory work along with a new press and stitcher for catalog production. Our joint venture with Bell Atlantic in providing photocomposition for their directories is showing highly satisfactory progress. As previously stated, our Group organization has brought about more autonomy, but there are many examples of inter-Group operations. One such concerns the new addition to our directory plant in Portland, Oregon which enjoyed a most successful start-up in producing computer documentation manuals, sales of which are the responsibility of the Documentation Services Group.

In face of a weak market, the Financial Group has continued to expand its share. As the name implies, our Common Financial System provides a national and international composition network for domestic as well as worldwide financial literature. New affiliations with printers in Canada and Australia have been established. London and Tokyo offices were active with Eurobond financing deals. Added domestic sales offices were opened in Boston and San Francisco, and a Los Angeles plant will soon be in operation to serve better the West Coast market. This Group is well positioned to take advantage of any upturn in its market.

The Documentation Services Group, newly established, is our fastest growing one. Rory J. Cowan was elected its Group President. We have four production facilities in the United States and three in Europe. One recently began production at Thorp Arch near York. The acquisition of Irish Printers, with plants in Dublin and Kildare, augments greatly our ability to service computer hardware and software customers throughout Europe. A Singapore operation will open in 1990.

The Information Services Group which was formally organized last year is responsible for managing new related businesses. One of its main efforts in 1989 was to accelerate the expansion and development of Donnelley's Business Services where we provide in-house printing and affiliated services for customers. Barton L. Faber is its newly elected Group President.

The International Group with headquarters in London continues to expand its York, England manufacturing facilities. It is in good position to take advantage of growth opportunities provided by the Europe of 1992. Its Ben Johnson unit was voted *Printer of the Year* in the United Kingdom. Jack D. Hansen was named CEO of Ben Johnson.

A Technology Group which includes Research, Engineering, and Communications was established so as to meet more effectively the challenges and changing demands in the graphic arts industry. W. Ed Tyler has been named Group President.

The integration of mailing list services provided by Metromail into our other operations is proceeding as planned. The precisely targeted gathering and binding capability of the Selectronic® system fits well with the sophisticated customer data provided by Metromail. James D. McQuaid has been named CEO following the retirement of Reginald C. Troncone.

Early in 1989, we acquired a substantial equity position in Alpha Graphics, an outstanding quick-printing operation. Its technological superiority and fine customer service bodes well for the future. Now we will be able to explore the quick-printing industry as such, and to integrate Alpha Graphics' capabilities with Donnelley Business Services and with our Financial Printing Group.

John B. Schwemm, Chairman of the Board, chose early retirement, but continues as a member of the Board. His contributions to the strength and well-being of the Company are well recognized and much appreciated. John R. Walter, President and Chief Executive Officer, was elected to the additional post of Chairman of the Board.

The Company faces the future with optimism and confidence under its new, young, and able leader. The various core businesses referred to above will be aggressively pursued. We have proven that our market share can be increased by continuing to provide top quality, service, and value to our customers, present and prospective. All of our other activities have potential for growth, perhaps even relatively more rapid. As always, it is necessary to direct our energies and resources toward the most promising goals since risk is ever present. There is also a constant search for new opportunities, spearheaded by the Corporate Development Group. We believe the ideal prospects for such expansion should have some relation to our present businesses, to our technology, and our skills. The most important element is, of course, the human factor. We feel truly blessed with the thousands of fine, dedicated men and women who make up the larger "Donnelley Family." To them and to our customers, suppliers, neighbors, and other friends who have contributed so much to our past success, we express our deepest gratitude and extend very best wishes of the season.

THE PUBLISHERS

Christmas, 1989

CONTENTS

List of Illustrations xxi
Historical Introduction xxvii

BOOK 1
RECOLLECTIONS OF MY BOYHOOD
by Jesse A. Applegate

Editor's Comments 3
   I. From the Mississippi to the Columbia . 11
  II. Down the Columbia to the Willamette . 79
 III. Our First Winter and Summer
    in Oregon 123
 IV. Experiences in the Willamette Valley . 151
  V. We Move to the Valley of the Umpqua . 171

BOOK 2
BY OX TEAM TO CALIFORNIA
by Lavinia Honeyman Porter

Editor's Comments 185
Author's Introduction 189
   I. Preparations and Farewells 193
  II. Novice Ways 205
 III. Kansas and Nebraska 217
 IV. Buffalo Country 227
  V. Indians 239
 VI. Trials of the Spirit 253
VII. Infant Denver 273

VIII. The Cherokee Trail to Laramie . . . 285
  IX. Stress and Hardships 295
   X. Back on the Overland Road 309
  XI. Getting Along with the Red Men . . 333
 XII. Salt Lake City 345
XIII. Desert Travel 357
 XIV. Friends Along the Way 369
  XV. Journey's End 381

Index 403
List of The Lakeside Classics 411

ILLUSTRATIONS

Emigrants Crossing the Plains . . . *Frontispiece*

Map: *The Routes of Jesse Applegate and*
 Lavinia Porter . . . . xxiv–xxv

RECOLLECTIONS OF MY BOYHOOD

Jesse A. Applegate 2

Lindsay Applegate 5

Charles Applegate 5

Jesse Applegate 5

Elizabeth "Betsy" Miller Applegate 17

Independence Rock 29

Fort Bridger 35

Chimney Rock 39

John Charles Fremont 47

Fort Hall 53

Richard Grant 57

Fort Boise 65

Dr. Marcus Whitman 75

The Whitman Mission 75

Fort Walla Walla 81

"The Wonderful Escape of Young
 Elisha Applegate" 103

Fort Vancouver 113

Jason Lee's "Old Mission House" 121

Chief Halo 177

By Ox Team to California

Lavinia Honeyman Porter 184
Hannibal, Missouri in 1857 199
St. Joseph, Missouri in 1853 199
Fort Kearney 223
Stampeding Buffaloes 229
Sioux Indians 243
A Deserted Pawnee Indian Village . . . 249
Cooking on the Plains with Buffalo Chips . . 257
Overland Stages at the Cottonwood
    Springs Station 265
Denver about 1860 275
Ferriage of the Platte River 297
Fort Laramie 311
The Black Hills in Wyoming Territory . . 319
Laramie Peak 319
View from the Summit of
    Independence Rock 323
Emigrants Attacked by Hostile Indians . . 327
Salt Lake City about 1853 351
Cabin in the Sierra Nevadas 387
Chinese Coolies in the Gold Fields . . . 395

Westward Journeys

*The Routes of
Jesse Applegate and
Lavinia Porter*

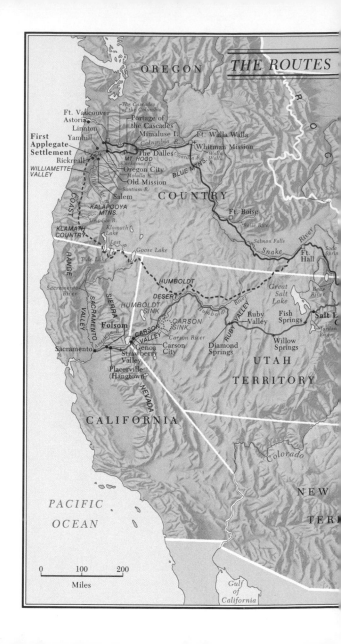

gate Route ——— Porter Route -----Applegate Trail

N

G
R
E
A
T

NEBRASKA

TERRITORY

Sweetwater River
Independence
Rock PLEASANT
VALLEY
LARAMIE
PEAK
andy R.
Ft. Laramie
Chimney Rock
Ash
Hollow
*Chugwater
Creek*
Cheyenne
Pass
Bijou
Denver

UNORGANIZED

TERRITORY

MINNESOTA

IOWA

Council
Bluffs

Cottonwood
Stage Station

North Platte
Ft. Kearney
Fremont
Springs
Little Blue R.
Platte River
Big Blue R.

St.
Joseph
MO.

Caw R.
Independence

KANSAS TERRITORY

P
L
A
I
N
S

M
O
U
N
T
A
I
N
S

UNORGANIZED

TERRITORY

TEXAS

HISTORICAL INTRODUCTION

IN THE early years of the twentieth century two quite different individuals—Jesse A. Applegate of Oregon and Lavinia Honeyman Porter of California—published memoirs of their pioneering journeys on the Overland Trail.[1]

Neither Applegate nor Porter qualify as a professional writer, but both tell compelling stories and both, in intimate ways, have much to say about this special experience in their lives. Neither boasted nor exaggerated unduly in an effort to make a personal book into a major historical document. Nevertheless, both books are not only interesting but have become important because they offer more information than dozens of other such accounts.

The Applegate and Porter narratives complement each other in several ways. Jesse Applegate describes his 1843 trip as part of a 900-person caravan. It was a time when no one had yet taken a covered wagon through the northern Rocky Mountains to Oregon, and in that early period it would have been

---

[1] There were a variety of routes that made up the Oregon-California or Overland Trail. In this text when the term is used for the Oregon Trail it includes the Platte River routes, Fort Laramie, South Pass, Fort Bridger, Fort Hall, Fort Boise, the Snake River Trail, and the Columbia. When the term is used for the California Trail it includes the route to Fort Bridger, then to Salt Lake City, the Humboldt River and through the Sierras.

an act of incomprehensible audacity and bravado to defy geography, nature, and the Indian for one family to try to make the overland journey alone. Large-scale migration was still in the offing; very little support existed along the trail to help travelers in need of food or supplies; there were no bridges or ferries at stream crossings; and the outcome of the Anglo-American contest over the ownership of Oregon was still uncertain.

Lavinia Porter's experience was substantially different. At the time of her trip in 1860, many rivers had been bridged, ferries were in regular service, the wagon road had been surveyed to make it shorter and safer, freight shipments and stagecoach travel were commonplace, and although an overland traveler still faced many dangers and inconveniences, it was possible for a family to undertake the journey alone. The amount of trail traffic was not so great as during the heyday of the gold rush, but there were enough parties on the trail during the spring and summer months so that one family rarely felt completely alone. Nevertheless, the Porters, like all others, needed a full cup of courage; and they also needed cash because toll charges at ferries and the price of goods purchased en route reflected what the traffic would bear. Moreover, Applegate went to Oregon when virtually all of it was underdeveloped while Porter made the trip a decade after the gold rush and California was already a state with urban centers and a substantial economy.

Like most travelers who kept journals or diaries or wrote memoirs, Jesse Applegate and Lavinia Porter never thought of themselves as famous or even especially noteworthy. But as years passed, they realized that they belonged to a remarkable company of men, women, and children—several hundred thousand strong—that had journeyed overland to the Far West before the advent of the railroad. They were involved in a powerful, dynamic movement on the American frontier, and they wanted their families, friends, neighbors, and later generations to understand what it was like to travel across half of the continent, when virtually all of it was unsettled.

Although they told about the people, places, and events that they remembered after half a century, neither really had sufficient perspective to understand the significance of their experiences or how they came to be an integral part of an American epic—the Overland Trail. They did know, however, because of their family histories, that westering was an American way of life.

The opening of the Overland Trail stemmed directly from American interest in what was then known as The Oregon Country. Viewed in retrospect, although it did not appear obvious at the time, American ownership of what is today the Pacific Northwest was inevitable despite an early English presence. By the end of the Revolutionary War, the population of the United States began to grow rapidly. After the War of 1812, American pioneers were quickly occupying the states east of the Mississippi River, and the habit to move repeatedly in search of cheap virgin land brought about a persistent westward movement. On the other hand, Canada was lightly populated; and British interests in the Pacific Northwest, tied primarily to those of the Hudson's Bay Company, centered on control of the fur trade with the Indians. There was little likelihood that Canada's population would either increase or migrate fast enough to outpace American growth and expansion. The English would have preferred to keep the United States from becoming a transcontinental power for geopolitical reasons, but their capability to hold back the Americans was limited.

The ink had scarcely dried on the 1818 Anglo-American Treaty of Joint Occupation that left Oregon open and free to settlement by citizens of both nations before Americans began to agitate for immediate ownership. Virginia Congressman Dr. John Floyd assumed the title "Father of Oregon" because of his enthusiastic advocacy of American possession. In 1822 Floyd introduced a bill that would have made "Origon"—his was the first use of the word—a territory of the United States when its population reached 2,000.[2] In the debate on the mea-

[2] Ray Allen Billington and Martin Ridge, *Westward Expansion: A History of the American Frontier*, Fifth Edition (New York, 1982), p. 454.

sure Floyd's critics claimed that the overland road
to Oregon was too hard to travel, that Oregon was
too far away to be part of the Union, and that the
Pacific Northwest would someday be a separate re-
public. In response Floyd pointed out that in 1775
there were people who asserted that Kentucky was
too far away to ever be part of the Union. And even
if Oregon would never be part of the United States,
he argued, it should be settled by liberty-loving
Americans. Floyd rightly believed that the ownership of Oregon would not be settled by force of
arms but by pioneering families who would occupy
Oregon's Willamette Valley. Despite Dr. Floyd's
spread-eagle oratory and the logic of his argument,
a less than visionary Congress voted down his bill
100 to 61.[3]

Succeeding Floyd as the lead-horse for American occupation of Oregon was a Harvard-educated
school teacher from Massachusetts, Hall Jackson
Kelley. Like Floyd, Kelley had become an advocate
of American ownership of Oregon after learning
about the experiences of Lewis and Clark. By 1826
he had launched a letter-writing campaign to Congress, and in addition to making speeches in support of his cause Kelley prepared a blizzard of
pamphlets, broadsides, and circulars to win public
support. In 1831 he founded the American Society
for Encouraging the Settlement of the Oregon
Territory, and in 1832, believing that Congress
    [3] *Ibid.*

would fund his effort, he issued a call for volunteers to rendezvous in St. Louis for the overland trek to Oregon. When governmental assistance was not forthcoming, Kelley's backers drifted away; and his grandiose, colony-planting scheme failed. Nevertheless, Kelley made his way to Oregon, where he received a polite but frigid response from Hudson's Bay Company officials who looked with distrust on anyone who threatened to disturb their hegemony over the region. Although Kelley failed, his activities heralded an era of "Oregon Fever."

There was a drum beat of propaganda insisting that the road to Oregon was easily traveled. Kelley quoted Joshua Pilcher, a well known fur trader, who felt that the Rocky Mountains presented no barrier to wagon traffic. Pilcher stated, "Nothing is more easily passed than these mountains." [4] David Jackson, William Sublette, and Jedediah Smith, on returning from their annual western trading trip, advised Secretary of War John H. Eaton: "This is the first time that wagons ever went to the Rocky Mountains; and the ease and safety with which it was done prove the falicity [sic] of communicating overland with the Pacific Ocean." [5] Pro-expansionist newspapers, such as the St. Louis *Beacon*, Philadelphia *National Gazette*, and the Washington *Daily*

[4] John D. Unruh, Jr., *The Plains Across: The Overland Emigrants and the Trans Mississippi West, 1840–1860* (Urbana, 1979), p. 29.
[5] *Ibid.*

National Intelligencer, echoed the idea that overland trips to the Pacific would be danger-free in a
few years. And Missouri Congressman Lewis F.
Linn, who had followed Floyd as Oregon's leading
boomer in the House of Representatives, issued a
report stating that the overland route through the
Rockies was so gentle that it could be traveled by
even "delicate females." [6]

The pro-Oregon enthusiasts who boasted of the
ease of overland travel to Oregon did not go un-
challenged. Early opponents pointed out that Lewis and Clark had never claimed that there were easy
passes through the mountains to Oregon. In fact,
their expedition was scarcely free of hardship, and
it had left a residue of ill-will among some Indian
tribes. Furthermore, the explorations of the High
Plains to the east of the Rockies—one led by Lieu-
tenant Zebulon Pike and the second by Major Stephen Long—had concluded that the plains were an
uninhabitable American desert.

British commentators, some like Dr. John Mc-
Loughlin who should have known better, but who
were doubtlessly reassuring themselves about the
minimal American threat to British control of Oregon, emphatically denied that large scale overland
migrations to the Northwest area were attainable.
McLoughlin, who lived in Oregon and managed the
Hudson's Bay Company activities at Fort Vancouver

[6]Michael B. Husband, "Lewis F. Linn and the Oregon
Question," *Missouri Historical Review*, 66 (Oct., 1971), p. 7.

on the Columbia River, was quoted as saying that Americans would as soon travel overland to Oregon as "undertake to go on to the moon."[7] In 1843 the *Times of London* labeled as nonsense an American plan to build a chain of forts from the Missouri River to Oregon. The Manchester *Guardian* felt that Britain had nothing to fear in Oregon because it would take half a century before American settlement would pass through the Rockies. That same year, the *Edinburgh Review* published an article stating that for six months of the year the region between the United States and Oregon was "a howling wilderness of snow and tempests" and a wasteland infested by Indians for the remainder of the year.[8] Ironically, just as the British press was ridiculing the efforts of American pioneers to settle in Oregon, the Applegate party, an expedition so large that it had to be divided into two columns, brought the first settlers through the Rocky Mountains and into the Pacific Northwest.

As large wagon trains of emigrants began moving west via overland passage, the feeling of Manifest Destiny, quite often referred to by expansionists, swept the nation. Newspapers and politicians alike boasted that the United States or American-style democracy was destined to rule the continent. This expansionist militancy led President James K. Polk to provoke a war with Mexico that resulted in the

[7]Unruh, *The Plains Across*, p. 21.
[8]*Ibid.*, p. 32.

American conquest of the Southwest and California.[9] It also encouraged President Polk to demand by ultimatum that the English withdraw any claims to the Pacific Northwest.

American ownership as we know it today, began to take shape in 1845 when the Hudson's Bay Company abandoned its headquarters on the Columbia and moved to what is today Vancouver Island in Canada. There was some wrangling over the location of the United States-Canada boundary which culminated in June 1846 when Lord Aberdeen, the British Foreign Minister, offered a treaty that fixed the line at 49° North. The United States now owned the Oregon Territory which eventually would split into the states of Oregon, Washington, and Idaho.

More than a decade before the boundary question was resolved, a most unlikely man played a key role in the settlement of Oregon and the establishment of the Overland Trail. Nathaniel J. Wyeth, a Boston ice merchant, influenced by Hall Jackson Kelley's propaganda but convinced that Kelley would not succeed, planned to challenge the Hudson's Bay Company fur monopoly in the Pacific Northwest. His first expedition in 1832, guided by the famed Sublette brothers, visited the Hudson's Bay Company posts at Fort Walla Walla and Fort Vancouver.

[9]For conflicting views on the coming of the Mexican War, see William H. Goetzmann, editor, "Historical Introduction," George Ballentine, *Autobiography of an English Soldier in the United States Army*, (the 1986 *Lakeside Classic*), and N. H. Graebner, *Empire on the Pacific* (New York, 1955).

His second expedition in 1834 included large supplies of livestock and trading goods, and to protect his wares, Wyeth built Fort Hall near the confluence of the Pontneuf and Snake Rivers. Defeated in his efforts to contest the Hudson's Bay Company, Wyeth sold all of his assets, including Fort Hall, and returned to Boston.

His second journey is also noteworthy because he took with him a party of Protestant missionaries—Jason Lee, his nephew Daniel Lee, and Cyrus Shepard. The party's journey west on the trail proved uneventful, except that the missionaries were surprised by the alcoholic excesses and bawdy behavior of the fur-trapping mountain men. To Jason Lee, the guides were "perfect savages." The Lees established Oregon's first American settlements.

The most noted of Oregon's several missionary colonizers was Dr. Marcus Whitman, who, in 1836, brought with him a party consisting of his wife, Narcissa, the Rev. and Mrs. Henry Spaulding, and a farmer/mechanic named W. H. Gray. Narcissa Whitman and Mrs. Spaulding were the first white women to reach the Pacific Northwest via the Oregon Trail. The Whitman's mission at Walaiipu became a major resting site for later settlers until the post was attacked by a horde of Indians and all the Whitmans massacred.

There is some irony in the fact that the Indian danger to emigrants increased as larger numbers of them began to go to Oregon in the early 1840s. The

Indians became restive because hunters with over-land parties killed or drove off game. Added hard-ships occurred when overlanders misjudged the supply of forage, provisions, and apparel; accepted as gospel the popular guide books that frequently passed along bad advice; and overestimated their own capacity to cope with problems brought about by a changed lifestyle.

Until news of the California gold strike was wide-spread, the national press devoted most of its atten-tion to the Oregon Trail. After 1849, the California Trail became the "hot story" for overland news. As the magnitude of the gold discovery at Sutter's Mill captured the national consciousness, the mania for California gold soon exceeded, by far, the "Oregon Fever" that had swept an earlier generation. As a result, more people crossed the continent in 1849 than in all previous years combined—upwards of 25,000—and in the next five years close to 150,000 headed to California and about 35,000 to Oregon.

The economic impact of these tens of thousands of gold seekers buying supplies, mining equipment, wagons, and animals had an immediate and pro-found effect on the towns that served as "jumping off" places for the argonauts. Independence, Mis-souri, the long-time starting point for Santa Fe and Oregon, suddenly faced intense competition from St. Joseph, Missouri, whose merchants realized that huge profits could be made in outfitting the young men going to California. Both of these Missouri towns with populations of fewer than 3,000 people were hardly larger than villages.

This did not, however, limit their aggressiveness when they competed for the overland business. The St. Joseph and Independence newspapers not only praised the low cost, quality merchandise available in their towns and the friendly treatment offered to the gold seekers, but also lied about the people, goods, and conditions in the other. The *Expositor* in Independence claimed St. Joseph was cholera-ridden, while the St. Joseph *Gazette* charged that the merchants of Independence were in league with those of St. Louis to mislead naive travelers. Each town used endorsements from well-known frontiersmen attesting to its advantages as the best starting place because it was served by more bridges and cheaper ferries, and pointing out that the route was shorter or had better grass for animals. St. Joseph beat out Independence because it was better located on the Missouri River, but its standing was short-lived. Kanesville (later renamed Council Bluffs), where the Mormons began their overland trek to the Great Salt Lake Valley, and which boasted of better access to the North Platte route, good grass, Mormon-operated ferries, and many more supply posts, surpassed it.

There was a good deal of "hard lying" in the western press concerning the competition for supplying the gold rushers with goods and services, but the press also played a highly constructive role as well. When newspaper editors lacked a commercial self-interest, they quite often dispensed sound advice. Since so many of the gold-rush overlanders were town dwellers and young professional men rather than farmers, they knew little about animals and equipment. The newspapers published articles that discussed the techniques of trail travel, warned against taking unnecessary provisions, and cautioned the overzealous travelers about exhausting their animals by trying to move too fast at the outset of the journey. They also advised travelers not to start before there was an adequate stand of prairie grass, but not to wait too long because of grass shortages and the hazards of being caught in the Sierra snows. Even though they carried advertisements urging that overlanders purchase goods, the editors also pointed out that the Mormon settlement at Salt Lake City offered an opportunity to replenish supplies and trade-in jaded animals.

The newspapers also explained the Indian situation in prudent terms. Following the hard winter of 1848–49, for example, editors warned that impoverished Indians were likely to attack isolated travelers, attempt to steal supplies, or become aggressive in begging for food and clothing. Small parties needed to be especially careful because they were vulnerable both to attack and to theft of horses and oxen, and even large parties should avoid contact with Indians. The editors advised that Indians were to be treated with kindness and tact, but repeatedly warned that they constituted a genuine danger, especially after sportsmen and food-seeking overlanders had killed off large numbers of game animals. These instructions made sense because so many of the argonauts had no experience with life on the High Plains and many of them held unrealistic ideas about Indians. Moreover, the newspapers campaigned ceaselessly in support of establishing military installations along the Overland Trail to protect travelers.

There is little doubt about why the argonauts went west—they wanted to strike it rich and return to their homes in the East—but there is no simple explanation as to why thousands of men and women were prepared to travel 2,000 or more miles of rugged trails to the Pacific in search of a new home when the Mississippi Valley still had countless acres of fertile unoccupied land. Perhaps the most reasonable answer is that Americans had developed a westering tradition that quickened an urge to pull up stakes in the hope of finding something better. Americans, according to this view, had itchy feet. Their diaries, letters, and memoirs provide a bevy of reasons why they left well-established homes. There were compelling and expelling forces. Some desired to run from financial problems, to improve their economic condition, to find a healthier climate, to achieve political success, or to support a patriotic movement. Others wanted to renounce a slaveholding society, to avoid the law, to do missionary work among the Indians, or to forget a personal romantic attachment that had failed.

These explanations in combination or alone express the presence of forces that drew people to the West and also expelled them from the East. The Far West offered an opportunity that did not exist at home. The West was depicted in superlative terms. Everything was bigger and better. California and Oregon were seen as places of renewal, hope, and especially self-betterment—the West was that wonderful place where dreams came true.

Successful propagandists created this image of the Far West. Dr. John Floyd, Hall Jackson Kelley, and Jason Lee contributed to making Oregon the farmer's frontier of choice, while Richard Henry Dana's *Two Years Before the Mast* presented life in California as so easy going that even Americans would succumb to its pleasures. However, there was a practical side to these utopian notions: Congress offered all the Oregon settlers one square mile of virtually free land, and in California, in addition to gold, a mild climate and excellent land awaited the energetic pioneer. According to one historian, Oregon attracted sturdy and respectable folks, while California appealed to gamblers and risk takers.

Why people moved west often determined how they traveled. Gold seekers willingly paid higher prices for speedy and comfortable transportation. Many were gulled into spending substantial sums to travel by stagecoach when no company was yet able to fulfill its contracts. Visions of luxurious travel to California faded when passengers were asked to look after livestock, drive wagons, and fend off Indians. Angry disagreements followed in the wake of unfulfilled promises and lawsuits resulted.[10]

Because they were in a hurry, unlike Oregon-bound settlers, most of the California gold seekers bought horses and mules rather than oxen. Wagon trains with mixed draft animals almost always broke up. Mule and horse owners quickly lost patience with a caravan when its pace was set by ox team. Westward moving settlers, however, learned that the slow, self-willed, perverse oxen, although often despised because of their general intractability, proved to be the most durable of beasts. The oxen, which could thrive on prairie grass and survive on scanty vegetation were less subject to exhaustion and cheaper than horses or mules. Before the cross-country journey was over many overlanders no doubt shared Lavinia Porter's enlightened view of oxen. She remembered how difficult it was to train wild oxen but how she and her husband developed a true appreciation and affection for the beasts that became as "docile and kind as kittens ... and ate out of our hands. ..."

The eagerness of the gold rushers was also evi-

[10]The best discussion of law on the Overland Trail is John Phillip Reid, *Law for the Elephant: Property and Social Behavior on the Overland Trail* (San Marino, California, 1980). See also, Juanita Brooks, editor, *On the Mormon Frontier: The Diary of Hosea Stout* (Salt Lake City, 1964), II, p. 378.

dent in their attitude toward employing guides to shepherd them safely to California. The use of former mountain men as guides had virtually ceased by the late 1840s. The Applegate party in 1843 paid John Gannt $1 per person to lead them to Fort Hall, but by 1845 the need for such pilots was on the decline. By that time there was almost always someone who was making the journey for the second time—perhaps bringing a wife and family west—who could captain an expedition. Moreover, since much of the trail was so clearly marked and previously traveled, prudent overlanders, aided by a good guidebook and advice gained along the way, could make the trip safely without assistance.

The gold rush produced a sharp increase in the cost of travel equipment and supplies. Prices had been rising steadily before the upsurge of traffic to California, but the '49ers changed the market. Most settlers spent perhaps two weeks at a jumping off point making purchases and preparing for the journey. The impatient argonauts refused to wait that long. Their impact on the small-town markets of Independence and St. Joseph accelerated a seasonal price cycle. Normally, prices were low in the winter, rose during the spring, peaked by late May, and then began a steady decline as fewer overlanders appeared. With cash to buy what was needed to make the trip, the gold seekers drove up prices so rapidly that merchants sold through street auctions where open bidding among argonauts determined prices. Little wonder that Oregon-bound settlers came to believe the merchants were price gouging.

Once they had left the towns in the Mississippi Valley, people going westward, especially after the mid-1840s, often encountered eastbound travelers who were returning from Oregon or California or who had given up before reaching the West Coast. The latter, frequently a mine of valuable information to overlanders, were deluged with questions about the road ahead and what it was like where they came from. Men returning from the California gold fields tended to be justifiably secretive if they were carrying home the rewards of their luck or hard work in the mines. Crime was no novelty on the trail, and men were murdered for gold. Married men returning from Oregon to bring their families west, although often in a hurry, were generally sociable and helpful to travelers by providing information about ferry costs, available grass, and safe river crossings.

The so-called "turnarounds" who had given up on the journey were quite often a depressed lot and tended to exaggerate the difficulties of the road ahead when asked for information. The tragedies and fears that had caused them to retreat were often co-mingled with rumors of potential disaster that awaited the westward bound. The most frequently spread warnings concerned Indian disorders, cholera outbreaks, and shortages of grass. Of course, there were those who came back for good cause: the death of a spouse or child, robbery, serious illness, and the loss of draft animals.

Information passed along by eastbound travelers was taken seriously by overlanders because the risks of the trail were too serious to ignore. Even the wildest rumors required thoughtful assessment. Lavinia Porter's account demonstrates this when she writes about Indian attacks she had heard about but for which no evidence can be found. Rumor may have been the bane of overland travel, but that was a conclusion reached by travelers only after they had separated fact from fiction.

Most overlanders, whether traveling in smaller groups or large wagon trains, elected officers to command and pilot their companies, and drafted constitutions to determine rules of behavior, including provisions against immoral conduct. These constitutions were in effect private assurances that business contracts would be honored. When disagreements resulted because some overlanders withdrew from a wagon train, and since there were no courts on the trail to settle arguments, only the westerners' respect for private property and the law made for largely equitable solutions.[11]

The moral aspects of these wagon train constitutions tested the religious commitment of the overlanders when they faced frontier conditions. The best example of this is obedience to the Biblical injunction: "Remember the sabbath day, to keep it

[11]See Reid, *Law for the Elephant.*

holy." (Exodus 20:8) Travelers were compelled to choose between a speedy crossing and stealing a march on other parties while they stopped or maintaining regular East Coast religious standards.[12]

Maintaining a sacred Sabbath may have been a matter of choice for travelers, but good health was a necessity if overland parties were to make the journey safely. Trail life was arduous, even under the best of circumstances, and an injured or sick companion could threaten the success of a whole party because of delays. Moreover, physicians were rare among overlanders before 1848.

The gold rush, however, attracted a large number of doctors, which was fortunate for the overlanders especially during the early stages of the journey, because in addition to the normal trials of overland travel they faced the threat of a severe cholera epidemic. According to Bayard Taylor in 1850, who wrote for the New York *Tribune*, cholera had been brought up the Mississippi River and reached St. Louis when overland parties were readying to leave for Independence. The disease was soon widespread on the High Plains and especially virulent

[12]Many emigrant guidebooks suggested that overland parties stop on the Sabbath. See Joseph E. Ware, *The Emigrants' Guide to California* (St. Louis, 1849), p. 14. For the attitude of some women as to the Sabbath, see John Mack Faragher, *Women and Men on the Overland Trail* (New Haven, 1979), pp. 95–97, and Sandra L. Myres, *Westering Women and the Frontier Experience: 1800–1915* (Albuquerque, 1982), p. 127.

just east of Fort Laramie, where crowded wagon
trains, careless argonauts, and poor sanitary conditions allowed it to reach epidemic proportions. For
the first three or four hundred miles beyond Independence, Taylor reported, the trail was marked
with graves, and many overlanders were so frightened by the disease that they even refused to help
bury its victims.[13]

Physicians were welcome members of any overland expedition, even when epidemics were not a
problem. There were always teeth to pull, children
to deliver, broken bones to set, amputations to per-
form, and illnesses to treat. Gunshot wounds were
a special problem. Some overlanders who were unfamiliar with weapons suddenly had them for the
first time, and there were many injuries resulting
from accidental discharges. Some overland groups
were known to assess individual members to pay a
physician to travel with them.

Contrary to the myth that overlanders, especially
gold seekers, were intensely individualistic, most
parties on the trail recognized that their success
depended on cooperation and mutual assistance.
Trailing equipment such as ropes and chains were
often shared; stalled wagons were dragged from
mud holes by passing strangers; unsolicited help
was offered to round up lost or stolen cattle; and, of

[13]Bayard Taylor, *Eldorado* (New York, 1850), II, p. 37. He
states a questionable estimate that 3,000 to 4,000 people
died of cholera on the California Trail during 1849.

course, assistance was rendered in the event of Indian threats. With so many companies on the trail after 1848 there was much trading of equipage when wagons broke down or household ware wore out. In fact, it was rare that any family or individual completed the trip without some traded supplies. Although there were reports of barbaric behavior on the part of some gold seekers—such as abandoning friends or travel companions stricken with cholera—most men did not forget their sense of civility nor women their familiar role as a supporting sisterhood when it came to helping one another. Children orphaned by the death of their parents were either sent back home or taken along, and widows were able to recruit assistance if they wanted to continue westward.

Sometime during the first several weeks of the overland journey, eager gold seekers and many settlers felt overwhelmed by the amount of material they brought with them. The young, single men heading for the gold fields quickly sold off, at great financial loss, such excess goods as guns, clothing, and even food, to buy more horses or mules that could travel faster. When the burden of overloaded wagons became too great, the travelers had to discard possessions they had hoped to use in the future. This caused the trail to become littered with abandoned goods. Stoves, plows, furniture, and even food, all dear to its owners, had to be left behind. Toward the end of the trail, as the California-

bound overlanders faced both the Utah-Nevada deserts and the Sierras, the last expendable items were
either sold off at absurdly low prices, given away, or
simply left behind because the draft animals were
so weakened by the journey that they could not carry the load. In fact, virtually the length of the trail
from fifty miles beyond Independence, Missouri, to
the foot of the Humboldt Valley was strewn with
carcasses of overworked draft animals—mules, horses, and even oxen—and the abandoned belongings
of overlanders.

There were scavengers galore ready to take advantage of this situation. The merchants in Independence and St. Joseph went out late in the season
to gather up what could be salvaged and sold to the
following year's overlanders. Travelers along the
way simply stripped sound, but abandoned, wagon
gear for their own use, swapping for it their own
inferior items. Because of the serious shortage of
fuel on the plains, they also broke up and burned
wagons or other wood products. Anything was fair
game from axles to wagon boxes. Indians on the
plains picked over and donned abandoned clothing
to appear in bizarre finery while they feasted on the
carcasses of dead draft animals. The Mormons in
Salt Lake City also sent out expeditions to pick up
what could be refurbished, refitted, and sold to
overlanders who came into town hoping to replace
worn out equipment. They also traded fresh animals for the exhausted horses, oxen, and mules that

had been driven too hard or starved for grass during drought years. Even some Californians made a profit crossing the mountains to cash in by picking up material surrendered at the eastern approaches to the Sierras.

Some overlanders underestimated how much to discard and faced acute food shortages near the end of the trail. Wagon trains headed for California were less well off than those going to Oregon. The Indians in Oregon could often sell fish while the lowly Paiute Indians of the California desert were themselves often nearly destitute. Some California-bound gold seekers became desperate when their animals collapsed and left them stranded. In these circumstances food prices, already high, often skyrocketed.[14] In some instances travelers, especially single men during the gold rush who had made serious miscalculations, were reduced to begging for their meals.

Most travelers found that other overlanders were prepared to share what they had at critical times during the journey. Some even extended their humanitarian spirit by paying to send water wagons to meet parties coming through the desert without adequate supplies, and to keep the few California price gougers from charging them $5 per drink and $10 per gallon.

[14] Milk and liquor were especially valued. A family with a productive cow or an overlander with a whiskey barrel was always popular as Lavinia Porter discovered.

The overland emigrant's contact with Indians remains interesting and contradictory. The earliest emigrants found Indians willing to trade, provide information on the route ahead, and sometimes accept employment. Because they often begged for tools, ornaments, and clothing, and were hopelessly curious, it was quite common for them to walk off with what pleased them. Many felt the Indians were more a nuisance than a threat. Emigrants used Indians as guides and, despite the tragic experience to the Applegate family, Indians became almost indispensable to Oregon-bound emigrants who used them to furnish canoes and lead them through the treacherous passages on the Columbia River. Most Indians were sharp traders, especially for horses, and overlanders who thought that they were dealing with naive "savages" were not only disappointed but often fleeced. In a larger sense the life style of both the whites and Indians proved intriguing to each other, and their frequent contacts remained relatively peaceful during the decade that preceded the Civil War.

Unfortunately, the immediate and long-term legacy of this generally pacific pattern of Indian-white relations faded in the face of accounts of scalping, massacres, and fights. There were numerous instances where whites, feeling racially superior, simply reacted with uncontrolled hostility to situations where had white been dealing with white there would have been no negative response at all. The

Indians, for their part, had many just causes for developing feelings of great animosity. As a result of two decades of overland travelers meeting and dealing with Indians, the stage was set for the post-Civil War military subjugation of the tribes. Moreover, possibly as a by-product of their contact with the overlanders, the Indians drastically underestimated both the military power of the United States and its determination to enforce its will upon a dependent group of people.

The Indians realized almost immediately that the overlander represented a direct assault on their survival. From the 1840s the Indians who lived on the eastern edge of the plains demanded a tax or tribute on all west-bound emigrant trains passing through their lands. Those Indians living closest to the Missouri River made the best case by pointing out that the emigrants killed or drove off game, polluted water holes, and reduced the meager supply of timber that was available. By the time of the gold rush, their demands for payment had markedly increased as had emigrant hostility to paying them.

The Indians, avid defenders of their rights, insisted that the "Great White Father" live up to agreements guaranteeing the sanctity of reservation lands and protection from white incursion. The Federal Indian agents for these tribes, in support of these claims, warned that only bloody conflict would follow in the wake of repeated violations of Indians' lands by overlanders who felt they had every right to go west. When the government failed to respond to frequent reports from Indian agents calling for action, it was little wonder that the Indians grew annoyed and demanded compensation from emigrants for damages done along the trail, while at the same time the emigrants argued that the Indians were little more than highway robbers. Some overlanders, who found it extraordinary that Indians claimed lands that they believed belonged to the United States, simply ignored requests for payment for passage, and marched ahead threatening the Indians with force. The results were often bloody skirmishes between overlanders and Indians as well as the theft of livestock.

Hostility also stemmed from Indian-operated toll bridges. Had these bridges been owned by whites, the overlanders may have grumbled, avoided them, or simply paid the charge. But when the bridges were Indian-owned, some emigrants refused to pay the tolls, forced the Indians aside, and forged ahead. Needless to say, violence often resulted. The Indians would chase the offenders, wait until nightfall and run off with their livestock, leaving the party stranded. Quite often, too, angry Indians took retribution by demanding excessive tribute from later overland parties or by attacking them.

The contemporary press, especially in Oregon and Missouri, often published exaggerated accounts of Indian fighting and unsubstantiated rumors of massacres. As a consequence, the newspaper editors also demanded that the army protect the emigrant trains and annihilate hostile tribes. But the presence of rumors does not mean that there were no tragic episodes, although they scarcely fit the stereotype portrayed in popular fiction and adventure stories. Most of these Indian attacks took place near the eastern part of the trail where whites first encountered Indians, or near the far end in Oregon, or on the Humboldt River.[15] By the 1850s relations between whites and Indians had thoroughly soured. Encounters were often violent, but they were few, indeed, as most Indians avoided the trail and the large numbers of whites almost insured their self-protection. In fact, many emigrants became so secure and self-confident that they often traveled unarmed or with their weapons unloaded. However, had Lavinia Porter and her husband traveled without escort eight years earlier, they would have assumed a much greater risk.

Accurate statistics on the number of whites and Indians killed on the Overland Trail simply do not exist. Estimated data for the years prior to 1849 indicate that only twenty-five Indians and thirty-four whites were killed. During the bloodiest years, those immediately following the discovery of gold in California when the trail swarmed with arrogant and careless argonauts, 148 overlanders died along

[15]There is a good deal of evidence that many of these so-called Indian attacks were the work of "white Indians," renegades who dressed as Indians to rob and rape.

with 276 Indians. All told, 362 emigrants and 426 Indians were killed in fighting along the Overland Trail.[16] These numbers seem almost insignificant— perhaps as low as one tenth of one percent—when compared with the approximately 350,000 emigrants who traveled the trail. But regardless of how few the number of killings, they are a lasting legacy of the overland experience and had a far greater impact on government policy and today's television writers than the thousands of peaceful contacts between whites and Indians.

Thomas Fitzpatrick, a long-time Indian agent, early pointed out that the government only had a choice of two policies to deal with the Indian problems that arose from overland travel. "The policy," he argued, "must be either an army or an annuity. Some kind of inducement must be offered to them greater than the gains of plunder, or a force must be at hand, able to restrain and check their depredations. Any compromise between these two systems will only be productive of mischief." [17] Neither Congress nor the several presidential administrations recognized the wisdom of Fitzpatrick's observation. Indian agents, who tried to protect their

---

[16]See Unruh, *The Plains Across*, p. 185, who qualified his figures by stating that they probably include attacks by "white Indians," but are also an undercount because many episodes may not have been reported.

[17]Quoted in Robert M. Utley, *Frontiersmen in Blue: The United States Army and the Indians, 1848–1865* (New York, 1967), p. 55.

charges from unprincipled white men who wanton-
ly cheated, murdered, and insulted them, constantly pleaded for funds to negotiate treaties that would
both compensate the tribes for damages and separate them from areas of emigrant passage. Money
for these activities was rarely adequate or forthcoming because both were subject to political pressure,
and also because of policies, based on white racial
attitudes, that questioned the merit of dealing with
the Indians in this way. Even the most humane of
Indian agents believed that the surge of population
moving west meant that the Indians had to either
give way and change or they would be swept up and
perish in the advance of white civilization. Time
and again Indian agents traveled along the Overland Trail in their districts urging peace, distribut-
ing gifts, and trying to mollify justifiably aggrieved
Indians. They had some successes, but in the end,
for practical, political, and racial reasons, the task
of pacifying the Indians fell to the army. As a result,
by 1860 about 7,000 enlisted men and officers—90
percent of the army—were stationed in the West.

As early as the 1840s when Americans began
their trek to the Pacific, there was basic agreement
that a military presence was essential to protect emigrants, but there was no consensus as to what that
presence should be. The House of Representatives'
Military Affairs Committee favored the establishment of a chain of forts along the trail, a policy that
was strongly urged by editorial writers. President

James K. Polk agreed, but also suggested that a force of mounted riflemen be garrisoned in the West. The Congress, unconvinced that forts were necessarily the best solution to guarding the trail, hesitated to pass legislation appropriating money to build them. The anti-fort faction could rely on the advice of Colonel Stephen W. Kearny, who had led a military expedition along the trail to South Pass, and firmly believed that it would be more cost effective to overawe and punish errant Indians than try to defend the emigrants from fixed positions. Kearny's column of 300 dragoons moved west in 1845 during the late spring when Oregon-bound overlanders were en route, providing them with a partial escort, but he also met with Pawnee, Sioux, and Cheyenne Indians and warned them against molesting the emigrant parties. Since he had no way of knowing that within a few years the gold rush would send thousands of people along the trail, he felt that a military thrust into the plains every few years would guarantee an open and peaceful route all the way to the Pacific.

As is often the case in military matters when Congress is divided on an issue, it decides to compromise and give each faction something. In due time, Congress rejected any one solution to maintaining peace on the trail and embarked on a policy that included an Indian reservation system, peace treaties, gifts, established forts, military patrols, military escorts for overlanders, punitive expeditions, and even maintaining and improving the road itself. Within a decade and a half, the army, which had been practically non-existent beyond the Missouri River before 1848, soon became the largest Federal organization in the West.

Major military posts were established at strategic points in the West to defend the overlanders and intimidate the Indians. The army in 1848 built its first major post, Fort Kearny, at Grand Island on the Platte River. Emigrants from Independence, St. Joseph, and Council Bluffs rallied there. The second bastion, Fort Laramie, was already an oasis for travelers and the place where overlanders refitted their equipment before moving into the mountains. It was purchased in 1849 from the American Fur Company for $4,000. By 1850 the Oregon Trail Permanent Defense Establishment was completed with construction of Camp Drum at The Dalles on the Columbia River. The California Trail did not have a post comparable to Camp Drum, although secondary posts were established near the foot of the Humboldt River and near the Great Salt Lake. Since both California and Oregon-bound caravans passed through Fort Kearny and Fort Laramie, they were able to rely on these stations for protection during almost one third of the journey. The two posts also attracted colonies of settlers to provide services for the troops and travelers and became bustling, if nondescript, communities.

Forts Kearny and Laramie were a godsend to

overland emigrants and gold rushers. Their post physicians tended injured and sick travelers and the military hospitals were opened to overlanders too weakened to continue on their journey. During the peak of the gold rush, the commanding officers distributed information to emigrants and argonauts about food and grass shortages and dispensed supplies to needy individuals. Overland parties that started too late in the season often wintered at Kearny or Laramie for both protection and assistance before gaining an early start in the spring. Post commanders were also plagued with demands that their Blue Coats apprehend criminals, find lost or stolen livestock, and adjudicate legal disagreements among argonauts when their companies broke up.

A by-product of the large military presence in the West, the number of people traveling along the Overland Trail, and the growing settlements in California and Oregon, was the need for better communication. The earliest emigrants had depended on returnees, fur traders, even Indians to carry news to the East, and also on a variety of improvised means of getting messages passed along the trail. But these unreliable methods were, of course, inadequate for the soldiers stationed in the forts or on the trail, and for emigrants and argonauts who, in 1849, demanded more government support. As a result, Congress appropriated funds, and bids were let for private contractors to carry mail from the Missouri Valley to California. Salt Lake City became the hub for the mail service which until 1858 operated along the trail on a monthly basis (albeit irregularly) between Independence and Sacramento. In 1859, weekly service was introduced, but economies forced cuts in service from time to time. In 1860 the firm of Russell, Majors, and Waddell began the remarkable Pony Express, which failed because it could not compete with the soon to be completed telegraph. It was possible in 1860 for travelers like Lavinia Porter to hope to find mail addressed to her in care of general delivery at Salt Lake City, a vast improvement from what confronted Jesse Applegate only seventeen years earlier.

The steady increase in overland travelers provided an incentive for businessmen to invest in enterprises that served emigrants while they were on the trail. There was a direct correlation between the growth in the number of travelers and the expansion of trail businesses. The same was true for the developing Federal presence. The first businessmen to capitalize on the opportunities offered by overland traffic were mountain men and the fur trading company agents who operated the several existing posts. For them the costs of entering the overland business were minimal because they already were well situated and needed only small increments in their stock on hand to supply the demand.

As the number of overland emigrants increased, and news of the profits that could be earned selling them supplies spread, many competitors entered the market. Traders primarily from New Mexico set up shop at key points on the trail. Rather quickly an entirely new and disreputable element, comprised of gamblers and liquor dealers, opened shop wherever travelers paused, if even briefly, on their journey. They congregated not only near the forts but also at popular ferry crossings, where they made up the beginning population of new, nameless, transient communities. Drunk and impoverished overlanders became a new phenomenon on the trail. Although many of the questionable characters who sold liquor and ran gambling dens were former mountain men, it is undoubtedly true that some scoundrels went west primarily to mine the miners for gold rather than dig it from the soil. But there were also legitimate entrepreneurs who could visualize the profits to be made from the sale of alcohol. Other enterprising operators altered their plans and began offering ferry service where none had existed or went into competition where the market seemed excessively lucrative.

By 1850 the number of travelers reached 50,000 which certainly met or exceeded the expectations of the businessmen along the trail, but the financial returns were mixed. Forewarned of possible shortages and exorbitant prices charged by merchants and speculators, the argonauts overloaded their wagons and pack animals with food and other supplies. As a result, instead of buying, the overlanders tried to sell their surpluses to the merchants at the forts and, failing in that, either abandoned them or gave them away. Prices and profits fell.

While 1850 brought mixed financial results, 1851 proved to be a disaster. Businessmen, hopeful that a swell of gold seekers would create a market, were sadly disappointed. Rumors of Indian war, word of the deadly cholera epidemic, and a host of other factors reduced the number of people trailing west to California to a trickle. Only the strongest enterprises withstood the retrenchment. Speculators simply gave up, while many of the troublesome element moved on to the California gold fields or returned to the East.

By 1860, as Lavinia Porter discovered, one did not escape all of the hardships of wagon travel, but certainly the roughest years of the Overland Trail had come and gone. Both the government and private entrepreneurs played a role in developing and protecting the way west. By the eve of the Civil War, when new gold finds were being made in other parts of the West, and prospectors were moving to newer areas, the Overland Trail was a well-worn road.

The thousands of individuals who walked or rode on the Oregon-California Trail, whether as settlers or argonauts, not only never forgot their experience but also had a significant impact on national development. The Applegates and the others who went on to Oregon assured the peaceful transfer of the Pacific Northwest to the United States because farmers, not force, proved persuasive in dealing with the British. The California caravans of gold-rushers and settlers were resolute in their insistence to be part of the Federal Union, and they did much to consolidate the American presence on the Pacific.

Many of the overlanders had a sense of destiny; they knew that they had done something unique. Those who opted for California used an expression that somehow came to characterize the nature of the journey. It was called *seeing the elephant.* And, it made no difference whether one gave up in the face of adversity or made it all the way, everyone spoke of *seeing the elephant.* The origin of the expression is lost in time, but its meaning is clear. It applied as much to Oregon as it did to California. The many people who conquered the Overland Trail proved to themselves, to their countrymen, and to generations to come, that they, like their forebears, had the courage to subdue a continent.

MARTIN RIDGE

The Huntington Library
The California Institute of Technology
August, 1989

1

Recollections of
My Boyhood

by
Jesse A. Applegate

Jesse A. Applegate
Courtesy Oregon Historical Society

2

Editor's Comments

JESSE A. APPLEGATE, the author of *Recollections of My Boyhood*, was descended from a distinguished pioneering family. His grandfather, Daniel Applegate, who was reared in New Jersey, was a fifer in George Washington's army during the American Revolution and later settled in Kentucky where he married Rachel Lindsay. In 1821 he decided that he could make a better living in Missouri and soon moved his family to land just outside of St. Louis.

Daniel Applegate's spirit infected his children. In 1832, several of his adventurous sons who were seeking new opportunities migrated as a family-group to the so-called "Platte Purchase" in Missouri's Osage River Valley.

Jesse was born on November 14, 1835, during his family's stay in the Osage Valley. His father, Lindsay Applegate, named him Jesse out of respect and affection for his younger brother. To distinguish between them, the boy was named Jesse Applegate Applegate—the double use of the family's surname was unusual—and he was called Jesse A. or Jess. As a child he suffered the loss of an eye, pierced—family legend records—by a scissors when he was a toddler. Family legend has it, too, that he was to escape

3

death on the Columbia River because his mother, fearful for his safety after the earlier accident, refused permission for him to travel with his brothers Elisha and Warren and his cousin Edward, as they shot the river rapids. When their boat capsized, Edward and Warren were lost, and only Elisha, who could swim, survived.

The Applegates, successful grain farmers in the Osage Valley, were restless pioneers and leaders. Highly patriotic, taken up with the cause of the American claims for the ownership of Oregon, and well aware that the first settlers on that farthest frontier could secure as much as one square mile of virgin land at no cost, the Applegate brothers, Lindsay, Jesse, and Charles, in 1843 decided to move west. They joined other land-hungry patriots who made up the largest overland party to Oregon yet organized, perhaps one thousand emigrants, and played a key role in its journey. Uncle Jesse, who had assumed command of the slow-moving cattle herd that followed the main overland party in 1843, wrote in 1876 a classic account of his experiences, *A Day with the Cow Column in 1843*, that ranks among the best westering narratives.[1]

Even after the Applegate families arrived in Oregon, they did not stay put. Always on the make, restless in search of fortune, the clan, led by Uncle

[1] Jesse Applegate, *A Day with the Cow Column in 1843*, *Quarterly of the Oregon Historical Society*, Portland, December, 1900.

Lindsay Applegate (father)
Courtesy Southern Oregon Historical Society

Charles Applegate (uncle)   *Jesse Applegate (uncle)*

Jesse, moved to the southern part of the territory where they finally established themselves as a first family. Uncle Jesse, a resourceful frontiersman with literary talent, a surveyor's skills, and unflagging energy, served in the legislature, and, although his brothers could not match his abilities or accomplishments, Charles and Lindsay, too, fought in Indian wars, and they helped cut a major road—to be known as the Applegate Trail—through the mountains by-passing the treacherous Columbia River so late-coming settlers would have an easier time reaching the fertile Willamette Valley. It was a time when energetic men could make their mark, and the Applegates earned lasting recognition in early Oregon history.

Years later, when he was in his late seventies, Jesse A. recalled his overland experiences, reflecting on the most critical event not only in his life but also that of his family. The Applegates had moved to Oregon when only a handful of Americans lived there, and the feat of crossing the plains and mountains required personal courage and physical stamina. This awesome journey also demanded that they leave behind a comfortable certainty and confront the perils of travel and the labor of beginning anew. They also moved into a region where ownership was contested by the United States and England and where the Indian menace was genuine.

Yet, Jess did not choose to write about these things, which would have been uppermost in the mind of an adult. Instead, he decided to relate his own childhood experiences. Therefore, his memoir is almost devoid of comparisons with the things an adult would have known.

To recapture his own story, Jess had to recall his western crossing through the eyes of a seven-year-old child, whose imagination rather than knowledge of the past fashioned his image of the world around him. Events and personalities that fascinated him as a child are highlighted in his narrative, while the usual statements that crowd the diaries of bone-weary and concerned adults who traveled overland to Oregon or California—such things as distance, available grass and wood, water, and interpersonal conflict—are almost absent from his story. It was not his intention to provide an interesting story based on the perspective of others. The exception from this pattern is when he describes the tragic drowning of his brother and cousin during the Columbia River passage. In these pages, he betrays the kind of knowledge that could only have been gained by repeatedly hearing about the event from adults who saw it and by their hindsight. Nonetheless, even in his depiction of the tragedy, the style and tone of his writing remains uniformly that of a boy.

Although the Applegates migrated to Oregon to open a new country and gain land, Jess's life did not confine itself to farming. Along with the children of other family members, he completed his primary education in a one-room school that was also used as a Presbyterian church. He earned a classical education at Bethel Institute. When he was seventeen, Jess was a soldier fighting against the uprising Indians in the Rogue River War. He later taught and was superintendent of schools in Polk County where he also read law. In 1863 he married Virginia Watson of Spring Valley, Oregon and settled in Salem where he practiced law for more than thirty years. Only failing sight in his remaining eye compelled his retirement. In 1907 he published *The Yangoler Chief: The Kommema and his Religion*,[2] which has remained a valuable ethnographic source on Oregon's Yoncalla Indians and also demonstrates Jess's fine knowledge of Klamath Indian poetry.

Jesse Applegate Applegate died at age eighty-three on January 4, 1919, and is buried in a family plot in Jacksonville, Oregon. He was survived by six of his seven children.[3]

[2]Jesse Applegate, *The Yangoler Chief: The Kommema and his Religion*, Roseburg, Oregon, 1907.

[3]For more information about Jesse A. Applegate and an analysis of his memoir, see Joseph Schaffer's, "Introduction," *A Day with the Cow Column in 1843* by Jesse Applegate. *Recollections of My Boyhood* by Jesse A. Applegate, Oregon pioneer, Chicago, 1934.

I

From the Mississippi to the Columbia

MY FATHER was born in Lexington, Kentucky, my Mother in East Tennessee, but from the time of my earliest recollection we had been living on the Osage River in Missouri. Our house stood at the edge of the woods which skirted the river bank. The prairie country from the house lay westward and up and down the river, and was vast in extent. Our house was of hewn logs closely joined together, and the spaces between were filled with limestone mortar. There were two buildings, one story and a half, under one roof, and a porch all along the west side of the building. There was a hewn stone fireplace and a chimney for each building. There were two doors and probably four windows opening on the porch, and a door towards the river, opening on a short walk to the small house containing a loom where cloth was woven. Near the river were several corncribs in a row, and sheds for stock. West of the house was a sizeable cornfield, cotton and tobacco patches, and garden. I have no recollection of any orchard, probably because as yet it had not supplied me with any fruit. Of forest trees between the house and river, I can name three kinds of hickory: black, shellbark, and pignut—the last producing a soft-shelled nut. This variety was found between the dwelling house and the corncribs. Several large walnut trees grew between the corncribs and the river, also a very large bur oak. Water oaks, persimmon, slippery elm, and sycamore trees, grew along the margin of the river. Of timber classed as brush, there were redbud, sassafras, willow, line-bark, and hazel. I saw red cedar, chinquapin oak, pawpaw, and pecan trees growing on the other side of the river. In the autumn season we always gathered several bushels of walnuts, pecans, and hickory nuts. There was a wild plum of this country which for sweetness was equal to the petite prune, while its flavor was superior. When ripe it was pale yellow, but frosted over with a white, flour-like substance. It was a size larger than the petite prune. Wild grapes of good quality were plentiful; a wild vineyard of the kind called Summer Grape grew along the brow of a hill about a mile from the house and in a "ruff." The ripe berry was black, nearly as large as the domestic Catawba, and as sweet and well flavored as that grape. But there was an herb growing in the woods, the root of which became so firmly fixed in my memory, that should I live to the age attained by Moses of old, I would not forget it. It was known as "Injun Fizic" (Indian physic), the technical name of the plant being epecaquane. Its usefulness as a medicine was learned from the natives. A dose of this physic brewed from the root, for a boy, was a tin cup full; it was brought to the patient at bedtime steaming hot and as black as coffee; no cream, sugar or salt, or anything else was put into the liquid, lest it might modify its perfect nastiness. When the boy saw the cup, and a whiff from the odors of the contents took his breath, he was seized with a fit of trembling more or less violent, and cold sweat was formed on his forehead, but kind hands now supported him, and encouraging words somewhat restored him, and it was considered that he was now prepared for the worst. Whereupon he was seized by the nose, and when, in gasping for breath, his mouth flew open, the physic was poured down his throat. The boy now, not being able to stand, was put to bed. I have thought that if Socrates would have had to take a dose of "Injun Fizic" instead of the cup of hemlock, he would have concluded to take the advice of his friends, when they told him arrangements had been made so that he could escape from Greece to another country where he could live in safety, and besought him to embrace this opportunity to save his life. The probabilities are that the old philosopher would have skipped, not to save his life, but to avoid the dose.

In those days nothing was accepted as medicine unless it was offensive to one's taste, and disagreeable to the stomach, and the more offensive and nauseating, the greater its medicinal virtues were supposed to be, therefore there was no discount upon "Injun Fizic" as a medicine. The opinion also seems to have been general that the surest way to cure a man of disease was to reduce him almost to the point of death; that the less life there was left in a man, the less disease there would be. Where the disease was said to be in the blood, the blood was to be drawn off, leaving enough blood in the body to keep the spark of life burning until new blood could be supplied. In those days I think it would have been difficult to find a man or woman without scars from the lance.

Wild turkeys were plentiful in the woods and we often heard them calling and gobbling near the house. They were highly prized as a game bird and a hunter could generally bag all he wanted in a few hours. I often trapped for quail and other small game; the trap was a small box made of boards set up on triggers in such a way that pulling at the bait, which was attached to one of the triggers, would allow the box to fall and enclose the game. One morning I determined a rabbit had been in the trap but had gnawed its way out and escaped. What surprised me, though, was the great size of the hole he had cut in one side of the trap to crawl out; it was large enough for a coyote. He probably considered himself much larger than he was. I knew it was a rabbit by the tracks in the snow. At another time, I visited my trap and, looking through the cracks from the top of the box, discovered I had caught a redbird, about the size of a jaybird. I was delighted when I saw what I had caught, for it is a very pretty bird and I had often wished I had one; so I raised one side of the trap just enough to allow me to put my right hand under and seize the bird. The bird, though, was quicker than I, for he seized me first with both his feet and made a swipe at my thumb with his beak, taking out quite a slice. His claws were like crooked thorns, his bill was as sharp as a tack and cut like a pair of scissors. I took hold of the bird with my left hand, but could not get it to let go of my right. While it dug its claws into my hand, it worked with its bill on my thumb and fingers, but I soon stayed the havoc he was making with his beak by securing his head with my left hand, grasping very lightly though, so as not to aggravate him. This much accomplished, I could do no more. The situation had become desperate. I would have gladly surrendered and given the bird his freedom, but the fight was on and I could not get the enemy off my hands. Realizing now that I must have help, I ran to the house, which was not over a hundred and fifty yards away, holding the bird up as if for exhibition. As soon as I got into the house the folks, seeing my bloody hands and agonized pose of countenance, came promptly to my assistance, and by carefully withdrawing each talon, as though it had been a thorn in the flesh, succeeded in separating me and my prize. I was told afterwards that they managed to give the bird its freedom without causing more bloodshed. That ended the sport.

My brothers, Elisha and Warren, the first about

four and the second about two years older than I was, and James, a cousin about the age of Warren and myself, were often about the river fishing, wading, wallowing in the mud and sand, and trying to swim. And yet I think we were often advised and even commanded not to go in swimming, as there was danger of being drowned.

One early spring day the snow and ice were melting and a rivulet, which poured into the river near the house, was full of roaring and foaming muddy water, of course about as cold as ice itself. But the sun was shining quite warm and we boys were having a jolly time, wading and floundering around in the angry waters. The excitement had thrown us off our guard, and we were taken with a sudden surprise and almost overcome with a feeling of wretchedness when we discovered Mother standing on the bank among our clothes with a long switch in her hand. No threat of punishment or cry of despair was heard above the dashing waters, but every boy, blue and numb as he was with cold, stuck his toes and fingers into the muddy bank and made a dash for his clothes. But I do not think we were much afraid of actual punishment, although fairly caught in an act of disobedience, for I had never known Mother to cause a child to suffer pain, however alarming her threats might have been. If she had been stern enough to punish us, as she probably be lieved she would, this was her real opportunity for all of us were naked and, being thoroughly wet,

Elizabeth "Betsy" Miller Applegate (mother)
Courtesy Douglas County (Oregon) Museum

could not get into our shirts. My brother Elisha had thrust his head and hands into his shirt, and though he made frantic efforts to get under cover, the garment stuck fast. Mother, probably considering him to be the most responsible one, thought she would make an example of him and actually gave him a swipe across the shoulders with the switch, which made him dance around and redouble his comical efforts to get his shirt on. But the ridiculous and pitiful spectacle had now overcome her resolution, and a smile was seen to start at the corners of her mouth, a harbinger of mercy our eyes were not slow to detect. She finally assisted us in getting into our clothes, and then warned us that the *next* time we would be punished to the full extent of the law.

My Mother bribed me with wild plums to go to school. I rode to school on the teacher's shoulders, sitting astride of his neck. I was wearing my first trousers with suspenders; it was playtime at school, and the teacher happened to be a fiddler as well as a pedagogue. I never had seen or heard a fiddle before. While he was playing, I ventured to approach very near the instrument, thinking I would be able to account for the wonderful and strange sound issuing from the flat box with the crooked neck; but I could not, and trembling with fear said, "Where does the noise come from?" Someone answered, "The devil makes the noise." Frightened almost into fits, I fled from the house and, running down the hillside probably thirty yards, took refuge in a small cave. Some of the children came after me and, by assuring me that the devil was gone, persuaded me to return to school.

The schoolhouse was a rough log cabin, and had a fireplace and flue built of rocks, clay, and sticks. The children used to pick clay out of the logs and eat it. When I came out of the cave, I looked up and, on the top of the little hill about thirty feet above the cave, I saw a man standing. He was not a white man nor a Negro. As I remember him now, he was dressed in buckskin and carried a tomahawk in his belt. I was told he was an Osage Indian, and before we started to Oregon, I saw a few other Indians said to be Osages. They looked like the first one I had seen and they were hunting horses.

It seems to me now that for a long time before we left for Oregon, the journey was talked about. Of course I did not know anything about Oregon, which was, in my mind, a country mighty far away, and I understood that to get there we would have to travel through a country swarming with wild Indians who would try to kill us with tomahawks and scalp us. Some girl cousins older than I would take a coffee cup after drinking the coffee and turn the mouth down, and after it had set a short time, look into it for pictures of future scenes. This was often done, and we thought we could see covered wagons and Indians scalping women and children. How little we guessed of what the future held in store for those wagons of courageous people. Little did we dream of the weary days and weeks and months of that long and toilsome march towards the land of the setting sun, a test of courage of soul. I give here a list of the names of heads of families and of young men considered old enough to do a grown man's work. This is a copy made from the original roll which was made by a young man of the party, J.W. Nesmith, later to be Senator from Oregon. There were several hundred in the wagon train; men, women, and children, who began that six-month journey in the Spring of 1843 into an unknown country; through the valleys, across the trackless plains, and over lofty mountains; ever on the watch for savage foes, and with a courage almost sublime, they moved always onward towards the promised land, and in the end,

> *"They toiled and builded on the western shore*
> *An empire that shall last for evermore."*

Applegate, Jesse	Brooks, John P.	Broadman
Applegate, Charles	Brown, Martin	Baldridge, Wm.
Applegate, Lindsay	Brown, Oris	Carson, F.C.
Athey, Wm.	Black, J.P.	Carson, Jas.
Atkinson, Jno.	Bane, Layton	Chapman, Wm.
Arthur, Wm.	Baker, Andrew	Cox, Jno.
Arthur, Robert	Baker, John G.	Champ, Jacob
Arthur, David	Beagle, Wm.	Cooper, L.C.
Butler, Anson	Boyd, Levi	Cone, Jas.
Brooks, Geo.	Baker, Wm.	Childers, Moses
Burnett, Peter H.	Biddle, Nicholas	Carey, Miles
Bird, David	Beale, Geo.	Cochran, Thos.
Brown, Thomas A.	Braidy, Jas.	Clyman, L.
Blivens, Alex	Beadle, Geo.	Copenhaver, Jno.

Caton, J.H.
Chappel, Alfred
Cronin, Daniel
Cozine, Samuel
Constable, Benedict
Childs, Jos.
Clark, Ransom
Campbell, Jno. G.
Chapman
Chas, Jas.
Dodd, Solomon
Dement, W.C.
Dougherty, W.P.
Day, Wm.
Duncan, Jas.
Dorin, Jacob
Davis, Thos.
Delany, Daniel
Delany, Daniel, Jr.
Delany, Wm.
Doke, Wm.
Davis, J.H.
Davis, Burrell
Dailey, Geo.
Doherty, Jno.
Dawson
Eaton, Chas.
Eaton, Nathan
Etchell, Jas.
Emerick, Solomon
Eaker, Jno. W.
Edson, E.G.
Eyres, Miles
East, Jno. W.
Everman, Ninimon
Ford, Ninevah
Ford, Ephram
Ford, Nimrod
Ford, Jno.

Francis, Alexander
Frazier, Abner
Fowler, Wm.
Fowler, W.J.
Fowler, Wm.
Fairly, Stephen
Fendall, Chas.
Gaunt, Jno.
Gray, Chiley B.
Garrison, Enoch
Garrison, J.W.
Garrison, W.J.
Gardner, Wm.
Gardner, Samuel
Gilmore, Watt
Goodman, Richard
Gilpin, Major
Gray
Haggard, B.
Hide, W.W.
Holmes, Wm.
Holmes, Riley A.
Hobson, Jno.
Hobson, Wm.
Hembre, Andrew
Hembre, A.J.
Hembre, Jas.
Hall, Samuel B.
Houk, Jas.
Hughes, W.P.
Hendricks, Abijah
Hays, Jas.
Hensley, Thos. J.
Hollery, B.
Hunt, Henry
Holderness, S.M.
Hutchins, Isaac
Husted, A.
Hess, Joseph

Haren, Jacob
Howell, Jno.
Howell, Wm.
Howell, Wesley
Howell, G.W.
Howell, Thos. E.
Hill, Henry
Hill, Wm.
Hill, Almoran
Hewitt, Henry
Hargrove, Wm.
Hoyt, A.
Holman, Daniel
Harrigas, B.
James, Calvin
Jackson, Jno. B.
Jones, Jno.
Johnson, Overton
Keyser, Thos.
Keyser, I.B.
Keyser, Pleasant
Kelley
Kelsey
Lovejoy, A.L.
Lenox, Edward
Lenox, E.
Layson, Aaron
Looney, Jesse
Long, Jno.
Lee, H.A.G.
Legur, F.
Linebarger, Jno.
Laswill, Isaac
Loughborough, J.
Little, Milton
Luther
Lauderdale, Jno.
McGee
Martin, Jas.

Martin, Julius
McClellan, Alex.
McClellan, F.
Mills, Jno. B.
Mills, Isaac
Mills, Wm. A.
Mills, Owen
McGarey, G.W.
Mondon, Gilbert
Matheny, Daniel
Matheny, Adam
Matheny, J.N.
Matheny, Josiah
Matheny, Henry
Mastire, A.J.
McHaley, Jno.
Myer, Jacob
Manning, Jno.
Manning, Jas.
McCarver, M.M.
McCorde, Geo.
Mays, Wm.
Millican, Elijah
McDaniel, Wm.
McKissie, D.
Malone, Madison
McClane, Jno. B.
Mauzee, Wm.
McIntire, Jno.
Moore, Jackson
Matney, J.W.
Nesmith, J.W.
Newby, W.T.
Neuman, Noah
Naylor, Thos.
Osborn, Neil
O'Brien, Hugh D.
O'Brien, Humphry
Owen, Thos. A.

Owen, Thos.
Otie, E.W.
Otie, M.B.
O'Neil, Bennett
Olinger, A.
Parker, Jesse
Parker, Wm.
Pennington, I.B.
Poe, R.A.
Paynter, Samuel
Patterson, I.R.
Pickett, Chas. E.
Prigg, Fred
Paine, Clayborn
Reading, P.B.
Rogers, G.W.
Russell, Wm.
Roberts, Jas.
Rice, G.W.
Richardson, Jno.
Richardson, Daniel
Ruby, Philip
Ricord, Jno.
Reid, Jacob
Roe, Jno.
Roberts, Solomon
Roberts, Emseley
Rossin, Jno.
Rives, Thos.
Smith, Thos. H.
Smith, Thos.
Smith, Isaac W.
Smith, Anderson
Smith, A.
Smith, Robert
Smith, Eli
Sheldon, Wm.
Stewart, P.G.
Sutton, Dr. Nathan'l

Stimmerman, C.
Sewell, Henry
Sharp, C.
Summers, W.C.
Stout, Henry
Stout
Stirling, Geo.
Stevenson
Story, Jas.
Swift
Shively, Jno. M.
Shively, Samuel
Stoughton, Alexan'r
Spencer, Chancy
Strait, Hiram
Summers, Geo.
Stringer, Cornelius
Stringer, C.W.
Tharp, Lindsey
Thomas, Jno.
Trainor, D.
Teller, Jeremiah
Tarbox, Stephen
Umnicker, Jno.
Vance, Samuel
Vaughn, Wm.
Vernon, Geo.
Wilmot, Jas.
Wilson, Wm. H.
Wair, J.W.
Winkle, Archibald
Williams, Edward
Wheeler, H.
Wagner, Jno.
Williams, Benj.
Williams, David
Williams, Jno.
Williams, Jas.
Williams, Squire

Williams, Isaac	Watson, Jno (Belly)	Waldo, David
Wilson, Wm.	Walters, Jas.	Waldo, Wm.
Ward, T.B.	Winter, Wm.	Zachary, Alexander
White, Jas.	Waldo, Daniel	Zachary, Jno.[1]

The day we started on our journey to Oregon I do not remember, but before we reached the Caw River I can recall to mind Harmony Mission and Grand River as being the name of a place and river on or near our route. We came up on the south side of the Caw River and camped below and near an Indian town of the Caw tribe. There were huts and cabins ranging along the river on either side of a street. It was said those Indians grew corn, beans, and pumpkins. I admired several of the Indian men I saw here. Many of them were more than six feet tall, and moved with a proud step. They wore blankets wrapped around their shoulders and leggins. Their hair was cut to the scalp except for a thing like a rooster's comb on top of the head, colored red. I remember standing and gazing up into the face of one of those tall Indians, probably to see if he were a good or bad Indian. I was not afraid of them. I had lived near the Osage River and I saw

[1] This party, which numbered about 900 people in all, was part of the great migration of 1843. Because of its size the train broke into two groups: a "light column" of wagons and a "heavy column" that brought up the cattle. The captain of the "light column" was Peter Burnett. That column was the first to take wagons beyond Fort Hall. Prior to that time travelers relied on pack animals. The story of the second column is best recounted in Jesse Applegate's, "A Day with the Cow Column," *Overland Monthly* (August 1868).

that the Caw River looked to be hardly half as wide. The current was slow and the water, I thought, was very deep. The men in some way made the wagon boxes watertight and used them as boats. In crossing the river the Indians assisted us by swimming with our cattle and horses. I noticed that the Indians did not swim like white men, but with an overhanded stroke, "dog-fashion" they called it. Those Indians were friendly and accommodating. They said we would soon reach the country of the Cheyennes and Pawnees, and that they were bad Indians.

One afternoon, when the sun seemed to be about three hours high, and we were traveling along at an ox-team gait over a level prairie, John East, a good, honest man, also from Missouri, who was walking and driving his team, was told that we were then crossing the Missouri line, whereupon, he turned about facing the east, pulled off his slouched hat, and waving it above his head shouted, "Farewell to America!"

I think it was the second day after we had crossed the Caw River, we met a war party of Caws marching afoot. There were about a hundred of them, painted and feathered, and armed with bows and arrows, war clubs, tomahawks, and knives. Some were wounded and limping, some had bloody faces; others had arms in slings and bandages round their heads. They seemed to be tired and in a hurry. They told us they had been out on a buffalo hunt and had been attacked by a war party of Pawnees

and had a fight with them, but that they had defeated the Pawnees and killed many of them. That evening or the next, we reached the battleground, and
went into camp. Several dead Indians were found,
and I heard men say they were Caws. If they were,
the Caws were defeated, else they would not have
left their dead.

There was a Mexican in our train, who cut off an
Indian's hand at the wrist and hung it on a stake
about three feet high in the encampment. I saw it
hanging there myself, and was afraid of it, for I saw
it was a man's hand. An indignation meeting was
the result of this ghastly exhibition, and the Mexican was compelled to leave the company.

On this long journey there were many days of
marching and camping, of which I have no recollection. I cannot remember places in the order in
which we came to them, but the next that comes to
my mind is Ash Hollow,[2] which appeared to be
only a depression in the usually level plain, where
were scattered ash timber trees. It appears to me
now that after we crossed Ash Hollow, the prairie
stretched far away to the west, and as we traveled
along, making a wagon road through the high grass,
we saw at a distance of probably a mile, a horseman galloping across the prairie. Some said he

[2]Ash Hollow was among the more famous landmarks on
the trail. Sometimes called the gateway to the high plains, it
was located north of the ford on the South Platte River
on a broad prairie in southwest Nebraska.

was a Pawnee on a pony and that he had tiny bells in his ears. I thought I could hear them ring.

In this part of the country we crossed the Big and Little Blue Rivers; the Little was small and the Big not a large river. I had heard of the Blue Rivers many days before we reached them, and expected to find the water really blue, and my recollection now is that the water was of a blue color.

We arrived at the Big Blue about sunset, and forded the stream. It was not deep, as I remember it. We went into camp on the west slope not far from the river. The weather was fair, and early in the evening I went to bed in a tent with an old man by the name of Alexander McClellan, whom I will now introduce to you. He came to our house in Missouri when I was quite an infant, too young to remember when he came. But I was told that when he came I was almost dead with a fever. The old man was familiar with the herbs and roots used by the Indians in sickness, and at once took charge of me and soon restored me to health. He was then between sixty and seventy years of age; had been a soldier; had been crossed in love and never married. The first tune I learned was of a song he sometimes sang when he had me on his knee. It was called "The Rosetree." This is the first verse:

> *"A rosetree in full bearing*
> *Had sweet flowers fair to see;*
> *One rose beyond comparing*
> *For beauty attracted me."*

Well, I went to bed with the old man, "Uncle Mack," we called him. I had always slept with him before my earliest recollections, when he was with us, as he almost always was. How long I had slept I do not know, but sometime during the night, I suddenly awoke. The rain was pouring down into my face, my eyes were blinded with the glare of lightning, the wind was roaring like a furnace, and the crash of thunder was terrible and almost continuous. I could see nothing but what looked like sheets of fire, and hear nothing but the wind, the pouring rain, and the bellowing thunder. For a minute I was dazed and could not understand the situation, and before I had totally found my senses, Uncle Mack picked me up and put me into the hind end of a covered wagon, and I well remember scrambling around in there among pack saddles, etc. I remember no more of this night, but in the morning the little river had overflowed its banks and the entire camp was flooded.

The next object that seems to have claimed my boyish attention, and a place on the tablet of memory, was Independence Rock.[3] It was just beyond a small stream which seemed to wind around its base. We passed quite near it and though I can now see

[3] Independence Rock, located on the Sweetwater River in central Wyoming, was named by men of the Rocky Mountain Fur Company. Father Pierre Jean DeSmet, the Jesuit missionary, later called it the Great Registry of the Desert because of all the emigrants and fur men who had carved their names on it.

Independence Rock
as drawn by J. Goldsborough Bruff
Courtesy The Huntington Library

Independence Rock and the Sweetwater River
as drawn by Frederick Piercy
Courtesy Missouri Historical Society

29

the picture of it on the pages of memory, I cannot describe it in a way satisfactorily to myself, but it looked to be oval on top and in the highest part quite smooth and slick, as I imagined, so that a person would slide off it. It was of a light gray color, as high as a house at the middle, tapering down both ways, and as long as a city block.

A man by the name of Lovejoy came to us somewhere in this part of the country, relating what I thought was a very funny story. He was traveling with a party of fur trappers and they had just set up camp in the neighborhood of Independence Rock. Mr. Lovejoy went to explore and examine it, and while there he was marking his name on the rock, and just as he was writing "joy" a party of skulking Indians captured him. They took him to the encampment of his party and sold him to his friends for ammunition and tobacco. Mr. Lovejoy was a very clever and good-looking young man and wore a slouch hat. He joined our party and came on through to Oregon.

It seems that the next object that made a lasting impression on my memory as we traveled westward was Fort Laramie of the American Fur Company.[4] I recall that the fort looked white as we approached it.

[4]Built originally in 1834 as Fort William, a fur trading post at the junction of the Laramie and North Platte Rivers in eastern Wyoming, it was acquired by the American Fur Company in 1836. By the 1840s it was a major facility on the overland trail. It was sold to the United States government in 1849 and made into a military post.

I think we were now traveling through the country of the Platte Rivers, a country of level plains it now seems to me and very little timber. We saw many herds of buffalo, some grazing quietly on the prairies, and others marching, and moving and bellowing, and the great herds making a roaring noise as they tramped along a half mile or a mile away.

Of the Platte Rivers there were the South Platte, Laramie's Fork, and the North Platte. At times we traveled along the banks of the rivers which were low, and the water often seemed spread over a wide surface and shallow. The pasturage was fresh and abundant, and I do not remember that we endured great hardships journeying through this part of the country. Buffalo and small game were plentiful and the men had great sport hunting. We had an abundance of buffalo meat and venison. Some mornings buffaloes were found scattered among our cattle, quietly grazing with them. One day as we were traveling along the bank of one of the Platte Rivers, a buffalo was seen swimming the river and coming in the direction of the train. Some of the men got their guns and when he came up the bank, attacked and finally killed him near the wagons, but they had to shoot so many times to bring him down that the firing sounded like quite a battle. I think they said he was an old bull. He had very large shoulders rising to a hump, which was covered with long dark hair, and he had an ugly, burly head. I thought him a very dangerous looking beast. While traveling through this country of rivers and broad plains, we were never out of sight of wild game.

I remember crossing the two Platte Rivers. One crossing where we forded, the river seemed to be very wide and quite rapid; the water was so deep in places that it ran into the wagon boxes and a single team and wagon would have been swept away, so they formed the entire train in single file, and attached the teams and wagons to a chain extending through the entire length of the train. The crossing severely tried the courage and endurance of the men, for they waded the river alongside their oxen, at times clinging to the ox yokes, and swimming; at some deep places the teams seemed to swim and the wagons to float, being held up and in line by the chain to which they were attached.

Whether at this crossing or another, I do not remember, but at one place where we forded one of the rivers, Mother, myself, and the other children were in a wagon, which we called the "little red wagon." It was drawn by one yoke of oxen, and it appears to me now that our wagon was attached to the last end of the train. As we were just getting up the bank from the ford, our team broke loose and wagon and team backed into the river. Being swept below the ford, the team swam and the wagon sank down, and was drifting on the sand; and I remember the water came rushing into the wagon box to my waist, compelling me to scramble upon the top of a trunk or something of the kind. But several men came to our assistance immediately, and by swimming held up the wagon, and soon assisted us to the shore. Probably this was at the fording of the North Platte.

It seems to me now that the next point of note on our route was Fort Bridger,[5] but I do not call to mind the appearance of the buildings or anything happening thereabout, unless it was the great number of Sioux Indians I saw either around this fort or at Laramie. I saw several very pretty squaws with cheeks painted red, wearing beaded moccasins and beautiful red leggins, fringed along the outer seams. Some of them had papooses almost white and very pretty. Some were wives of white men at the fort, and others belonged to the great war party I saw there mustering to fight the Blackfeet. As I remember this horde of Sioux warriors, all of them were mounted on fine horses; bucks and squaws all painted about the face, and armed with bows and arrows encased in quivers slung on the back. Some had spears, some war clubs, but no guns, or if any, very few. This war party, as I see the picture now, looking back sixty years, marching or halting in close array, covered several acres of prairie. They were a savage-looking lot, particularly when a squadron of those warriors would break away from the main

[5] Fort Bridger, located at the Black Fork of the Green River, was intended to aid overland emigrants rather than as a fur post. Established by James Bridger and Louis Vasquez, it was sold to Mormons in 1855 and became a United States army post in 1858.

*Fort Bridger about 1853
from a lithograph by Ackerman*
Courtesy Missouri Historical Society

body and come toward us shouting the war whoop, urging their ponies at full speed, I thought it a grand display, indeed, although I fancied I could feel the hair rise on my head. Several of the Amazons from this war party visited our encampment. They were dressed and painted and armed like the men. Some of them were very fine of figure, had pretty faces, and eyes as soft and bright as the antelopes on those wild plains. They were all young women, and, as I thought, made love to our young men with their eyes like city damsels, but in the excitement of battle I suppose they became furious and those doe-like eyes flashed fire. Their small, shapely hands and small feet clad in beaded moccasins were admired even by our women, and I fear our men, bold as they were, were almost captured by those lovely warriors.

The train had been moving westward across a level country for days where no tree was to be seen, but looking ahead, far in the distance, I saw a bush, which, as we moved along, continued to grow until the shades of evening began to darken into night and we went into camp. The following morning about the first object that attracted my attention was that bush, which now appeared to have grown to be quite a sapling. By noon it had grown to be a tree, and about sunset we were under its branches, and, I believe, went into camp near it. It was a very large pine tree, the round, straight trunk towering up like a great column and supporting a spreading top. This was the "Lone Pine." [6] For several years after, I heard about the Lone Pine from emigrants following our trail, but later I was told that it had been cut down for firewood.

I can remember incidents, places, and things that I find I cannot locate. In attempting to do so I may be several hundred miles off. Where was Chimney Rock? [7] Somewhere on the plains. It was near the line of march and we could see it, it seems to me, for several days before we passed near it. At first we could only see a pinnacle afar off, looking much akin to a chimney flue or church steeple, but as we traveled on, it appeared to be somewhat divided into two or three points at the top, but one pinnacle was much higher than the others. Nearer, we could see that the chimney-like pinnacles were on the top of a mountain or high hill, and that beyond and not far from it was an irregular range of mountains. I could not form an opinion as to the heighth of this Chimney Rock, but it seemed to me to touch the sky. We went into camp not far from it. Some of the young men that evening visited the Rock and returned quite late at night. They declared it was ten

[6]This is probably a reference to "lone tree" because "lone pine" is a site in Oregon. The exact location of the tree is uncertain, and more than likely more than one tree was called lone tree by overlanders.

[7]The name Chimney Rock appears in an 1827 report. The formation is located on grassy plains of the western part of the Nebraska panhandle south of the Platte River. Diarists mentioned it more frequently than any other geographical site on the overland trail.

Chimney Rock
as drawn by J. Goldsborough Bruff
Courtesy The Huntington Library

miles away. Emigrants who followed told me that Chimney Rock had continued to crumble and fall away from year to year until now there is scarcely anything left of that far-famed landmark that was so very appealing.

We must have traveled across vast stretches of almost level country where there were no forests of timber and, in fact, where there was very little timber. Where we camped we sometimes had to use small willows for firewood, such as we found growing along the margin of streams and around springs. At other times, and quite often too, we had no wood of any kind and used "buffalo chips" for fuel. What we called "buffalo chips" was the dried dung of the buffalo.

I had quite an adventure one evening while gathering "buffalo chips." Several of us boys were out from camp some little distance, picking them up and throwing them into piles. Our party had a pile and other parties had their piles, and as we were not far apart, it seems that we had claimed certain small districts adjacent to our respective stacks of chips, and we had to guard against trespassers. We were working hard and had become considerably excited, when, I remember, a boy about my size with yellow sunburnt hair and freckled face (at that time I thought he had scales or scabs on his face), came over into our district and attempted to get away with a large chip, but I caught him in the act and threw another into his face with such violence as to knock off a scale and make the blood come. I think I was urged to this by the elder boys, for I remember they laughed, when I could see nothing to laugh about.

I think it was in this part of the country we found the prairie dog towns. The prairie dogs seemed to prefer city life, for we always found them living in towns and cities.[8] The population of some of their cities I should think was as great as that of New York. The dog is about the size of a very young puppy dog. As we would pass through or near their towns they would come out of their holes and sit up straight on their hind quarters, always near their burrow, and utter something like a yelp, or so it seemed to me, and on the slightest alarm drop into their holes. I saw owls sitting among them, and it was said that prairie dogs, owls, and rattlesnakes lived together in the same holes.

It seems that matches were not in use when we crossed the plains, for I remember that to get fire a man would rub a cotton rag in powder and shoot it out of a musket, or put it in the pan of a flintlock gun, and then explode the powder in the pan; often a flint steel and punk were used. I think many of these guns were flintlocks, but I know some were what they called percussion, with nipple and cap; they were all muzzle-loaders.

[8] These tawny ground squirrels—*cynomys ludovicianus*—weighing as much as two pounds, yelp and hold their bodies erect to look out for enemies.

Antelopes and long-eared rabbits seemed everywhere. Father had two black dogs called greyhounds; they were very fast runners, and could soon pick up a rabbit, but when they chased an antelope it was quite different. One day an antelope had in some way been separated from the herd, and ran through the train. One of the dogs, Fleet by name, pursued the antelope, and the chase led across a level plain. The black dog, as he sped on with all his might, looked like a crane flying along the plain. We were all excited, for the dog was gaining on the antelope at every bound, and would no doubt soon overtake him. The dog thought so too, for when he was within a few yards of the antelope and expected in another bound or two to seize his prey, he gave a yelp, but that yelp seems to have been a fatal mistake, for that antelope, in a few seconds after that bark, was fifty yards away from the dog, and flying over the plain as if he had been shot out of a gun. He actually passed over several yards before we could see the dust rise behind him. The dog was so astounded that he stopped short, and after gazing at the antelope for a moment, no doubt amazed beyond expression, turned about and trotted back to the train. It was said that dog would never chase an antelope afterwards.

At another time, we were traveling over a level plain and on our right hand many miles away, were high mountain ridges, almost of uniform height, and almost or quite devoid of timber, stretching away southeasterly in the direction, as I have since been told, of Yellowstone Park. They said these were the Wind River Mountains. While we were traveling in sight of them there was a continuous and disagreeable wind blowing, which I in some way associated with the name of the mountains.

I cannot now locate the great sage plains, as we called them, but they were vast in extent and not well watered. In crossing them, at times we traveled until late at night to reach water, and a few times we had to camp without it. Those plains were thickly set with sagebrush and greasewood shrubs, growing nearly waist-high to a man, and as we had no wagon road to follow, we had to break a road through this shrubbery. It was hard service for the teams in the lead, so the strongest teams were put in the van, but these were changed everyday. Part of the time we followed a train of pack animals and horsemen.

One day, as the train was slowly tramping along over a wide plain, a party of horsemen appeared in our front about a mile from us, coming down a little hill toward us. A man of our party was riding a quarter of a mile in advance of the train when those horsemen came in sight, and he, supposing them to be a party of hostile Indians, came galloping back, lashing his horse with his hat, which he carried in his right hand, and shouting at the top of his voice, "Injuns! Injuns! Corral! Corral! Corral!" The corral was soon formed and all in readiness to do battle, but there was some excitement and confusion. I was then riding in the little red wagon with Mother, and I noticed she had a bright brass pistol in her hand. I did not know that she owned a pistol, and when I looked at her face, I thought she was a little pale but not scared. The party we thought were Indians soon came up to us. They were mountain men or trappers, so the train was soon on the march again.

One afternoon when the teams were tired and some of the oxen limping with sore feet, I found myself looking far away in the direction we were traveling, across a dreary sage plain that to every appearance extended to the end of the earth, and I got to wondering where we were trying to get to. I asked the question and was told "to Oregon." I did not learn any more yet I was satisfied, and I decided then and there not to ask that question any more, but to wait and not draw out an answer which afforded me no information. To me, "Oregon" was a word without meaning.

After traveling a long way over a vast level country almost without timber, we saw broken country and hills far off in the direction we were traveling. I heard it remarked that somewhere in the hilly country was the Sweetwater River. This was good news to me, for I fancied that when we got to that river I would have all the sweet water I could drink. When we came to the river, which was a small shallow stream flowing gently over yellow sands, I ran down to the water's edge, and resting on my hands, took a large mouthful, but was greatly disappointed for the water was quite ordinary, and surely was not sweet.

The color name of the next river that comes to mind interested me somewhat, too. I was anxious to see it. The name was Green River, but when we came to it the water was of a white crystal clearness, and not a dark green river, as I had expected to see it, running across the country like a broad green ribbon. It was small and easily forded.

It seems to me now that for several hundred miles of travel through this part of the country, there was scarcely anything so unusual in incident or accident or feature of the country as to make a lasting impression on my memory.

The Soda Springs seem to come next in the order of my recollection.[9] We camped very near one of these springs and nearly a quarter of a mile from Bear River, a rapid stream about the width of Green River. Here we met Fremont[10] with his party, and I thought their large tent, which was spread near our encampment, a very nice affair. There was a soda spring or pool between the camps, and Fremont's men were having a high time drinking soda water. They were so noisy that I suspected they had liquor mixed with the water.

[9]Soda Springs, located on the Bear River in Idaho, was inundated by the Soda Point Reservoir. It was a hot spring that erupted occasionally and produced carbonated water.

[10]John Charles Fremont was a distinguished cartographer and western explorer, military officer, and the first Republican candidate for the presidency of the United States.

John Charles Fremont
Courtesy Oregon Historical Society

Fremont had a cannon, the first one I had seen; a six-pounder, they said, and made of bright shining brass. It was resting on a low carriage, which was standing between our camp and Fremont's, and near the soda spring. I admired this cannon very much and examined it very closely several times. I discovered a touchhole near the breech, and looking in at the muzzle could see the ball, or thought I could. After Fremont's men had been drinking soda water from that spring, and enjoying it greatly for nearly a full day, one of our company fished out an enormous frog from the pool, almost as large as a young papoose, and falling to pieces with rottenness. Soon after this discovery, we noticed that the hilarity inside the Fremont tent suddenly ceased.

I thought Fremont was a very fine looking young man. In fact, all his party were pretty well dressed, and jolly fellows. I don't remember seeing Fremont at any place other than Soda Springs.

We probably remained at this camp a day or two. Several of the women took advantage of the opportunity offered by plenty of hot water here at the springs to wash a few things. While at this camp, some of our party visited the river, and found near the bank of the stream, a spouting soda spring. Like all the geysers, it threw up water convulsively. This spring would heave up about every three or four minutes. The mouth of this spring was at the top of a rim-like formation raised up about eight inches from the common level. This rim was composed of deposit from the water. The mouth was nearly a foot across, and nearly round. There were puffs of steam issuing from the mouth. Also eight or ten feet from the mouth there was a hole in the ground four or five inches across, and whenever the spring went into convulsions and commenced throwing up water, gusts of hot steam and spray would issue from this hole with a noise like that from the escape pipe of a boiler. This hole evidently connected with the spring. The boys seemed to regard it as of more interest than the spring. Some tried to keep it from puffing by closing it with dirt and with grass, but whenever the spasm came the caulking would be thrown out. One young man had a wool hat which he placed over the hole, and held there with his hands and knees planted firmly on the brim. This I suppose was generally regarded as a "corker," but when the puff came, the hat crown stretched for a moment and then burst at the top. This spring was called the Steamboat Spring[11] since it appeared to puff like a steamboat.

As we returned from this spring to our camp, we passed by a rock or some compact substance, standing up six or seven feet above the ground, of funnel shape, three feet across or more, and nearly the same at top and bottom. I think it was as hollow as a gun, and I saw there was a hole in one side. This

[11] It is also reported as sounding like a steam whistle. John C. Fremont says he named it the Steamboat Spring, but it probably had been called that by previous travelers.

was the "Bellowing Rock," for we were told that at one time it bellowed like a bull. How long since it had bellowed I did not learn, but I visited this, to me, inspiring rock twice while at our soda spring camp, and stood a long time near it, listening and thinking it might conclude to bellow again. I remember very little else about this part of the country, but it seems to me the face of the country was broken and in many places rocky. There were also some scrubby trees, probably red cedars and hard pine of stunted size, growing among the boulders.

After leaving the springs, we moved on to Fort Hall, but I can recall nothing about the trip.[12]

At Fort Hall we were probably in camp a day or two. Captain Grant was in command at the fort.[13] It was a Hudson's Bay trading post, and a resort for trappers, mountain men, Indians of probably the Shoshone or Snake tribes, and others. The fort was built of sun-dried bricks called "adobe." The walls

[12] Fort Hall, located on the Snake River near the mouth of the Portneuf in Idaho, was established in 1834 by Nathaniel Wyeth, a Boston ice merchant, who entered the fur trade to compete with both the Rocky Mountain Fur Company and the Hudson's Bay Company. Fort Hall was the first American owned fur trading post west of the Continental Divide. Financial problems forced Wyeth to sell it to the Hudson's Bay Company in 1837.

[13] Richard Grant devoted his life to the fur trade, first with the North West Company and later with Hudson's Bay, rising to be a chief factor. He assumed control of Fort Hall in 1842 and remained there until he took early retirement in 1851. He did not return to Canada but started ranching at Camp Loring, an abandoned army post. He died in 1862.

were solid on the outside except for portholes and a gate or two. There was a square court inside, and the houses opened facing this square on the four sides. I visited the people in the fort with Mother and other folks, and found women and children living there. They were very kind and sociable. I think the women living there were Indians or mixed bloods. I noticed some very pretty moccasins and other garments from deer and antelope skin, tanned and dressed. The garments were ornamented with needlework, beads, and porcupine quills of different colors, the moccasins having red and blue colored instep pieces. Those women wore bracelets of gold or brass on their wrists, broad rings of gold or brass on their fingers, and a profusion of bright colored, mostly red, ribbons on their garments. Those bright colors I thought were in beautiful contrast with the brown skin and glossy black hair of the women. Conversation between the visitors and these women and children was difficult, but by the use of signs and a few words, it was accomplished.

There had been no wagons beyond this fort, and I think it was the opinion of the people here that it would not be practicable to take them further; that we had better leave the wagons and resort to pack animals, but the emigrants, after a thorough investigation of the subject, determined to move on with the wagons.

Though there was no scarcity of wild game, there was a very large and fat ox slaughtered here by the

Fort Hall
as drawn by J. Goldsborough Bruff
Courtesy The Huntington Library

Inside View of Fort Hall in 1849
Courtesy Oregon Historical Society

emigrants. I don't know whether they had bought the ox from the people of the fort, or whether the people had made us a present of him. But he was slaughtered about one hundred yards from camp, and during the afternoon we boys were at the place where the ox had been killed and found the stomach, or paunch as we called it, lying there on the ground; the weather being warm, it was swollen to the size of a large barrel. The game we played there with the stomach of the ox was both original and uncanny, and I am sure we never played it afterwards, for it very nearly ended in a tragedy. The sport consisted of running and butting the head against the paunch and being bounced back, the recoil being in proportion to the force of contact. The sport was found to be very exciting and there grew up a rivalry between the boys as to who could butt the hardest. There was a boy by the name of Andy Baker who was much taller than I. He was slender, had a long neck, and his hair was cut very near to the scalp. This boy was ambitious to outdo all the others, and backed off so as to have a long run for it. He backed off much further than anyone had before, and then upon lowering his small head, charged the paunch at the top of his speed, and when within a couple of yards of the target, leaped up from the ground (the boys yelling, "Give her goss, Andy!") and came down like a pile driver against the paunch, but he did not bound back. We gathered around to see what the matter was, and discovered that Andy had thrust his head into the stomach, which had closed so tightly around his neck that he could not withdraw his head. We took hold of his legs and pulled him out, but the joke was on Andy, and "Give her goss, Andy" was a favorite joke among the boys for a long time.

Many years after we had settled in Oregon, he became a candidate for sheriff of Yamhill County, and I went down from Polk County and told this adventure of his on the plains. Andy was elected.

And now I recall to mind a long march across a dry and level plain, thickly set with sagebrush and greasewood, through which the breaking of a road was very heavy work for the now somewhat jaded teams; and the boys walking behind the wagons were frequently under the painful necessity of sitting down and pulling the thorns of the prickly pear out of their toes. This evening we traveled until late at night, probably ten o'clock, and camped as near as we could get to the Snake River, for the riverbed was in a groove cut more than a quarter of a mile deep in the plain. In the morning we could see the river from our camp, so far down that it looked like a small stream. The slope down to the river was very steep, but there was bunch grass in abundance and some of our cattle were grazing on the slope and along the river. Some boys were rolling rocks down this slope into the river. They did not seem to consider the danger to the cattle below them, and were thrilling to the sport of seeing the

Richard Grant
Courtesy Oregon Historical Society

large stones rush and bound down the long and steep declivity and plunge with a tremendous splash into the water, sometimes throwing water twenty-five and thirty feet high. How long this sport had been going on, I had not noticed, not having been invited to take a hand, but it was going on when the train was ready to take up the line of march. Just at that time a boy known by the name of Wame Hembre had started a large stone which went with the velocity of a cannonball in the direction of a yearling calf grazing near the foot of the slope, and just as the rock struck the calf, Wame was heard calling it to get out of the way. Of course the calf was killed as dead as if it had been struck by a bolt of lightning.

We were now approaching Salmon Falls in the Snake River, and heard the roar of the waters a long time before we saw them.[14] The first sound that struck my ear seemed to jar the earth like a crash of thunder. As we approached, many Indians were seen, and long lines of something of a red color, which I thought were clothes hanging out to dry, attracted my attention; but as we came nearer I learned that those lines were salmon which the Indians were drying in the sun. The company made a halt here, whether for noon or overnight, I don't remember. Many Indians visited our camp, bringing fish, both fresh and dried, which they exchanged for

[14]Salmon Falls was located about 160 miles downriver from Fort Hall.

old clothes, and a number of them strutted around dressed in their newly acquired garments, seeming to enjoy their often absurd appearance as much as we did, for when we would laugh, they would laugh and jabber among themselves. They were almost naked, some of them quite so. When one would get a garment he would put it on at once. A naked Indian would put on a shirt and step around as though he thought himself in complete dress; then another seemed delighted with nothing but a vest; while yet another with only a hat on would grin and seem as pleased as if he were "dressed to kill." This was grand sport for us children, and the Indians did not seem to object to our fun at their expense. The fish which the Indians brought no doubt were very acceptable to the emigrants, as I do not remember having any before, except at Bear River, where the men caught an abundance of very large trout.

These Indians were Snakes and Shoshone, and our visit with them had been pleasant and entertaining. But when getting away from this place we had a narrow escape. We had to follow the "Devil's Backbone," and it may have been a mile or more. It is a very narrow ridge with a gorge a thousand feet deep on the left hand and a sheer precipice on the right down to the Snake River, which looked as though it might be a mile or more away. Indeed, it was so far away that it looked like a ribbon not more than four inches wide. The danger was so great that no one rode in the wagons. As I walked behind a wagon, I would often look into the gorge on the left and then down to the river on the right, and as I remember it now, at many places there was not a foot to spare for the wagon wheels between the bottomless gorge on the left and the precipice down to the river on the right. The Bible says:

"Strait is the gate, and narrow is the way, which leadeth unto life. But wide is the gate, and broad is the way, that leadeth to destruction, and many there be which go in thereat."

But this Devil's Backbone was worse than either, for it was both narrow and crooked, and it was hard to tell what it might lead to. But we passed it in safety, and soon again were slowly tramping along over a broad and level expanse of sagebrush and greasewood.

One afternoon somewhere in that level country, when there were only Father's three wagons in the party—I think there had been a dispersion and confusion of tongues soon after passing the Devil's Backbone, and Father had pulled out, preferring to face the dangers of the wilderness alone, to civil warfare—we were aware that horsemen were coming toward us from an easterly direction. When we first saw them, the ponies looked no larger than grasshoppers, and there were only a few of them visible, but directly more appeared in sight, and the numbers continued to increase until the plain was swarming with them. They approached us at a gallop and

gathered into a hoard as they came nearer. They
did not whoop nor gesticulate as they approached;
they were not painted and had no weapons in their
hands. They did not slacken their pace until they
had completely surrounded our little party. They
were in such great numbers and crowded so closely
about the wagons and teams that we could not move
on. But they were very friendly and we learned in
some way that they were visiting us to see white
women and children, for they had never seen any
before. They peered into all the wagons from the
ends and both sides, and caught hold of the wagon
covers on the sides and raised them so they could
look in. There was a host of them around the wagon I was in, lifting the sides of the cover and peep-
ing in at Mother and us children. We were not
afraid of them for they all looked pleasant and
much interested. Some were squaws, riding astride
of saddles which had very high horns before and
behind. The women's saddles were decorated with
large headed brass tacks, and long flowing fringes.
Some of the squaws had infants encased in sacks
made of a dressed hide of some kind, with a board
attached so as to fit on and support the back of the
child. They looked like cocoons of some kinds of
insects and were swinging from the front horn of
the saddle like a holster pistol. There was nothing
to be seen of the papoose but its little, round, chub-
by face. While they were crowding about our wagon, a squaw, with a youngster hanging to her saddle

bow, was trying to get a peep into the wagon when a horseman swung his horse against the child, which commenced crying. This drew forth such a volley of Snake lingo that the offender appeared very suddenly to lose all interest in the show and got away from there in a hurry. Besides a desire to see women and children, it seems they wanted tobacco, which was given in small quantities to a few, who appeared to be big Snakes. We were not detained by them more than thirty minutes, I should think. Finally they rode away and we traveled on.

Our trail most surely took us through the Rocky Mountains, but when or where I am not able to say. I do not remember climbing mountains until we came to the Blue Mountains. Several times before reaching Fort Boise[15] I saw mountains at a distance, and at one place I saw what might have been a mountain range quite near the line of our route. A mountain almost without a tree, nearby and on our left hand, seemed to ascend to the clouds and its slope to be within a few degrees of perpendicular. The sides in many places were broken into crags, at other places, smooth. In some places were enormous gorges and canyons, dividing the immense walls and peaks. These may have been the Rocky Mountains, but I do not remember ever traveling

[15]This post, built in 1839 by the Hudson's Bay Company to compete with Wyeth's Fort Hall, was located at the mouth of the Boise River and the Snake River, sixty miles from the current city of Boise, Idaho. It was destroyed by a flood in 1853.

through any canyon here, or over any very steep or rough country. I think we must have reached the divide or backbone of the Rocky Mountains by a very gradual ascent of hundreds of miles, seeming to be generally level, but gradually rising. However, the descent was probably not so regular, for I remember going down several steep and long hills.

It must have been in this part of the country that a grizzly bear was killed, also an animal they said was a mountain sheep. I did not see the carcass of the bear, but I ate of the meat and I did not like it for it seemed to be almost all fat and its strong flavor was new and unpleasant to my taste. The carcass of the mountain sheep was brought into camp and I saw the animal myself, but I was disappointed in its appearance for I could not recognize it as a sheep. The horns were like those of the ibex, yet it was not covered with wool, but hair. However, the flesh when cooked was about as good as the best of venison.

Upon our arrival at the Boise River, we were again with a considerable company. The river we found to be about a hundred yards wide, quite rapid, and too deep to ford, though the banks were low and not precipitous. How the crossing of the river was handled I do not remember, but it must have been difficult and very dangerous for one man was drowned. When we had crossed the river, we were at Fort Boise, which was a Hudson's Bay post. It was most probably while camping near this fort that we

Fort Boise on the Snake River
Courtesy Oregon Historical Society

children were much surprised and delighted to find beads, generally small and white in color, in the ant hills. We picked up many of them, but while searching for more, we soon came to a place where the ground was white with them, and looking up discovered that we were under a broad platform raised on posts seven or eight feet high, and that the platform above our heads was thickly strewn with the decayed corpses of dead Indians. We knew then where these beads came from. Many of the bodies were yet rolled up in blankets and robes. Some had been torn into fragments by carrion crows and other scavenger birds, and skulls and other bony parts of the body lay bleaching in the sun; a few had fallen to the ground. After this ghastly find we did not tarry long for the shades of evening were quickly creeping along the ground and the Bannock, Shoshone, Crow, or Blackfeet spooks may have been already congregating to hold their nightly "wake" at this Golgotha. We fled to camp with the jackrabbit speed of barefoot, backwoods children to report our strange discovery and exhibit our beads. We were greatly disappointed that our report did not create a sensation in camp and decidedly grieved that the "old folks" did not admire our beads, but reproved us for having them and made us throw them away. I don't remember another time on the plains when I thought the parents as unreasonable as on this occasion about the beads. It was so upsetting to me that I did not sleep well that night, and several times

I almost made up my mind to run away and go home. I knew the place where I had thrown the beads, and had not given up hope of being allowed to get them again. For in a case when Mother had all the facts before her and fairly tried the case on its merits, I regarded her judgment as very nearly infallible. So I concluded that in the morning I would very easily convince her that she had made a mistake by showing her that as the Indians who owned the beads were dead, they would have no use for them any more, and that so far as the ants were concerned, there were plenty left for them. But as the morning came, probably some new adventure diverted my thoughts from the things of the day before for I have no further recollection of the beads.

Our family had a very strong wagon we called the meat wagon. It was heavily laden with provisions, the bulk being flour and bacon. It was drawn by a team of two yoke of oxen, driven at the time I now speak of by a man by the name of George Beale, a dark-skinned, black-eyed young man, the son of a slave owner in Missouri. Mother told me not to ride in this wagon, but one day while we were traveling through this part of the country, I was walking, as I frequently did, and climbed into this wagon and up beside the driver on the top of a skin covered trunk, which was placed against the foregate of the wagon bed. The lid of the trunk was quite slippery and rose several inches above the foregate. The day was warm and the oxen were walking slowly. George

Beale was drowsy and in some way I got hold of the ox whip, which had a stock about five feet long, and a lash six or seven feet long. Feeling now the importance of my position as teamster, I swung the whip around and then forward with all my strength to make it pop over the oxen's backs. But the effort to jerk it back pulled me forward and I slid off the trunk, over the foregate of the wagon, and fell down between the oxen's heels, and the front wheels of the wagon, one of which ran over the small of my back. I tried to escape the hind wheel, but it rolled over my legs. I now saw the team that was behind and only a few feet away approaching me, and made several vain attempts to get onto my feet. The man driving this team was walking and, upon seeing me, stepped quickly forward, picked me up, and put me into a wagon. I am not now able to say whether he put me into his wagon or the one I had fallen out of. I was badly hurt and soon became very thirsty and felt very uncomfortable. It was in the afternoon, and I waited anxiously for the train to go into camp. But I think I suffered more mental than physical pain for I had disobeyed Mother and got hurt by it, and I feared that I was so badly hurt that I would not be able to conceal the fact, and Mother would find out all about the accident. The disobedience did not seem to trouble me much until the danger of exposure stared me in the face, and this is not saying much for my honesty.

The train went into camp soon after sunset, and

the place was fresh and grassy. The wagon I was in seems to have been one of the hindmost for several wagons were already there and people were busy at their evening camp chores when we arrived. I saw Mother on her knees, sorting various things from some baggage that had been taken out of the wagon. She was only a few yards from where our wagon stopped, and I kept an eye on her, resolving at the same time to behave myself in such a way that she would not suspect that anything unusual had happened to me in consequence of my disobedience, which probably she was already aware of. As soon as the driver had taken the team from the wagon, he lifted me out and put me down by a forewheel, to which I caught for support, as I discovered that I could not stand alone. Mother now looked over at me, but I straightened up and made a great effort to appear in fair condition as usual. When she took her eyes off me, I caught hold of the front of the wagon box and thus supporting myself, managed to reach the wagon tongue and straighten up just as Mother looked at me again. My last desperate effort was to walk along the wagon tongue, having it for a support. But my scheme failed, for at that moment Mother rose quickly to her feet and after uttering a cry of alarm, caught me in her arms. Oblivion claimed the remainder of this day, this accident, and this encampment because my memory fails to recall another thought or impression.

Having found it convenient to mention George

Beale in my story, I will say further of him that he continued to Oregon, but I do not remember seeing him after the day I had the misfortune to supercede him as teamster of the meat wagon. However, about twenty-five years after arriving in Oregon, George Beale and a confederate named Baker (not Andy) were convicted of the murder of an old man by the name of Delaney, who crossed the plains in 1843. The murder was committed for money, and Beale and Baker were hanged for the crime in Salem, Oregon. This man Beale taught a little school near our house in Missouri when I was about four years old, and had struck me with a switch because I could not distinguish between the letters "B," "P," "Q," and "D." When he struck me, I was very much frightened and grabbed the stick, broke it, then jumped out the door, ran home, and never returned to that school. This was the only time I was ever struck in school and I don't remember that I was ever insulted in school by a teacher but this one time. After George Beale was hanged, I sometimes stated that the only teacher that ever dared to switch me was hanged. My children, when they were attending school, heard me say this, and one day while we were living in Salem, one of my little boys spoke up and said, "Pa, why don't they hang my teacher; she struck me today with a ruler, and you said that the teacher that struck you was hung?"

After we descended a steep grade into Grande Ronde Valley so late in the evening that we had no view of the valley, we camped near a small river. Early the next morning, looking in a northerly direction several miles away, we could see a column of steam rising from the ground like a white cloud. This they said was from a hot spring. I thought this was quite a good country, though it was then inhabited only by Indians.

Several things about the crossing of the Blue Mountains I remember quite well. The timber had to be cut and removed to make a way for the wagons. The trees were cut just near enough to the ground to allow the wagons to pass over the stumps, and the road through the forest was only cleared out wide enough for a wagon to pass along. I think we made one camp in the mountains and probably it was at this camp that the men so admired the abundance of fine timber. The people of this emigration even talked about the possibility of a railroad being built across the plains, and yet there were few of the party that had actual knowledge of what a railroad was. John East, who I have mentioned in connection with the Missouri line, pointed to a very fine grove of fir or pine timber and remarked that when they got to building the railroad he wanted the contract of making the rails, and said he, "I will split the rails right there in that grove."

In passing across these mountains, we were overtaken by a heavy snowstorm which made the passage very dismal. I remember wading through mud and snow, and suffering from the cold and wet. But the camp on the Umatilla was a pleasant place; this we soon reached after passing the mountains. The Umatilla was a small stream with sandy banks and bottom. The stream was lined with quaking aspens and black hawthorns. I distinctly remember noticing the quaking asp trees here for the first time. A campfire on the bank of the creek was burning near one of these trees and as the sparks and smoke went up, the great wriggling among the leaves attracted my attention as I lay on my back looking up into its foliage, and I asked someone the name of the tree. None of the trees were large, but they were shapely like orchard trees and afforded a pleasant shade.

The fruit of the black haw was in demand for we had not had any berries for a long time. They were black and near the size of buckshot with a single seed, very sweet and otherwise pleasant to the taste. It was a thorny tree and grew ten, fifteen, twenty, and even twenty-five feet high. Our party ate large quantities of this fruit. It was told for a fact in camp that a woman died during the night we stayed there from the effects of a gorge of black haws. I ate about all I could get my hands on but experienced no bad results—they were ripe and mellow.

The Indians in this country were the Kiuse (Cayuse), who had many horses and some cattle, however the grass was scarce. The Kiuse were quite friendly and even sociable and brought vegetables from their gardens to trade for clothes and trinkets, scraps of iron, and ammunition, when available. There were pumpkins and potatoes; the former I call to mind with fond remembrance. Naturally, there was no set price on anything; they would take all they could get. One Indian wanted much more. He had a yellow pumpkin not larger than a man's head, which first one and then another made a bid for, until the Indian's head was completely turned as to the value of his vegetable. After refusing a new suit of clothes worth twenty-five dollars, he went away with the pumpkin under his arm. Many old-timers will remember the saying, "Just like the Indian with his pumpkin," even unto this day.

On account of the lateness of the season—we already had a snowstorm—and the scarcity of feed, we probably did not stop at this place more than one night. Journeying from our camp on the Umatilla, we passed across what seemed to be a kind of sandy desert with at times rocky ground, sagebrush, greasewood, and occasionally a few willows.

We passed Whitman's Mission (some called it a station)[16] situated in such a country as last above described. There was nothing cheerful nor inviting about this place; a low and quite modest looking house or two, the doctor in the yard and one or two

[16]Dr. Marcus Whitman and his wife Narcissa established this mission among the Indians in 1836. Emigrants used it as a rest site in the 1840s. The mission was attacked by Indians on November 29, 1847, the Whitmans and others were killed, and a large number of women and children were taken captive. They were eventually ransomed by Peter Skene Ogden, an agent of the Hudson's Bay Company.

Dr. Marcus Whitman

The Whitman Mission
Courtesy Oregon Historical Society

other persons about the premises, are about all I re-member of this historic place where the slaughter was to be three years later. I think we did not halt here but just passed along by the place. Some years after reaching the Willamette Valley where the Applegate families settled, I heard this same place, Whitman's Mission, or station, called Wailatpu, or saw it printed Wailatpoo.

After passing Whitman's, the aspect of the country-side continued about the same to the Columbia River. Drifts and hummocks of dry sand, sagebrush occasionally, and everything dry, dusty, and dreary all the time. Nearby on the Columbia was another Hudson's Bay post, Fort Walla Walla.[17] It was built mainly of sun-dried bricks, and the plan was about the same as the Hudson's Bay forts we had passed on our journey.

[17]Fort Walla Walla, originally Fort Nez Perce, was established in 1818 by the North West Company, the Hudson's Bay Company's Canadian competitor until the two companies were forced to merge.

II

Down the Columbia to the Willamette

O UR TRAIN which arrived here at this time was a
detachment of the company which came out to
Oregon this season and numbered ten families and
probably twenty wagons. The entire emigration of
1843 has been computed at about a thousand souls.
This detachment included the three Applegate families; families of three brothers, Charles, Lindsay
and Jesse. I call to mind also the names of Alexander McClellan, Wm. Wilson, Wm. Doke, Robert
Smith, Benjamin Williams, Mr. Clyman, John G.
Baker, Elijah Millican, Thomas Naylor, Almoran
Hill, Miles Carey, and Daniel Holman.

Besides the oxen of the teams, there was a small
herd of stock cattle. Jesse Applegate had probably
thirty head and others had a few cows and calves.
There were also a few horses. This train of wagons
corralled for the last time about one hundred yards,
so it appears to me, up the river from the fort and
very near where the Walla Walla River flows into
the Columbia.

A train of wagons with their once white, now
torn, grease and dust stained covers, parked on the
bank of the Columbia River, was a novel spectacle.
Such had never been seen there before. The faithful

oxen, now sore-necked, sore-footed, and jaded, which had marched week after week, and month after month, drawing those wagons with their loads from the Missouri River to the Columbia, had done their task, and were unhitched for the last time. I hope all recovered from their fatigue and lived to enjoy a long rest on the banks, "Where rolls the Oregon and hears no sound save his own dashing."

Mr. McKinlay[1] was in charge of the post of Walla Walla, and was very kind and accommodating to the emigrants. There were many Indians around: bucks, squaws, and papooses, and these were often visitors at our camp. Some of the bucks talked English fairly well, and all were quite adept at sign language. There had been mission establishments at this place, both Catholic and Protestant, and this trading post had been for several years in this part of the country, and so the Indians were to some extent accustomed to modify their manners and dress. They were not naked like some Indians we had been among before.

A young Indian whose English name I think was Ellis, and whose dress was like that of a white man, had his hair shingled or cut short, and was very civilized in his manners. It was said he had been sent East to school when a boy and was well educated. I believe he was a son of the high chief of the Nez

[1]This is a reference to Archibald McKinlay who, after he retired from the Hudson's Bay Company, became a leading sheep rancher.

Fort Walla Walla about 1843
from a painting by John Mix Stanley
Courtesy Oregon Historical Society

Perce tribe, and would succeed his father. He appeared to realize the fact that he was an important man, and conversed fluently in English with our best talkers.

The Indian tribal names were Cayuse, Nez Perce, and Walla Walla, and we had many visitors from all these tribes. I think there was no hostile feeling among these people against us, but some of the emigrants were prejudiced against Indians of whatever kind, and were annoyed by the familiarity assumed by them in their dealings with whites. This probably came near leading to very serious consequences. I believe the boys were more or less tinctured with this prejudice, and besides, we did not realize the fact that to arouse a spirit of vengeance among this horde of barbarians, who could muster a thousand painted warriors on any night, meant certain destruction to every man, woman, and child in our little party.

The first unpleasantness was between us white boys and the Indian boys. One day we were trading nails and scraps of iron of all kinds to the Indian boys for a root they called *yampa*—a small root half an inch thick, or less, and two or three times as long as thick—which, when dried, was almost as white as chalk, and easily ground between the teeth. Of the parsnip family, it is swect and rich and very pleasant to the taste. This barter was going on atop the sand drifts some three feet above the common level, and was proceeding quite sociably. All of us were

munching *yampa* with great humor and filling our
pockets with the surplus roots. But some of the
boys did not have pockets (some mothers will not
make pockets in their boys' trousers because if boys
have pockets they fill them so full of rocks, strings,
tops, nails, dead beetles, dried fish worms, chewing
wax, toy pistols, crulls, doughnuts, fishing tackle,
bullets, buttons, jews-harps, etc., that the strain on
the suspenders often becomes too great), and were
holding the surplus roots in one hand up against
the stomach. When one's hand was full of *yampa*,
they would spill and fall to the ground, and this
much I know to be true. I saw some fall and picked
them up and put them into my pockets for I did not
want such valuable property to "waste its sweetness
on the desert air." I saw other boys, both white and
Indian, picking up something, and then I saw an
Indian picking himself up.

It appeared from the official report of this battle
afterwards that the Indian who was picking himself
up had stooped down to pick up a *yampa*, when
one of our boys attacked him in the rear with his
foot, and the young warrior toppled over on his
head. A race war broke out instantly and the battle
soon became general. Cries of vengeance arose from
the whites and yells of defiance from the reds. It
was now a hand-to-hand fight for we were all mixed
up together when the battle began. How we became
separated I never knew, but presently we were some
distance from the enemy and throwing pebbles

about the size of black walnuts and Irish potatoes at
them. They returned the fire with arrows and pebbles. The arrows at first alarmed us a little, and to
admit the truth, I believe that if the Indians had
charged us just then, we would have been routed,
but we very soon discovered that we could see the
arrows approaching and dodge them, as the range
was not very close. As we pressed forward towards
the enemy, throwing finger stones with great fury
and dangerous precision, they fell back to the shelter of the potato house. Since we had no field artil-
lery heavy enough to batter down a sand hill, we
charged over and around the ends of the potato
house, taking on the enemy in front and on both
flanks. This assault was made at a speed of about
four double quicks, and was so impetuous as to be
irresistible. The enemy now became demoralized
and fled into the fort through an open gate. But we
were not far behind and entering the courtyard of
the fort, gathered up more dangerous weapons and
proceeded to slay and spare not. We found a pile of
pack saddles, and one of the boys armed himself
with a cinch, with which he attacked an Indian,
striking him on the head with the iron ring on one
end of the cinch, and another Indian boy was cut
on the head by some kind of a projectile, put in
motion by the sinewy arm of one of our boys. But
this ridiculous affair was not allowed to proceed
further for McKinlay, the commander of the fort, in
some way, very suddenly pacified us and sent us to

our corral. Our boys began the fight, as before stated, but it was claimed that the Indians were picking up the *yampa* that fell to the ground and selling it to us again. Whatever the true situation, relations between us and the Indian boys became so strained by this affair that we got no more roots.

The boys also had a skirmish with a young buck who was mounted on a pony. This was on a sand flat some distance from the camp, and I only remember that the Indian came galloping his pony towards us with his spear poised in his hand and pointed towards us; that we gave him and his pony a volley of finger stones; that he threw the spear in our direction and it stuck fast in the sand. I also remember that he got away from there as fast as his pony could carry him and left his spear behind.

After the battles of the "tater-house" and atop the sand flat had been victories for the kids, we noticed that the Indians visiting our camp were sulking and not talkative. One evening after the campfires had been burning some time, and it was fairly dark, Indians began to drop in singly or by twos, with a noiseless tread peculiar to such people. So snakelike was their approach that a big Indian with a blanket drawn around him would be seen standing or squatting near the fire before his approach had been noticed by us. After a while, there were a half dozen or more of them about the campfires and each one had his blanket over his shoulders and it completely enveloped his body. I don't know that this alarmed the whites or caused them to suspect danger, but the big bucks were sometimes standing and squatting in the way of people about the fires, and were indifferent to the fact.

One of our young men, who did not like Indians, gave a buck a push to get him out of his way, and when the Indian resisted, seized a brand from the fire and struck him a severe blow with it on the shoulders. I heard the blow and saw the sparks fly. The blow was probably aimed at the Indian's head, but he ducked and thereby saved his cranium. This rather rough affair, coming so unexpectedly, created some excitement in camp for a moment, but it was soon over, for a few of our party caught the young man, who was now fairly on the warpath, with his "brand snatched from the burning," and pacified him. The chances are that had not this been done promptly, there would have been a sanguinary battle fought then and there, for there were probably many Indians skulking near our corral, prepared for mischief and only waiting for a signal from the Indians in camp, who were spies and had weapons under their blankets. By the time the trouble arose in camp, I think the spies had discovered that our men were on the alert and prepared for anything the redskins wanted, and having become satisfied of this, they did not wish to precipitate a fight, so were willing to drop the matter as it was.

Probably this scrimmage at the campfire between the white man and Indian did not much alarm me for soon after quiet was restored, I became drowsy, went to bed, and went to sleep listening to a monotonous song and grunt accompanied by a tapping noise on the spoke of a wagon wheel. Years afterwards I heard the same song and noise made by Indians gambling.

The following day, the commander of the fort, McKinlay, visited our camp and remained quite a while. I understood afterwards that he invited, or rather advised, us to sleep in the fort as the Indians were not well disposed toward us. I can remember sleeping in the fort, and think it probable that the women and children retired to the fort during those nights when the men guarded the corral.

During the time we remained at Walla Walla, probably two weeks, the men were busy sawing lumber and building small boats. They called them skiffs and one of average size would carry a family of eight or ten persons. The lumber was sawed by hand with a pitsaw or whipsaw from timber that had drifted down to that place when the river was very high. To carry out the plan of descending the Columbia River to the Willamette country in those small boats, it was, of course, necessary to leave the wagons and cattle behind. The cattle and horses were branded with a Hudson's Bay Company's brand, "H.B." and the property was understood to be under the protection of that company.

I well remember our start down the river, and how I enjoyed riding in the boat, the movement of which was like a grapevine swing. Shoving out from the Walla Walla canoe landing about the first of November, our little fleet of boats began the voyage down the great "River of the West." Whirlpools looking like deep basins in the river, the lapping, splashing, and rolling of waves crested with foam sometimes when the wind was strong alarmed me for a day or two at the start. But I soon recovered from this childish fear, and as I learned that the motion of the boat became more lively and gyratory, rocking from side to side, leaping from wave to wave, or slipping down into a trough and then mounting with perfect ease to the crest of a wave, dashing the spray into our faces when we were in rough water, the sound of rapids and the sight of foam and whitecaps ahead brought only pleasant anticipation. Quite often, when the current was strong, the men would rest on their oars and allow the boats to be swept along by the current.

Children left to themselves and not alarmed by those they look to for protection do not anticipate danger; as a rule they do not borrow trouble. "Sufficient unto the day is the evil thereof," is their motto, and so when not goaded with hunger, yanked up with colic, or tortured by a stone bruise or sore toe, a boy on pleasant autumn days, who had been traveling all summer barefoot through the desert sands, through sagebrush, greasewood, and cactus, and had been often broken of his rest, mayhap being tortured by prickly pears between his toes, now haply being rocked as in a cradle at his mother's knee, might peradventure be overcome with drowsiness, and while dreaming of unromantic things, butter and bread for instance, pass in total ignorance of the presence of all that grand panorama-like scenery along the river, which so many clever tourists have admitted they were not able to describe. But I was aware of some ugly cliffs of rock, black and forbidding in appearance, close to the river banks, some high and some not so high, some rough, barren, and precipitous, while others were thickly set with timber and brush. Neither did the grown up people seem to be delighted with the scenery along the river. At least I never heard any expressions of admiration. A jaded emigrant, however, might gaze upon the face of a precipice a thousand feet high, with a crack extending from top to bottom, without being struck dumb with awe and admiration, or pass by a contemptible Indian and never realize that he had met one of Fenimore Cooper's noble red men.[2]

Now of nights we encamped on the bank of the river, sometimes on the north, and sometimes on the south side. I remember especially a camp we made on the south shore. There was a very narrow strip of sand and rock almost level, between the river and a high bluff, with a high mountain rising above it. Here we were, I well remember, with this

[2]This is James Fenimore Cooper, the American author who wrote *The Last of the Mohicans* and who popularized the idea of the noble savage in his fiction.

precipitous bluff and lofty mountain at our back and the broad river before us. We must have landed here quite early in the afternoon for the unusual occurrence which underscored this camping place on memory's tablet took place before the sun was low. Perhaps it may have been a nooning place. Now at a venture I will say that our people, for frontiersmen and women of those days, were unusually free from superstitious whims. I had never seen a horseshoe over the door; they never spoke of looking at a hog's melt for a forecast of the weather, did not believe in lucky or unlucky days, nor that dropping the dishrag was a sign that the family would have company at the house. But my Mother, meaning to make sport of any superstitious notions, no doubt, sometimes spoke of a belief among the people that seeing the new moon over the right shoulder was an omen of good luck, and to be candid I must admit that when I know the new moon is out, I sometimes put myself to a little trouble to get first sight of it over my right shoulder. That indicates a trace of superstition. Ghost stories, stories of haunted houses, of goblins, of witches and fairies, were current among the people in those days, but were not told as truths by our folks.

The unusual occurrence referred to was this. Although we were now several days on our voyage down the river, I had not heard of anyone complain of hardships or express fear of hardships or dangers to be encountered, and for my part I had come to feel as safe on the water as on land. But at this camp, I heard remarks that renewed my apprehensions of danger. There was a driftwood campfire burning and the womenfolks were around it doing the kitchen work and talking. I do not remember what they said except that my Aunt Cynthia, Uncle Jesse Applegate's wife, said, "There is going to be a death in the family," or something similar. She was standing and pointing upward and added, "See that raven flying over the camp?" I was lying upon the sand and, hearing the remark, looked up and saw a blackbird, a raven or crow, flying about one hundred feet above us and going in the direction of the river. Now this thing of reading the future from the flight of birds was then new to me, and as my aunt's countenance, gesture, and tone of voice, bespoke alarm and distress, the event made a lasting impression upon my mind. And yet the prediction must have been passed over lightly for when the calamity overtook us a few days after, I never thought of the omen and did not hear anyone speak of it.

Occasionally, we saw Indians on the river in canoes. Each canoe was wrought of a single log cut from a pine, cedar or fir tree, and excavated mostly by burning, but the finishing work was done with edge tools, originally of stone and bone perhaps, but now of iron and steel. The canoes I saw here on the upper river were shapely and neatly finished, but quite plain in appearance, and generally large enough for only two or three persons. One day, however, a large canoe carrying six or seven natives shot out of a little cove on the north shore, and passing across our bow slowed up, while the man in the bow of the craft, lifting his hand towards his mouth, spoke and said, "Smoke six!" which literally translated is "Tobacco, friend!"

The spokesman was a large, stout man with more black in his skin than a red man and an immense shock of grizzly, almost curly hair, which grew down to his ears and to within an inch of his nose, making his head seem unnaturally large. Some of our party gave them a little tobacco and they passed on. Now, who could this shock-headed heathen be? They said he was the son of a Negro man[3] who came to the coast with Lewis and Clark's expedition as cook, about forty years before the time of which I am speaking, and who, one might surmise, because of his black skin, woolly head, large proportions, thick lips,

> *"And lusty beauty*
> *Such as none*
> *Might safely dare*
> *To look upon,"*

was so petted by the squaws that he left the expedition in the Walla Walla country, and remained with the native daughters.

[3] His father was York, the slave of William Clark who with Meriwether Lewis were the first Americans to lead an overland exploration from Missouri to the Pacific Ocean.

I was now wide awake for I had expected to see something grand when we got in sight of Mount Hood. When we had reached a point on the river where they said we would get a first sight of it, I was on the lookout, but although I was scanning the sky in the direction where it was supposed to be, I did not see it. Finally, someone said to me, "What are you looking for away up there?"

"Mount Hood," said I.

"Well, it ain't up in the sky," someone said.

Now, I had never seen a snowpeak but had seen pictures of them and had been told they were very high, so I was looking for a kind of obelisk-shaped thing, towering up into the heavens almost as high as the moon, but upon this remark I began to look more towards the earth. I saw the tops of ordinary, forest-clad mountains, and looking again yet lower and not high above the tops of fir trees skirting the south side of the river, I discovered what appeared to be a mere hill. It looked so low, with a dome or rather hood-shaped top as white as a lump of chalk. And this appeared to stand on an immense mass of snow as wide across as the biggest cornfield I had ever seen. The mountain appeared to be only a few miles away, and yet the wide expanse of snow could frequently be seen shining through gaps between the hills. What I saw seemed to prove the point that Mount Hood was, after all, only a snow covered hill. How did I account for that hill being always snowclad, while the high mountains nearby were not? Well, I didn't account for it at all. It might be I never thought of that, or it may be I thought it was God's white throne or footstool, or that it was a miracle God had provided to show men His contempt for the Laws of Nature. Remember now, I was looking at this scenery through the inexperienced eye of a seven-year-old. The realization of what we see depends very much on what we already know. Of course, I was yet a novice in perspective. I saw as a child and my understanding was at fault.

We had an Indian pilot, probably selected by McKinlay at Fort Walla Walla, although I do not positively remember noticing the pilot before we entered the rapids we were now approaching. At the head of those rapids the river bears from a west course a little northerly, making a very gradual curve. As we approached this bend, I could hear the sound of rapids, and presently the boat began to rise and fall and rock from side to side. When we began to make the turn, I could see breakers ahead extending in broken lines across the river, and the boat began to sweep along at a rapid rate. The pilot squatted low in the bow. An old, red handkerchief was tied around his head and his long black hair hung down his back. Now there were breakers on the right and on the left, and occasionally foam-crested waves swept across our bow. The motion of the boat had never been so excitingly smooth before. It was an exaggeration of the cradle and grapevine swing combined. I began to conclude this was no ordinary rapid, but felt reassured when I noticed that the older people sat quietly in their places and betrayed no sign of fear. Rocked on the heaving bosom of the great river, and lulled by the medley of sounds, the two babies had fallen asleep in their mothers' arms. Our boat now was about twenty yards from the right hand shore, and when looking across the river I saw a smaller boat about opposite to us near the south bank. The persons in this boat were Alexander McClellan, a man about seventy years old, William Parker, probably twenty-one, and William Doke, about the same age, and three boys: Elisha Applegate, age about eleven, and Warren and Edward Applegate, each about nine years old. This boat now near the south shore, it would seem, should have followed our boat as the pilot was with us, and this was a dangerous part of the river. But there was little time to consider mistakes or to be troubled about what might be the consequences for presently there was a wail of anguish, a shriek, and a scene of confusion in our boat that no language can describe. The boat we were watching disappeared and we saw the men and boys struggling in the water. Father and Uncle Jesse, seeing their children drowning, were seized with frenzy, and dropping their oars sprang up from their seats and were about to leap from the boat to make a desperate attempt to swim to them, when Mother and Aunt Cynthia, in voices that were distinctly heard above the roar of the rushing waters, by commands and entreaties brought them to a realization of our own perilous situation, and the madness of an attempt to reach the other side of the river by swimming. This was sixty-seven years ago, and yet the words of that frantic appeal by the women, which saved our boat and two families from speedy and certain destruction, are fresh in my memory. They were, "Men, don't quit the oars. If you do we will all be lost." The men returned to the oars just in time to avoid, by great exertion, a rock against which the current dashed with such fury that the foam and froth upon its apex was as white as milk. I sat on the right hand side of the boat and the rock was so near that I thought if we had not passed so quickly I might have put my hand upon it.

Having escaped the danger at hand, the next thought, no doubt, was to effect a landing at the earliest possible moment, but the shore was rockbound with a rise of several feet vertically and presenting a serried line of ragged points against which the rapid current fretted and frothed, and the waves, rearing their foam-flecked heads aloft, rushed to destruction like martial squadrons upon an invincible foe. Ah! That half-hour's experience, this scene so wild, so commotional, so fearful and exciting, had not death been there was worth a month of ordinary life.

Further down the river, however, there was a break in the line of the shore and here the boat was landed, the women and children going ashore. It has often been said that "Truth is stranger than fiction," and it is true that an author manufacturing a story will avoid what would appear to be absurd, but in telling a true story, facts must be stated regardless of appearances. This is a case in point for it is a fact that just as our boat touched the shore, Father grabbed his rifle from its place in the boat to shoot our Indian pilot, but he had disappeared; a fact which, due to the excitement of landing the boat I presume, he had not noticed. In fact it seemed that no one noted his disappearance or knew what had become of him; we never knew. A suspicion seems to have been aroused only a few minutes before our boat landed that our pilot meant treachery, intending to lead us into these rapids with the expectation that the whole party would be destroyed. If there was evidence to justify this suspicion, I never heard what it was and can only attribute it to the delirium of excessive grief and the natural inclination to blame someone for the great calamity. I presume the first impulse was to hold the pilot responsible and execute vengeance upon him, and, carried forward by the intense excitement, there was no time for reflection.

From the south shore of the river there was a level tract of ground running back to the hill probably fifty yards wide and extending along the river a considerable distance. Many Indians were seen there, a few mounted on ponies and some in canoes along the shore, and were seen to set out so as to gather in the bedding, clothes, and various pieces of furniture from the foundered boat. It was said the Indians did not make any attempt or show any desire to assist our people in the water. William Doke could not swim and had taken hold of a feather bedtick which carried him safely to the foot of the rapids, between which and what was called the main Dalles there was a short interval of quiet water. Here Mr. Doke floated clinging to the bedtick. The Indians passed by him in their canoes, and though he called for help, they did not offer any assistance. He was picked up by one of our boats as he was about to go into the second rapids. Now, the appearance of so many Indians at the time may have encouraged the suspicion of treachery against the pilot, but I learned afterwards that there was a large Indian town in that vicinity, so the appearance of many Indians was not significant. A fact favorable to the good faith of our pilot is that but one boat was lost and that if it had followed the pilot it would have been safe. It is my opinion, probably founded on the explanations of those who were saved, that those who had the management of the boat intended to follow in the track of the pilot boat, but at the time they entered the rapids, their boat was caught in a strong current bearing towards the south shore, and when they saw they were being swept away from the safe channel indicated by the pilot boat, were unable, on account of the intervening shoaly bed of the river, to pass across to that channel.

After going ashore, the men remained with the boat and the little party of women and children climbed up the river bank, which at this place was not steep and only a few yards high, to a narrow plateau which ran parallel to the river. From this place we had a good view of the river, but could not see anything of the foundered boat or of those who had been in it. An Indian footpath ran along this plateau and we followed it down the river, very slowly, all the time searching the river with eager eyes. Now and then one would stop and point to the river and say, "I see someone's head there," and then we would all bunch up and look for the object pointed at. But it was only the top of a rock occasionally exposed by the ebbing of the waters. Several times we were deluded in this way. Mother and Aunt Cynthia were weeping. While we were yet walking along the river bank, someone came and told us that Parker, Doke, and brother Elisha were safe, but that McClellan and the two boys, Warren and Edward, could not be found. Then we understood that Elisha had saved himself by swimming. No doubt the fact that Mother had always objected to the boys going swimming now flashed across her mind, and as the fact appeared that he had learned to swim by disobeying her orders, and had thereby saved his life, she felt a momentary pang of remorse, poor stricken soul, for she said, "I will never object to the boys going swimming anymore."

Looking from where we were, a person could get

but a very imperfect knowledge of the tragic scene on the other side of the river, but those who escaped said that as their boat was being swept along down the rapids, it was caught by one of those currents which, whirling in its course like a cyclone in the air, increases in velocity as the radius of the circle diminishes, until, with a roaring noise, it seems to sink, forming an open funnel-shaped vacuum in the water to the bottom of the river, often called a whirlpool. After being spun around for a few seconds, the boat was swallowed up in the roaring vortex. The boat came up presently and all the crew except Warren Applegate succeeded in getting into it, but very soon after it was caught by another whirlpool and swallowed up again, to be seen no more. The last time the boat went down, end foremost, the boy Elisha, as it descended, climbed to the upper end and leaped as far as he could, to avoid being taken down with the boat. Towards the south shore, some distance below where the boat went down, there stood a lava-rock island which rose table-like from five to ten feet above the water, very rough and broken in appearance, and in an area of about a quarter of an acre. This island rock was connected onto the south shore by a narrow causeway of rock, and the north side of the island had been hollow so that part of the river flowed into it.

When Elisha rose to the surface, he discovered that he had one foot thrust into a pocket of his coat and while extricating it, sank and rolled in the water until he was almost exhausted; but as soon as his feet were free he struck out boldly for the upper point or head of the rock island, avoiding the force of the waves by diving under them.

William Parker, soon after escaping from the whirlpool, took hold of a feather bedtick floating near him, and being a strong swimmer, guided it towards the head of the island. It chanced that Elisha overtook Parker when near the shore, and taking hold of the tick they both together succeeded in reaching the island from which they with great difficulty, being very weak, followed the narrow causeway of rock to the mainland.

The boy Warren was never seen nor heard of after the boat went down the first time. The old man McClellan was seen the last time trying to reach the head of the island where Parker and young Applegate were. He had placed the boy Edward on a couple of oars, and carrying him this way, was trying to reach the shore, but being hampered with a heavy coat and boots, falling a little short of the point he attempted to reach, the old man and boy disappeared under projecting cliffs and were seen no more. The brave old soldier could have saved himself by abandoning the boy, but this he would not do. Of the three persons drowned no body could be found, and the search had to be given up. The boat was never seen after it went down into the roaring throat of the second whirlpool.

WRECKED IN THE RAPIDS.

"*The Wonderful Escape of Young Elisha Applegate*"
lithograph from F. F. Victor's The River of the West
Courtesy Douglas County (Oregon) Museum

That afternoon a windstorm with cold rain burst upon the wretched and broken-hearted women and children while they yet lingered upon the bank of the river. We camped that night at the Perkins' Mission.[4] During the late evening a man from Peter Burnett's[5] camp came to ours and said that a little Negro girl was lost. She had been sent to the river where the boats were to get a bucket of water. The storm had continued and the boats on the beach were wildly rocked and tossed by the waves. Some thought the girl had entered one of the boats to dip up the water, and had been thrown into the river and drowned. Others said the girl had been taken by the Indians. She was never found.

The next dangerous part of the river we had to pass was The Dalles. At that place, the banks of the river approach to within a few yards of each other, and are faced with overhanging cliffs of volcanic stone as black as pot metal, between which the river pours with fearful swiftness, and the channel is not only narrow, but crooked also, making this part of the river dangerous to navigation by boats or canoes. I cannot describe the picture I have in mind of that part of the river except to say it must have

[4]The Rev. H.K.W. Perkins, a Methodist missionary, arrived in Oregon in 1837 by sea. His mission was at The Dalles.

[5]Peter H. Burnett was the first elected leader of the Applegate wagon train to Oregon. He served as Chief Justice of Oregon's provisional government in 1845 and later became governor of California.

looked like the place the old Hebrew Elohim fixed his eye upon when "His wrath waxed hot and he said 'Anathema Maranatha!'"

Passing The Dalles was spoken of as "shooting the rapids." Only enough men to handle each boat were detailed to take them through that crooked and narrow way. Two boats, I recall, were manned by two men each, the one known as the "big boat" was taken through by Charles Applegate and L. Clyman. Uncle Charles was an athlete and stood six feet in his stockings, and was a bold and strong swimmer. The other boat, not so large, was manned by Tom Naylor and Hiram Strait, and they started down the narrow channel some time before the big boat. This was done to avoid danger of a collision. On account of the winding course of the river, the boats were often not in sight of each other. And so it happened that while the small boat had slowed up and tacked to follow a curve in the shoreline, the big boat rounded a point only a few yards above it, and was bearing down upon it with the speed of a toboggan on ice. Now, at this critical moment, when a collision seemed certain, and the lives of four men were in jeopardy unless the course of the big boat could be changed, the pin which held Clyman's oar in place, gave way. Clyman, with that high courage and steady nerve that goes to make the hero, threw the beam of his oar in front of Uncle Charles' big, immovable knee, and with a single stroke changed the course of the big boat enough to avoid the other. I have heard Uncle Charles say, "When Naylor and Strait saw us coming at them, their faces were as white as if they were dead."

I did not witness those boats passing through the Devil's Gullet (Dalles), but recalled that we had passed over the Devil's Backbone on the Snake River, and now boats had gone through his gullet.

We were following a footpath which ran along the north bank, but could not often see the river. We saw only one boat passing down the channel. Following the path, we children came out of the woods into a small glade, perhaps a hundred feet above the river and about fifty yards from it. At this place, we found a stick fire almost burned out. Throwing the brands together we soon had a cheery blaze. From this location we saw probably a hundred yards of the river. A boat was gliding down the river with only one man in it, and he seemed to be standing. While following the path down the river, we came to a thicket of wild rosebushes. They bore a large crop of seedpods or berries, which were ripe and red, and we ate of them freely. Poor as they were, they were fruit, and the girls carried a quart or two to camp. Aunt Melinda (Mrs. Charles Applegate) made a pudding of them for the children, using in the making what was still remaining of some homemade starch.

Farther on, the path led across the island known as "Mimaluse," which connected with the mainland on the north shore when the river is low. We passed

a pond or small lake on which were floating many
rafts made of logs on which were dozens of dead
bodies rolled in blankets or Klisques mats. While I
stood looking at the ghastly spectacle, my companions passed into the woods. Seeing I was alone with
the dead, I hurried after them. I came to a pen built
of logs and in this were bodies rolled up like those
on the rafts. This did not frighten me, but near the
pen was an object that did. A little, old black man
stood there. I took a long breath and stood for a
while to see if he were alive. He seemed to move,
and I ran for my life. Others who passed that way
across the island said they saw dead bodies everywhere, on rocks, on rafts, in old broken canoes. All
around were little wooden devils which, someone
said, were placed there to protect the dead, a sort
of scarecrow. No beast or bird would face that dia-
bolical array for the sake of a feast. Mimaluse Island
was the Golgotha of the Waskopum tribe.

Still following the path along the riverbank, we
seemed to be getting through the mountains, and
there was quite a stretch of beach sloping to up-
lands and foothills overgrown with shrubs and oak
timber. We passed a few native huts and a store-
house containing, among other provisions, acorns of
the white oak, which were sweet and quite palatable. We helped ourselves, and being very hungry,
ate many of the nuts. It was a fair day, and after our
acorn feast, we felt quite cheerful. We soon came to
a place where the Waskopum Indians were drying

fish eggs. The eggs were hanging in festoons atop poles that were supported by forks stuck in the ground. Of course, this smelly mess had no attraction for us, and we held our noses and fled.

Robert Shortes met us at The Dalles with supplies.[6] He came in a canoe with two Indians. He lived at Tum-Chuk (the falls), now Oregon City. I don't remember what he brought besides flour and sugar. I suppose the reason we children grew tired of sugar was because the quantity was too great in proportion to the supply of other food. Shortes did not come as a speculator, but as "a friend indeed to friends in need." He had made his home with the Applegate families before he came to Oregon then had written letters from Oregon to his friends, advising them to come to the new country, giving as reasons the healthful climate and mild winters of the northwest coast. His letters were published in the newspapers and widely read with that deep interest we always feel when we hear tidings of a better land. The "Oregon Fever" followed.

When we passed the Cascades, the river was at the lowest stage and the water covered only a part of the river bed. On the north side the stone floor of the bed was covered with green mosses. Being barefoot, I enjoyed walking upon this pillowy carpet,

[6]Shortes came to Oregon as part of the Peoria party of emigrants in 1839. He played a leading role in the development of the Oregon frontier and served as a member of the territorial legislature.

where in the early summer the waters roll fifty feet
deep. I passed men who were dragging a boat over
this moss-covered stone floor. Getting past this ob-
struction was called "The Portage of the Cascades."
The boats had to be drawn or carried over the rocks
a considerable distance. I remember meeting an Indian at this place. Someone must have spoken to
him for he stood still and striking one hand on his
breast said emphatically, "Waskopum!"

When the boats had been launched below the
Cascades, we had navigated the river from old Fort
Walla Walla to the head of navigation. Now we had
an open and safe waterway to the sea. Below the
Cascades there were seals in the river. None were
seen on the shore, yet I never saw one swimming.
We would see their heads sticking up out of the
water, but they would vanish before we could get
near. Yet I felt I knew something about them, for had
I not worn a sealskin cap three years until it was
almost as slick and hard as a steel helmet. And it
would have been almost as good as new had not the
brim parted company with it on the night of the
thunderstorm on the Big Blue.

Somewhere in this part of the country an effort
was made to get a colt for food. I saw the animal
they were bargaining for; it was fat and sleek and
almost grown. Someone said, "It will make good
eating." For some reason the colt was not secured;
why, I did not learn. We had been without flesh of
beast or bird for a long time. There were no cattle,

sheep or hogs in that part of the wilderness in those days. I cannot say that we had plenty to eat at all times, neither was there a time when we were in danger of starving, but we skirmished for food and ate what we learned the natives had found good to feed upon: berries, acorns, tender plants, the *yampa* and cammas, tubers, bulbs, and roots. We drew the line, however, at a few of the Waskopum luxuries and dainties, namely, caterpillars, the larvae of yellow jackets and tainted fish eggs. Emigrants were hungry all the time. Children seated in the boats would enjoy themselves for hours gnawing off the fat coating from the dried salmon skins. An emigrant not hungry was thought to be ill.

Now it was noised around that we were approaching Fort Vancouver, a Hudson's Bay station or trading post.[7] We had to pass Cape Horn on the way. We were told to pass in the night, as there would be less danger of a storm at that time. Sometime during the night the boats were moving slowly along near the north shore; there was no wind and the rain had moderated into a mist. It seems that I, alone, of all the children was awake. I was waiting for the show, and had just begun on another salmon skin, when Cape Horn was announced. Our boat passed within a few feet of the Horn. I could see it

[7]Fort Vancouver, established by the Hudson's Bay Company in 1825 on the Columbia River near the mouth of the Willamette River, was not only the major fur trading post but also governmental center of the Northwest. It was a major supply base for overlanders.

quite distinctly. It looked quite smooth, but seemed to be standing on end and sticking up out of the water. I could not see the upper end, however I was told it was a rock. Then I must have fallen asleep, for I awoke on the beach at Fort Vancouver the next morning. What I had expected to see before closing my eyes, tired, hungry and sleepy though I was, was a genuine horn sticking out of the riverbank, with a cape of some kind spread about it. This was my last and greatest disappointment on our trip to Oregon.

The first talked of place I had been anxious to see was Red River, a river not on our route. Next came the Missouri line, which I did not see, although I thought we must have crossed it somewhere. At "Ash Holler" I did not notice any ashes nor did I hear anything "holler." Later on I was looking for the Black Hills. Hills I saw, but none of them were black. Blue River had faded out, Chimney Rock was only a sharp pointed rock on the top of a hill, not a chimney at all. The "Devil's Backbone" was only a narrow ridge on the Snake River. Green River was not green, and Sweetwater was a disappointment, too, for I took a drink of it. It was brackish but not sweet. What a list of disappointments for a small boy who had his mind made up to see all these marvelous sights.

It was broad daylight when I awoke that morning at Vancouver. Our camp was near the river and the fort was a little farther inland. Breakfast was being served when I opened my eyes, and the roast fish

Fort Vancouver about 1845
Courtesy Oregon Historical Society

and potatoes were the first things I saw. I think it was the smell of something to eat that first aroused me. When I arose and threw back the covering, a mist seemed to arise from my body, there were puddles of water on the bed where I had lain, the bedding was as wet as if it had been dragged from the river, and yet I had slept soundly all night while a pouring rain had drenched my bed.

Dr. McLaughlin,[8] of the Hudson's Bay Company at Vancouver, had not known of our arrival until he visited our camp that morning. I well remember his kind face and pleasant manner. When he came near to where I was standing, smiling, bowing gracefully and talking pleasantly, he won me entirely. This was while he was being introduced to the young ladies and their mothers, who were but young women themselves. Of the young ladies being introduced, two were my cousins, Lucy and Rozelle, each about fourteen years of age. In those times girls from twelve to seventeen were young ladies. When they passed that age they were called old maids. Old maidenhood was frowned upon. Some "Inglorious Milton guiltless of a rhyme" had expressed the prevailing sentiment of the times in this little ditty:

> *"Old age is honorable but*
> *old maids are abominable."*

[8] Dr. John McLaughlin, the chief factor of the Hudson's Bay Company, ruled the Columbia District (Oregon) for England from 1824 until 1845, when he retired. He moved to Oregon City and became an American citizen in 1851.

Small families were not in vogue. A family of five or six children was considered small.

The doctor invited the emigrants to visit him at the fort, and some of them did so. He was a valuable friend to the needy. I never saw him afterwards, but always heard good reports of him.

The object here that fixed my attention, and that I gazed upon with admiration and astonishment, was a ship lying at anchor in the river a short distance below our camp. The hull was black and rose above the water, and the mast was like a tree. I had never before seen a watercraft larger than our big boat or a Chinook Kinnim.[9] So great was its size and beauty, I would have believed it to be one of the wonders of the world, had not someone told me it was only a schooner.

We were at this camp one day, and discovered that the river rose and fell two feet. We had reached tidewater and were on the western margin of the continent. Our small fleet of boats had kept within supporting distance of each other on the way down the river, but here there was a parting of the ways.

The Applegate families, with the Straits and Naylors started to cross the river from the camp at Vancouver intending to go direct to the mouth of the Willamette River, however there came such a storm of wind and rain, it was thought best to land the boats at Sovey's Island, where two or three deserted houses accorded shelter. Our departure from

[9] An Indian canoe.

Vancouver had been emphasized by an unpleasant circumstance. When the big family boat was passing beneath the bow of the schooner, the sailor boys tossed big, red apples to the oldest of the young ladies, Cousin Lucy. She tried to catch the apples in her apron but they all bounded into the river and were lost. I heard Cousin Lucy speak of this experience when she was over seventy. She said it was a disappointment to the children, who had depended on her, that made her failure painful to her then, and unpleasant to remember.

The Straits and Naylors parted company with us at Sovey's Island, where we remained three or four days. Passing across from Sovey's Island and near a low point of land on our left, our boats entered the mouth of the Willamette River. Continuing up the stream we passed the place where Strait and Naylor had established a camp on the west bank of the river. They called the place Linton. They told us Mr. Strait's daughter had died there. Soon after passing Linton we landed on the west shore, and found a campsite on the high bank where there was very little underbrush among the pine trees. No one lived there and the place had no name; there was nothing to show that the place had ever been visited except a small log hut near the river, and a broken mast of a ship leaning against the high bank. There were chips hewn from timber, showing that probably a new mast had been made there. We were at this place a day or two and were visited by two men from the prairie country up the river, then known as the "plains." These two men, Thompson and Doty, had been trappers but had taken native women for wives and settled down to steady habits. Doty had gone to the mountains with the Ashley party when a boy. Father and Doty were boys together and had started to the mountains with Ashley at the same time, but Father, falling sick, returned home.

Where we should locate was the all-absorbing topic of conversation at this camp in the woods. It appeared to be difficult to decide where to settle down in such a vast unappropriated wilderness. We were then actually encamped on the site of the city of Portland, but there was no prophet with us to foretell of the beautiful city that one day in the not too distant future was to take the place of that gloomy forest.

From this camp we were two days getting up the river to Tum-Chuk, now Oregon City. We passed the Klackamas Rapids on our first day up the river. The men, women, and children not needed to help in the boats went ashore at the foot of the rapids, and followed along the riverbank, while men with the boats, some poling and others on shore towing, brought the boats safely through the rapids. The camp that night was near the bank of the Klacka-mas River. The second day we reached Tum-Chuk, and the boats were hauled around the falls to the river above by a French-Canadian with one yoke of long-horned steers. We then made camp on the east shore nearly opposite the main cataract. There were less than a dozen houses at Tum-Chuk including a tinshop, blacksmith shop, sawmill, and probably a gristmill. We spent one night at this place. Then in the morning several Kanakas helped to launch the boats above the falls and to clear the rapids. In the evening of the same day we landed at Champoeg[10] and remained there one night in a long shed in one end of which was a bin of peas. I never saw our boats again, and do not remember how they were disposed of.

From Champoeg we traveled by land. The baggage was hauled on a cart drawn by one yoke of oxen. I think the cart was hired from a French settler. Mrs. Charles Applegate and four small children rode in the cart while the rest of our party followed on foot. All day we traveled and it was quite dark when we saw a light. The light was in a window at Doctor White's house.[11] It seemed to me we were a long time getting to that light, but upon arriving at the house I forgot I was tired, for the

[10]Champoeg was a strip of prairie bordering the Willamette River. It had been the location selected by Dr. John McLaughlin as a place where retired Hudson's Bay Company fur traders might settle. It later became the site of the first efforts to establish a government outside the control of the Hudson's Bay Company.

[11]Dr. Elijah White first arrived in Oregon in 1837 but returned to the "States" in 1840. He led a party to Oregon in 1842 after he had been appointed to his post as an Indian agent. He had become the first American government official in Oregon.

doctor, having notice of our coming, had a bright fire in the fireplace and supper on the table in the kitchen. The smell of frying pork was sweet to my nostrils. From Doctor White's place we had to travel another mile and our long journey was ended. We called this place the Old Mission. It was at this place that the first Methodist mission in the Willamette Valley was located. The missionaries must have lived here two or three years for there were peach trees there in blossom the next spring. When another location, called "The Mill," now the city of Salem, had been made farther up the river, this place was abandoned. The town of Gervais now stands on the site of the Old Mission. There were three log cabins under one roof at this place. We went into them on the 29th day of November, 1843, and here we passed our first winter in Oregon. It was our home until after the summer harvest.

Previous to this we had been in the rain most of the time for twenty days. Oh, how we could have enjoyed our hospitable shelter if we could have looked around the family circle and beheld all the bright faces that had accompanied us on our toilsome journey almost to the end. Alas, they were not there!

Jason Lee's "Old Mission House" about 1841
Courtesy Oregon Historical Society

III

Our First Winter and Summer in Oregon

THE absorbing thought of this winter was keeping up the food supply. The men were out at work in all kinds of weather, not for money, but for food. Father built a ferryboat for A. Beers or James O'Neil. He first caulked the openings between the planks in the bottom of the boat, and then poured in hot pitch. As it was a large boat, he used several bushels of literature he found in the old house. Tracts and other pamphlets that had been left there by the missionaries were forced into the cracks with a chisel and hammer.

For building the boat Father took his pay in provisions; pork and peas constituted the greater part of these provisions. The French settlers seemed to have grown peas extensively. I remember wading around in a large bin of peas for an hour or more while we were in camp at Champoeg. These peas were white and very hard. The Indians were very partial to peas, or "lepwah," as they called them. They used them for making soup which was called "liplip."

There was no place to obtain clothing or dry goods nearer than Fort Vancouver. Nor was there a place where shoes could be purchased. The older people wore buckskin moccasins purchased from the Indians, while the young ones went barefooted. Fortunately, this proved to be a warm winter, but wet, as a Willamette winter usually is.

I had already learned a number of Indian proper names. We saw Indians on the Columbia River who said they were Spokane. Others said they were Waskopum, Walla Wallas, Kince-Chinook, Klackamas, Klickitat and Chemomichat. After we had settled in the valley, we had visitors from many of the tribes living on the Columbia. When asked where they came from, or where they lived, the answer was "Katchutehut." I could speak those names just as they were spoken by the Indians, but it is difficult to tell the reader how they should be pronounced. We learned to speak the Chinook language that winter. The mission children spoke it as habitually as they did their mother tongue. We talked Chinook everyday with the Indians and half-bloods. There was one Indian who spoke both English and Chinook. He had a droll way of speaking in Chinook and then in English. He would say, "Nika tikeh chuck," "I want water." "Nika hyas olo," "I am very hungry." "Potlatch tenas piah sap-po-lil," "Give a little bread," and so on. But we could not have had a better teacher than this waggish Indian. There were a few missionaries and Canadian families in the neighborhood. There was a school that was kept during the winter close to where we lived. Children of the three Applegate families, with the

French and the mission children, made up a school of about twenty-five pupils. No Indian children attended this school. A pious young man, Andrew Smith by name, presided over this religious training school. As soon as a child could spell out words, however indifferently, he or she was required to read religious tracts, which were intended to make the child realize it was both wicked and in danger of punishment. These tracts were alarming, more alarming and most alarming. They were our first, second and third readers. Occasionally our teacher would select a tract containing a choice lesson and read aloud to the school. One evening he read one that alarmed me greatly. I can recall the substance of it, which was as follows. There was a little boy whom his parents had never taught to pray to the Lord before retiring to rest at night. He did not know how to ask the Lord to forgive his sins and protect him from the evil one whilst he slept. One night he went to bed and fell asleep. He never awoke and was lost. I was a very small boy and that evening, after I retired I was thinking of the lost boy. It seemed plain that I was in as much danger as he. The chances would surely be against me should I fall asleep. The thought of awakening and finding myself in the "bad place" kept me from sleeping. After suffering for an hour or two from this conflict between drowsiness and fear, I got out of bed and sat down before the hearth of the old fireplace. I scraped together a few live coals from the ashes, and intended to sit there until I could make up my mind what to do. My Mother's bed was in the same room. She had been watching all the while and now asked me if I were ill. I denied being sick and told her why I could not sleep. I do not remember her words, but the substance of her speech was this: that I was a good boy and there was no reason why I should be frightened; that I had done nothing to be punished for, only the wicked were punished. She told me to go to bed and think no more about it. I had confidence in Mother, and what she said was common sense, so I was soon back to sleep.

There were three cabins in close proximity for about twenty-five persons; men, women, and children. The three Applegate families, and three or four young men who came out with them as help. The wagons, teams, and all the cattle and horses had been left at Fort Walla Walla. Much of the furniture, cooking utensils, and bedding had been lost in the disaster on the Columbia River. The families had reached the place where they were to pass the winter almost destitute of furnishing goods or food supplies and without visible means of support. I am not prepared to say how nearly destitute they were, but I remember that Mother did her baking all that winter on a skillet lid found in the house.

There was in the neighborhood a small settlement of French Canadians, trappers, and mountain men, who had consorted with native women and become ranchers. They had cleared small farms and were growing grain and vegetables. They had hogs, horses, and chickens, and, being kindly disposed toward the emigrants, assisted them, through barter and otherwise, to provide subsistence; that is, the food sufficient to live upon, for luxuries were not thought of. The conditions were hard, yet due to the unflinching perseverance of those upon whom the burden fell, there were, of necessity, many days of fasting.

We found a tribe of Kalapooyas living along the river at this place. They were not numerous. There were a few families of them living in miserable hovels near us, and down the river, less than a quarter of a mile, was a small village. There were a few huts at other places, but little skill was made manifest in the design or construction of their houses. These Indians were poor in every sense of the word. A few miserable ponies were all the livestock they had— except for vermin and fleas. They were spiritless and sickly yet appeared satisfied with a miserable existence. Many died that winter, and the hideous wail of the mourners, as they conducted the funeral services, was heard almost daily. If any effort had been made to civilize or Christianize this tribe, there was no evidence of it. That they could hardly have been more wretchedly housed, poorer in property, more degraded morally or more afflicted mentally with demonology, was plainly to be seen.

When speaking of livestock, I forgot to mention the dogs with which these Indians were abundantly supplied. A canine adjunct to the family, of coyote descent, lean, lank, and cadaverous, they were neither useful nor ornamental. These people needed no watchdogs because the squalid and forbidding appearance of their hovels and the noxious fumes floating from them were a sufficient protection.

One evening in the early winter, while we were eating our frugal supper, a great commotion was heard in the direction of the Indian village: loud talking, screams of women, and barking of dogs. Then we heard the war whoop and the report of a gun. But before anyone had time to make a remark, the face of an Indian appeared at a small window back of the table where we were eating. When he saw we had discovered him he shouted "Billy, Molalla," "Billy, Molalla," and immediately disappeared. Billy Doke was a young man who made his home with us that winter. The Indian, who was from the village down the river, had learned his name and had rushed to warn us to prepare to defend ourselves from hostile Indians, the Molallas. All the light we had was furnished by the feeble flame from a twisted rag immersed in a puddle of grease in an old tin plate. This flame was snuffed out instantly, the doors and windows fastened, and preparations made for defense. There were five men to defend the house, and being pioneers, were ready to do battle.

The women and children went to the loft, where the children were put to bed on blankets and quilts spread on the floor. Efforts were made to put the little ones to sleep and to keep them quiet. One child, I distinctly remember, was hard to pacify and caused much anxiety. Some of the men kept watch below. Very few words were spoken, but I heard enough to know that the pioneers were not afraid to fight, but were afraid the Indians would set fire to the house. I must have fallen asleep as soon as the fretful child was quiet for I can recall nothing more of that night. Shortly after sunup next day, the Kalapooyas prepared to follow the Molalla raiders, who had taken a number of ponies. About twenty warriors made up the party. War paint was drawn on their faces, and some had tied cords and red bandages around their heads from which feathers of many kinds and colors waved and fluttered in the morning breeze. Feathers also decorated the manes and tails of their ponies.

I had seen a great army of the Sioux on the warpath against the Blackfeet when we crossed the Dakota Plains on our way west the summer before, and I did not think very highly of this war party of Kalapooyas. They returned that same day, having no scalps to show us. They failed to overtake the raiders. A few days after the raid mentioned we heard of a fight at Tum-Chuk in which a Molalla was killed. A white man by the name of Lebreton was shot in the arm with a poisoned arrow and died of the wound. A number of others were struck by arrows but not seriously wounded. We decided that the same Indians made the attack at both places. The stream which runs into the Willamette River a short distance above Oregon City is now known as the Molalla. In those times all the country roundabout the Molalla River and its branches, even to the great white mountain eastward, and far south of it, was the Land of the Molallas.

I have said our first winter was mild. I can recall but one snowstorm and this snow disappeared in a few hours. There was ice on a few mornings, but it was no thicker than window glass. I might have forgotten that little snowstorm, had I not been sent to the woods to find dry sticks and boughs for fuel. Picking them out of the snow made my hands ache, and when I went to the fire to warm them the agony brought the tears to my eyes. We had no team nor wagon and could not borrow. The home of the man who lived on the mission farm was less than half a mile from our place. This man refused to let Father use his yoke of oxen to haul a load of wood. He said he would not allow strangers to use them, as they might be spoiled.

I went to school that entire winter. We children followed a footpath that led through wild shrubbery higher than our heads. After a rain, we were well sprinkled from the wet bushes, and often ran into the schoolhouse thoroughly soaked. The schoolroom being a cold and cheerless place, we considered ourselves fortunate if we were dry by noon. I can remember no playtime and no games, not even tag.

The last school day I recall must have been near the close of the term, for I went from the old well near the schoolhouse door to the fence on the mission farm and found the wheat was as high as the fence.

Our people harvested on the mission farm, using sickles and scythes to cut the grain, which was afterwards bound into bundles or sheaves. My work was to stack the sheaves into shocks. A vine known as the ground blackberry had grown with the grain. When they cut the grain they failed to separate it from the vines, which were bent and twisted into loops all through the stubble, and were also in and around the bunches of bound up wheat and oats. My poor, bare feet had to wander in thorny paths and the scratches on my hands made me forget that I was tired and hungry. Sometimes I would find a sheaf securely bound to the earth by vines; in that case I had to pull the vines out of the ground before I could get the sheaf. By harvesting this crop we supplied ourselves with grain to take to the new settlement. The wheat was the red bearded variety.

Many families arrived in the Willamette Valley in November and December, and located in different parts of the country. The Waldos, Keysers, Looneys, and others went up the river and settled on the Waldo Hills, Chemeketa and valleys of the Santiam. The Millicans, Bakers, Holmans, Hembres, Hesses, Birds and others crossed the river and established settlements in the rich valleys of the north and south Yamhill.

When our families had been installed in winter quarters within the deserted mission houses, the country west of the river was explored, and places for settlement selected along a stream called Salt Creek, at the eastern base of the Coast Mountain range. In December, Uncle Jesse Applegate established himself there in a shanty or hut. Here he, with one or two young men, resided during the winter, making improvements and preparing a home for his family. The settlement in Salt Creek Valley was about three miles north of where the city of Dallas, Polk County, now lays. The three Applegate brothers located on three adjoining sections, since known on the township map as the donation claims of James Frederick, George Brown and A. H. Whitley.

When our families started west again, we crossed the river in the ferryboat which Father built during the winter. Taking a southerly course between the hills and the river to Salt Creek Valley, then west through a low gap in the range of hills six miles north of The Mill, now the city of Salem, we traveled west about nine miles and kindled our last campfire on the bank of a branch of Salt Creek under the brow of the Coast Mountain range. In order to make this move, a team had been hired or perhaps borrowed. There may have been more than one team, however I can recall but one. This was the beginning of the first road in Polk County. The road was laid out before there was a county. It was difficult to break a road through the prairie on account of the luxuriant grass. Wild game was not scarce, for that afternoon some of the young men killed a deer and a bear and the two carcasses hung on a tree in our camp that night. No other camp scene of pioneer days is so deeply impressed upon my mind as that of that evening, our first night in our new home.

Our camp was in a grove of large oak trees. The three campfires were close together and lighted the avenues between the trees up to a dark canopy of leaves overhead. We children played games in the grove early in the evening. One game I remember was "Miley-Bright." We chose sides and then one party called loudly, "How many miles to Miley-Bright?" The answer came from the other side, "Three score and ten." Then the question, "Can I get there by candlelight?" and the answer, "Yes, if your legs are long and your body light, but look out for the witches on the way." Then away we would go as fast as we could run on to "Miley-Bright."

Later we were gathered near the campfires when bedtime came, and a rustle of mighty wings was heard. Then an eerie voice came from overhead saying "Chuchounyhoof-ouf! ouf! ouf!" Again came that awful voice calling, "Who! Who! Who are you?" The three younger children, trembling with fear, clung to Mother's skirts, but she laughed and told us it was only an owl. That is what I believed, too, until I had become learned in the religion of the Kommema and was told all about the great Kalapooya goblin, "Chuchounyhoof."

Our second camp scene in the grove of oaks was brilliant while it lasted. Uncle Jesse Applegate's hut was covered with fir boughs which had become very dry. In the evenings it was his custom to read and write by the light of pitch splinters, a substitute for candles. While so engaged, quite late one evening, the volume of flame suddenly increased, the tongue of fire shot up and all at once the roof of boughs caught fire with an explosion like gunpowder. All the upper part of the shanty burned away before the fire could be checked. I doubt if Uncle Jesse considered this sudden combustion of the roof of his "study" as a capital joke, but I heard laughter in the grove after the illumination.

The native population in our neighborhood was a tribe of the Kalapooya and near and far, even to the sea, were the Tillamook, Tawalatin, Chemeketa, and Luckyuke, all appearing to be one tribe and speaking the same language. They were a degenerate and priest-ridden people, but their language was remarkably smooth and musical. It was a custom of these Indians, late in the autumn, after the wild wheat was fairly ripe, to burn off the whole country. The grass would burn away and leave the pods well dried and bursting. Then the squaws, both young and old, would go with their baskets and bats and gather in the grain.

It is probable we did not yet know that the Indians were wont to baptize the entire country with fire at the close of every summer; but very soon we were to learn our first lesson. This season the fire was started somewhere on the south Yamhill, and came sweeping up through the Salt Creek gap. The sea breeze being quite strong that evening caused the flames to leap over the creek and come down upon us like an army with banners. All our skill and perseverance were required to save our camp. The flames swept by on either side of the grove; then quickly closing ranks, made a clean sweep of all the country south and east of us. As the shades of night deepened, long lines of flame and smoke could be seen retreating before the breeze across the hills and valleys. The Indians continued to burn the grass every season until the country was somewhat settled up and the whites prevented them; but every fall for a number of years, we were treated to the same grand display of fireworks. On dark nights sheets of flame, tongues of fire, and lurid clouds of smoke made a picture both awful and sublime.

In the summer of 1844, the cattle, horses and wagons left at old Fort Walla Walla were sent for and the remnants arrived at the settlement late in the fall. Some of the cattle were not found. A few, it was supposed, had been appropriated by the Indidians. About fifty head reached the new settlement, a large group of which belonged to Jesse Applegate. What was recovered of the wagons I don't know, except that of the three left by Lindsay Applegate only four wheels were found and brought to us, and they were all hind wheels. Those wheels were used to make two carts.

Wagons were made wholly of wood. The wheels were without hub, spoke, or felloe; they were simply short sections of large trees, three or four feet in diameter, sawed off and holes made in the center for the axles. This wagon was called a truck, a very clumsy affair, which, without a load, a single yoke of oxen could not draw with ease even on level ground. The friction on the spindles in the wheels, though they were well tarred, was such that, even with a load of rails requiring three yoke of oxen to draw them, the truck did not need any brake going down a steep hill. Under a heavy moving load, the spindles, if not abundantly tarred, would send forth a fearful scream with variations that could be heard for miles. One evening after dark we heard loud screaming or yelling a mile and a half away across the prairie, and presently a fire was seen to start up like a flash. Someone said it must be a band of Indians on the warpath, whooping, and firing the grass, for it was autumn and the grass was dry. The facts were, as we learned next day, that Uncle Charlie's truck heavily loaded and drawn by three yoke of oxen was enroute across the valley and one of the spindles took fire and burned off before the teamster, who was busy with the cattle, noticed that anything unusual had happened.

Sleds were also used for hauling. They were very

heavy to draw on the ground and there was hardly ever any snow. Fifty green rails on a sled were a load for two yoke of oxen. As we had much fencing to do, the hauling of rails was a very common occupation. At times, we hitched three yoke of oxen to the sled and could haul a hundred dry rails, and with such a team we could haul all the firewood we could load onto the sled.

One day my oldest brother and myself were sent to haul a load of rock from a place in the hills a mile or so from the house, but we had never hauled rock before. As we had a team of three yoke, we piled rock on the sled till the bulk appeared to be about as big as a hundred rails. My brother had a long whiplash braided of rawhide with a buckskin thong for a cracker and with a straight, wild cherry sprout for a stock. When he whistled the whip around and applied it to an ox, the cracker popped like a toy pistol and cut the hair like a glancing bullet. The sled being loaded, my brother spoke to the oxen to move on and cracked his whip, but though the team surged forward a little, the sled did not move; then the long lash of the whip performed rapid circles through the air and the cracker became a terrible scourge. The oxen sprang forward, wavered, then stood still. But the sled had not moved an inch. That team had never balked before. We were indignant, and after a short consultation, concluded that the use of the whip was not sufficient for the occasion; so it was laid aside and we both went to a hazel thicket and cut switches about nine feet long. With these we attacked the team in the rear, on the flanks, and all along the line, shouting words of encouragement mixed in with threats that awoke the echoes of the hills far away to the spurs of the Coast Range. Every steer was by this time mad all over and resolved to move forward if he had to burst his yoke. Every ox at the same moment lowered his head, lashed his tail spitefully, and with all his ponderous weight and mighty strength advanced. The power exerted now was almost irresistible; something must give way or the sled move. For just one second there seemed to be a doubt, then the tongue separated from the sled. This trial of strength suggested a fact which we well knew, but had not made a practical use of in this case, namely, that a load of stone is much heavier than a load of wood of like bulk. Putting the team into position again, we attached the tongue to the sled with log chains and began throwing off rock; and after the load had been considerably reduced in this way, we started up the team again but as the sled did not move, we threw off more rock. We continued to reduce the load in this way until we had thrown off all but about two washtubs full of rock; and with this load we managed to reach home late in the afternoon. Since the broken sled could not be hidden, an explanation was demanded which led to our having to make a full confession of this very foolish affair.

The pioneers in the beginning had to make their own agricultural implements, such as plows, harrows, and all kinds of equipment to clear and cultivate the ground. My father, Lindsay Applegate, was handy with carpenter's tools of the few and simple kinds they had, while Uncle Charles was a rough blacksmith, who shod horses when it was necessary, made bars, shears, coulters and clevises for plows; rings and clevises for ox yokes, and repaired broken ironings of wagons; and generally speaking, did all kinds of frontier blacksmithing. Father did the woodwork in making plows and harrows and in repairing wagons. Every part of the plow was wood except the bar, shear, coulter and clevis. Tough oak was used in the beam and the mouldboard was of ash timber. Ash was also generally used in ox yokes.

The prairie lands fenced for cultivation were more or less heavily sodded and set with tufts of brushwood and strong roots of various kinds, and it was necessary to have very strong plows to break the lands. A strong, two-wheeled truck with a large strong plow attached to it, drawn by four yoke of oxen, was an outfit often seen breaking prairie. To the largest plow supported by a wheel attachment, which was of necessity very strong and heavy, I think they used a team of six yoke of cattle; and with this outfit broke three and four acres of prairie land in a day. Horses were seldom used to work in harness. In crossing the plains I can recall seeing only one team in which a horse was used. That team was made up of a yoke of milch cows on the wheel and an old roan mare in the lead. The outfit, I recall, belonged to Henry Stout and its uniqueness and economic makeup was not overlooked nor soon forgotten.

When we arrived at the place where we settled on Salt Creek in September, we had no time to spare from the building of cabins and other preparations for winter to make plows; and so it happened that the first plow to break ground in that country was one brought by Lindsay Applegate from the Old Mission where we had passed our first winter in Oregon. This plow was probably purchased from a missionary or French Canadian settler, but there were no names or figures discovered on it, telling where, when, or by whom made.

After the first rains had softened the ground, about the last week in November, 1844, prairie was broken with this plow for spring wheat and a garden patch, and I think plowing was done from time to time during the winter where the ground was a little rolling and not too wet.

The wild country I am now speaking of was afterwards named Polk County, and this plow being the very first to poke its nose into the virgin soil of that county, should be entitled to some distinction, and its mysterious origin, private life, and tragic end should be noted. The beam and handles were wood; all the balance was metal, cast in sections and fastened together with bolts and screws. The bar was one piece and the knee, shear, heel, coulter and nose were each separate. The first piece that broke disclosed the fact that it was pot metal. All of the pieces were of the same metal. Each had been cast in a mould. When one of the sections was broken a new section had to be hammered out of iron at the blacksmith shop. In the course of four or five years all the parts had been broken and replaced with wrought iron sections, except the mouldboard; and the beam and handles had been removed, but it continued to be the same plow; and as we had named it the "Cast Plow" in the beginning, we never changed its name, and it never changed its habit of trying at times to stay on top of the ground, or of trying to go to the center of the earth. It was this habit that made us boys wish it might sometime wear out; although the prospect was discouraging in view of the continued renewal of its parts. To cultivate old ground with it, where there were no sod and roots, was bad enough for it was like dragging an anchor since the mouldboard was never known to scour. But although the mouldboard was of such shape that sod rolled up before it like a scroll, it turned up its nose at every root that lay in its way and, unless prevented by the person at the handles, would glide over the top of it, or, if prevented, would try to go under it.

Now we boys knew all the tricks of this veteran implement, and one day in the early summer of 1849, we were required to break a small tract of sod ground with it. We had two yoke of heavy steers and their gait on a warm day, without urging, was quite slow. Several times when the plow had struck a root and was prevented from jumping out of the ground, it had turned its point downward and balked the team. There was only one thing we could do then: dig the plow out and take a new start. After several hours spent in stopping and digging up the plow, we talked the matter over and concluded that the team was stopped because of their slow movement, so the next time we were approaching a root of a large sunflower, I urged the team forward till the oxen were almost ready to break into a trot, while my brother put his arms under the plow handles and raised them to his shoulders to prevent the plow from jumping out of the ground. This time when the plow struck the root and turned its nose down, the team did not balk; it walked right along dragging a shattered plowbeam and the old "Cast Plow" was a total wreck. There we left its remains buried in the soil of the valley. If, as the pioneer plow of old Polk, it had anything to do with "Saving Oregon," it buried much better than it plowed.

The hills of the Coast Range rose like a continuous wall four thousand feet high along the line of the ocean. Covered over with a dense evergreen forest, vast, dark, and as yet unexplored, they marked the western line of our horizon. Being now comfortably fixed, Father concluded to go on a hunting and exploring trip into these mountains. Supposing the natives were in the habit of roaming through these mountains, Father wished to have one go with us as a guide. But no Indian wanted to go. Numerous as they were, no consideration would induce one to go with us into this vast wilderness. We went without a guide. Traveling west four or five miles, through open woods of white oak timber, we began the ascent of a spur of the Coast Range. By following a winding footpath made by wild beasts, the ascent was not difficult. Traveling through an unbroken forest all day, we made camp near the summit of the range just as the sun went down. There was a spring of good water here and a meadow covered with grass and clover which afforded good pasture for our horses. It may have been the fear of getting lost which caused me to take this precaution, but before sunset I took my hatchet and blazed a tree which stood near our campfire. I marked the tree exactly on the reverse side from where I saw the sun go down that evening. I was up early the following morning and soon dressed. I greased my feet with marrow from the shank of a deer, they being a little sore, and put on what was left of my sealskin cap, which was not much. The brim had been lost on the "plains," and we boys had used the crown a number of times for a target when practicing archery with our bows and arrows. I looked east, as I supposed, for the sun to rise, when it came up directly behind me. I went to my witness tree but no

blaze was there. I walked around it and found the
blaze on the other side. We left our horses in the
meadow and climbed to the summit on foot. In
some places the trees were so close together we had
to turn sidewise in order to pass between them. I
blazed the way as we went. We found a broad district of almost level country. At the highest point
on the summit, brother Elisha climbed a tree, and
from this lofty perch could see the Pacific Ocean.
We found a vast district of burned and fallen timber. The logs were covered with dewberry vines
bearing the largest and sweetest berries I have ever
eaten. We found also hundreds of acres of salal berries. Bears are very fond of these berries, but we
found them sweet and insipid. We returned home
after less than a week. That we returned unharmed
seemed to astonish the natives. They asked us many
questions as to where we went and what we saw.
Some of the Indians assured us, as their reason for
not going with us, that there was a very dangerous
goblin in the Coast Mountains, whose awful name
was Chuchounyhoof. When we expressed no fear,
saying we would shoot him if we found him, just as
we would a deer or a bear, they said, "Wake klietan
kokshot. Skin hyas kull kahkwa chickamin," that is,
"His hide is bulletproof; it is as hard as iron." Our
parents did not seem to regard this story as of any
consequence; they said it was only an Indian superstition. But my training in the school at the Old
Mission had developed the bump of curiosity in my

head and I absorbed this story eagerly. I had been taught that there was an evil spirit roaming about this earth, and I thought this goblin the Indians told us of might be it. I interviewed many Indians on the subject, but gained little information. I discovered that the low caste natives truly believed in the existence of the goblin and were frightened by it. Their priest, Dickadowdow, said that to fall into the hands of Chuchounyhoof would be a fearful thing.

Although slow in making the discovery, I eventually learned that there existed among the natives a professional class possessed of all the learning not considered necessary in the day by day affairs of life. These professors were known in the Chinook language as "Lamachin," that is, medicine men or doctors. The Klamath and Modoc name for these learned men was "Keyox," meaning one skilled in healing by the use of natural remedies or by magic. They were supposed to be learned in the law, and in every branch of a religious or superstitious character. I became acquainted with two or three professionals. But when I introduced Chuchounyhoof as a text to be expounded, I found them averse to discussing the subject without the assurance that I was not prompted by idle curiosity.

Of all the men of the priestly order the patriarch of the tribe we found inhabiting the country between the south Yamhill and north Luckyuke was probably the deepest learned in mythological and mystic lore. This was Dickadowdow. His forehead had been flattened when he was an infant; it retreated in a line from his brows to his crown and was as flat as the board against which it had grown. The flattening process had made his head unusually high above his ears. He had numerous wives, as polygamy was not prohibited by the Kalapooya code. Though well acquainted with the patriarch, I was not so with his family, and can now recall but one of his children, a daughter who had reached the age of young womanhood. This girl wore an ornament thrust through her nose and resting on her upper lip. The ornament looked like ivory, was about four inches long and tapered to a point at each end. All agreed in calling it a spindle, and so this ornament won for her the name of "Spindle" of which she was proud. I frequently saw various colored shells worn by the natives in similar manner, but this ornament worn by "Spindle" was unusual in shape and size. Dickadowdow, with his family and relatives, had permanent quarters on the Rickreol. It was here he had his winter house, and some of his relatives had a fish trap. There was a tradition that a long time ago, even before the patriarch had reached years of wisdom, the Cleopatra of the northwest coast lived at this old village. She was said to have been the child of Kalapooya and Mexican parents and very beautiful. She became known as La Creole. At this place, the Indians built their very best houses; and after moving from place to place during the dry season, returned to them as winter approached.

Father built his first cabin on the point of a ridge a hundred and fifty feet above the valley. He said that in the river bottom where we lived in Missouri we had chills and fever. He wanted to build where we could get plenty of fresh air. In this he was not disappointed for the sea breeze kept the boards on the roof rattling all through the autumn season, and the first storm of winter blew the roof off. I awoke that night to find the rain pouring down onto my face. I could see nothing overhead but darkness. The wind was blowing a gale while the rain poured down in torrents. The house being no longer a shelter or protection, we left it and retreated down the eastern slope of the hill to a big, black stump. This place was not so much exposed to the fury of the gale and a fire was kindled against the stump. There was an abundance of wood, logs, treetops and broken branches, and we soon had a roaring bonfire which lighted and dried the ground more than fifty feet around and made us so comfortable we children laughed in the face of the furious storm. Darkness fell before the blaze and stood like a black wall around our brilliant fire. We remained in camp here while the cabin was being made habitable.

We had had no bread since we had lived at the Old Mission where Mother baked her bread on a skillet lid. Father loaded a horse with two or three sacks of wheat, and taking as a companion a young man by the name of Alby Shaw, started a trip to a gristmill at the mission settlement on the banks of the Willamette River, about fifteen miles from where we lived. The weather was stormy and, since they had no tent, they camped beneath a fir tree on the bank of the river. Here they worked for two or three days making a canoe, as there was no way to cross the river. When the canoe was almost completed one of their axes struck a knot with such force as to make a hole in the bottom of the boat. This misfortune made them desperate, however they knew a new mission had recently been built across the river, so they started up a loud cry for help. After hallooing themselves hoarse, a miller came with a canoe and took them with their grain across the river; and when the grain was ground, brought them back again. Father returned at the end of a week, getting home late at night. We had all retired and I had been fast asleep, but was awakened by the aroma of baking bread. A sack of flour had been opened and Mother was making pancakes. This was my second realization of perfect bliss; the first had been the smell of frying pork at Doctor White's. The flour was coarsely ground and there being seven in our family, and two men employed on the place, our supply did not last long. Various substitutes for bread were tried. Wheat scalded with lye made from wood ashes was used as hominy. Some tried to provide flour by grinding wheat on a coffee mill, while others resorted to the mill used by the Indians. This mill was a stone basin and a pestle, but was abandoned after a few trials, as the flour was very coarse and the quantity obtained in this way was quite small.

The settlers now resolved to have a mill in the neighborhood, and it was through their influence that James O'Neil came to our house in the spring of 1845 to consult about the matter. Father went with him to show him the mill site on the Rickreol. The place is a mile above where the city of Dallas now is. The mill operated one run of stones. These stones were shaped from a granite boulder found about two miles from our home. A man by the name of Williams split this stone with steel wedges and made the pair from the halves. This was the work of an entire winter.

IV

Experiences in the Willamette Valley

I N THE course of three or four years after we began life in the wilderness of Salt Creek, we had pastures fenced, grain fields and gardens, small apple and peach orchards grown from the seed, comfortable log cabins, barns and other outhouses, plus quite a number of cattle, horses, hogs, and chickens. We had grain growing and in store, and vegetables in abundance. But many things we had always considered necessities were not to be had in the wilderness where we lived. Coffee, tea, and sugar were among these. Having an abundance of good milk, a family could do without tea or coffee, and even an old coffee drinker could be consoled by a beverage made of roasted peas crushed in a buckskin bag. Habitual tea drinkers quickly became reconciled to what was generally known as "mountain tea," a drink of a spicy odor made from the leaves of a vine found growing in the woods. Many people came to prefer this tea to any tea of commerce. But there was nothing to take the place of sugar. Father and Mother had seen the sugar camps in Kentucky and Tennessee and knew how sugar was made from the sap of maple trees. Our spring was surrounded by a grove of maple trees and though the sap was not as sweet as the sap of the sugar maple, they believed sugar could be made from it. The experiment was tried and proved to be a success, so we had plenty of sugar, syrup, and candy.

The problem of clothing had become a very serious one. Tents and wagon covers that had seen service from the Mississippi to the Columbia would shed rain when made into coats. Lined with the remnants of some old woolen garment, and with a broad collar and cuffs faced with the fur of beaver or otter, these garments would pass without criticism even though their ancestry might be known to everyone by indelible marks that had been on the tent or wagon cover. It would be a mistake to suppose that this was regarded as humiliating or a real hardship. Necessity demanded very plain attire among the first settlers and custom sanctioned it. Buttons for these coats were made of pewter cast in moulds cut in blocks of soapstone. Old spoons, plates, and other pieces of worn-out tableware that had seen service around many a campfire on the plains and in the mountains were used for buttons. Garments were sometimes made of the wool-like hair of the wolf. During the time we lived in Missouri, there was in almost every family a spinning wheel and loom, and the womenfolk spun yarn of wool and cotton out of which they knit socks, stockings, and other garments, and wove cloth for family use. They were, therefore, skilled manufacturers on a small scale in this line, but for some years after the family had settled in Oregon there was neither cotton nor wool to be had, so the hair of the wolf was used as a substitute for wool, but it was a poor substitute for the yarn spun of it was coarse and not strong. Another drawback was that wolves could not be fleeced so long as they were alive, and also a man could not kill a sufficient number of the kind that were common, the prairie wolf or coyote, in a month, to make a sweater. The yarn spun from the fleece of one pelt would hardly make a pair of slippers for a child. The attempt to provide clothing in this way was, of course, an experiment which was not successful. But my Aunt Melinda had brought a pair of wool cards with her from her home in Missouri. She had someone make a spinning wheel, and after carding the fleece from wolves into rolls and spinning these into yarn, she knit garments. One garment, a jumper or sweater, I often saw Uncle Charles wear. The skin of the deer, when tanned by the Indians, was soft and pliable and was used by the pioneers. Coats and trousers of buckskin were worn, but I confess to a prejudice against buckskin. I have seen poems printed on this material, notably *The Days of '49*, and I have heard men talk about having notes written on it to hold against parties usually slow to meet their obligations, for a note inscribed on buckskin will not wear out. In a climate where it never rains a buckskin suit might be comfortable, but in the climate where we lived, such garments often proved to be woefully disagreeable.

All trousers, after frequent wettings and dryings would assume a fixed shape that permitted no re-formation. This malformation did not appear when a man was sitting, which was, for this reason, his favorite posture; but when he arose the appearance to an inexperienced eye was that he was not yet up, for the knees of his trousers did not respond to the straightening of his legs but held the shape of the sitting posture, and the seat of the trousers did like-wise. We boys, ever heedless, were caught in the grasp of buckskin trousers about every other day all through the long winter season. Coming in wet and cold, we would naturally hurry to the fireplace to warm our hands and feet, and the wet buckskin would immediately begin to shrink as it began to dry and the result was anything but comfortable for us. After a time, a heavy unbleached muslin, com-monly called "factory cloth," could be gotten from Oregon City or at the Hudson's Bay trading posts. This my Mother and aunts dyed a light brown, us-ing for this purpose the bark of the alder tree which was boiled in water until the desired shade was ob-tained. This cloth was then used to make dresses for the girls and shirts and trousers for the boys. Hats were made of braided oat straw that were both com-fortable and becoming. Shoes, as I have said before, were not to be purchased, and the pioneers wore buckskin moccasins when they first settled in the new country, but after a time, an attempt was made to manufacture shoes of a rough sort. Someone in almost every family could hew out a last, make pegs and rough shoes which were a tolerable protection to the feet and fairly comfortable. But there was no competent tanner and the material used was rawhide, a very poor substitute for tanned leather. If we boys waded in mud or water these rawhide boots became soft and many sizes too large so that we sometimes left them sticking in the mud. When they were finally recovered it took many hours of drying and cleaning to make them fit to wear.

Notwithstanding our privations and many hardships, we children found much pleasure in life. We lived close to nature in the early days. We hunted and fished and gathered wild berries and nuts in the woods and along the streams. We dug the many toothsome roots found on the hillsides and in the valleys, and contrived in many ways to find amusement and pastime in inventions of our own. My brother Elisha, who was an inventive and mechanical genius, read an old book on mechanics, and was able to build a gyroscope after casting the heavy wheel in a soapstone mould. This toy, when in operation, astonished the children, and the Indians regarded it with superstitious awe. When the wheel was put in motion and one end of the axle placed on the upright support and they saw that the other end did not fall, although there was no visible support, they would gaze at it with open mouths and breathless attention. When the wheel and axle began to turn on a horizontal circle around the pivot, a deep grunt expressed their involuntary satisfaction. I believe they regarded the occult power they saw manifested as a hopeless mystery since only one of them ever asked to have it explained. Many Indians came to witness what was, to them, a wonderful creation.

My brother also cast a cannon of lead. It was about ten inches in length and weighed five or six pounds. It carried a ball the size of a buckshot and the touchhole was just large enough to admit a grain of gunpowder. Of course, we had it mounted on a carriage. We used two kinds of projectile; the regular buckshot and a long bullet we moulded especially for the cannon. We began testing the gun with very small charges of powder and as our confidence in the strength of the metal grew, the charge was augmented till we reached the maximum of the quantity the gun would burn. In all those experiments we loaded with only one ball. Having settled the question as to the maximum charge of powder, we entered upon a series of experiments to find the maximum weight of projectile or projectiles the metal would bear—two buckshot did not appear to make much difference. A long bullet and a buckshot was all right, so we loaded with a buckshot, several paper wads, some ashes, a wad, a long bullet and paper wad all being tamped into the barrel very tight. The gun stood this severe test without injury, but the recoil carried the carriage back about five feet, and though we suspected that this drawback saved the gun, we were satisfied with the tests and

that there was little danger in firing any ordinary
load. The testing took several days, because the
business had to be frequently suspended, on account of calls to do other work, and it consumed a
large quantity of powder. It was not safe to be near
the cannon when it was undergoing a test of its
strength. The gun was placed near the wall of an
unoccupied log cabin and our place of safety was
around the corner of the house, so that the corner
would protect us if the gun should burst. So a train
of powder had to be laid from the touchhole long
enough to reach a little distance past the corner, so
that we could reach it with a fire-coal on the end of
a long pole from our place at the end of the house.
Accordingly, a train of powder five or six feet long
had to be burned every time the weapon was discharged. The gun being safe, the next thing in order
was to find its range. We tried it at the side of a barn
a hundred yards away, but there was no evidence
that the projectile hit the barn, though we tried several tests at that distance both with buckshot and
the long bullet; in fact we could not tell where the
bullets went. Continuing our advance upon the target, firing occasionally as we approached, we hit the
barn several times with a round shot at a distance of
forty yards. We never could find where the bullet
struck, but we could hear it rattle. The chickens
might have suffered at short range, but we never
could get one to stand still long enough to get the
cannon unlimbered and sighted.

Finally, a circular powder stain about two inches big was made on a foot-wide board we put up for a target at a distance of twenty steps. We fired many shots at this target using both kinds of bullets, but only succeeded in piercing the board with three or four round shot. The long bullets never hit the board and we concluded that as soon as a long bullet left the gun, it began to turn end over end and both velocity and direction were lost in ricocheting. As luck would have it, this theory was verified by a mere accident. We had put a maximum charge in the gun, using a long bullet, and tamped the wad down on it very hard. Just then there happened to be an Indian coming up the path from the spring and when he was about twenty yards to one side of the target and about the same distance from the battery, the gun was very carefully sighted and discharged. The report had just reached the edge of the woods sixty yards away, but the echo had not had time to return, when the Indian came running toward us while crying out in a frightened tone of voice, "Mika tika pu nika pe kotta? Do you want to shoot me? For what?" We pointed to the target and assured him we were shooting at it, but he looked at it and then in the direction he had come, and said in Chinook and sign language "that the bullet was coming right at his head, but he heard it whiz just in time to dodge and avoid it." We were reloading and had put in the powder and wad and I had a long bullet in my hand when our visitor held out his hand and uttered, "Nuh! Nika nanich, Say! Let me see." Examining it for a moment, he offered a grunt of satisfaction or disgust, coupled with the remark: "Cultus piltin colitin nowitka. It is a bad, crazy projectile sure enough." We then discovered for the first time what the true, quick eye of the red man had seen at a glance. The long bullet was a bit smaller at one end than the other, a little bent and slightly beveled on one side of the larger end; it was almost a perfect model of the Australian boomerang, a veritable *boomeranglet*.

Having made this discovery, I put a round shot in the gun, for it was plain that the *boomeranglet* was liable to come back to the place it started from and we might not be so lucky in dodging it as the Indian had been. This shot missed the board, and the Indian, now in a good humor, being satisfied that the close call on him was an accident, and having his bow and arrows with him, strung his bow and as he did so, said, "Ulta nika pu. Now, I shoot," and the next instant the arrow sped. He was so alert I didn't even see him place the arrow in position, but it was launched with such force that it whizzed as it left the string. The board was split and fell in two pieces and the arrow passed on over the brow of the hill. The target had been hit nearly in the center. We all laughed, and as the Indian was a young fellow and had behaved so well after having to dodge one of our bullets, I gave him a plug of tobacco, about the size and shape of a squeezed lemon. I had

had the tobacco in press under the corner of the fence a week or two. This was when we were growing and manufacturing our own tobacco. The Indian, now very much pleased with his day's sport, for when he came to us he had been hunting and had several birds he had killed, left us and went home. The small village where he lived was only a quarter of a mile from our house, up on a bench of a hill, where there was a spring in a grove of wild cherry trees. He was truly one of our next-door neighbors. Someone in the settlement had named him Jacob, or Jake for short. He was a typical Kalapooya. The men of the Kalapooya tribe were not working men; they were either sportsmen or loiterers, while the squaws were industrious and did all the work. Aside from game furnished by the men, which they killed as much for sport as anything else, the squaws had to provide all the food. They had to get the wood; sometimes carrying great bundles of sticks on their backs for quite a distance. In moving from place to place they carried all the goods, provisions, wares, and "plunder" of every kind. It was not unusual to see a squaw with a pack on her back heavy enough for a pony, with a child riding on top of it, and trudging along behind a man mounted on a pony, who was carrying nothing but his bow and arrows, or an old "pil-pil musket"—a kind of short musket with a red stock which the Hudson's Bay people traded to the Indians for furs.

The only battle we were in, where our cannon

was taken onto the field, was an engagement with a skunk. Our dogs were very courageous and watchful for they would not permit an Indian to approach the house even in the daytime to within less than thirty or forty yards. Many times I have heard an Indian calling for protection against the dogs and would find him standing on the fence holding to a stake for support, or on top of a hog house on a bench of the hill, about forty yards from our dwelling. The dogs would fight a bear or panther, and two of them would kill a prairie wolf; but they would shun a skunk, though if under orders, they would make short work of one notwithstanding the disagreeable job.

One evening after supper, we were sitting about the fire, some engaged in a game of fox and geese, when one of the dogs came and stood in the door and, after wagging his tail and looking over his shoulder a time or two, uttered a couple of short yelps, which was to say, "There is a nasty thing in the yard you should be looking after, I don't want anything to do with it myself." When he felt we understood him, he turned and stood on the porch looking into the yard. The moon was brightly shining and as soon as we looked out, we saw a skunk nosing around in the yard. Our cannon was loaded with a maximum charge of powder, a wad, a buckshot, a wad, another buckshot and a wad on top of it; the long bullet, for reasons before stated, had been condemned. It was our plan to shoot at very

short range and kill the animal so suddenly that it
would not be able to retaliate; for the weapon a
skunk fights with was as much dreaded by us as by
the dogs. Speaking of the cannon being already
charged, suggests the remark that all our firearms
were kept loaded and ready for immediate use.
Game was liable to be seen near the house at any
time—dangerous wild animals were nearby at all
times. The deep basso growl of the gray mountain
wolf was heard of nights, as also the scream of the
prowling panther, cougar, and California lion. We
were few in number in the Indian territory, surrounded by their villages, never quite sure of their
friendship, and frequently had cause to fear their
hostility. Though we had tested the gun severely
and considered it safe, we did not care to be very
near it when it went off. The gunner, whose business it was to discharge the gun for that reason, always put the coal of fire used for that purpose on
the end of a very long and slim pole. When the
skunk saw us advancing, it turned about and with
its tail waving over its back came toward us hopping
backwards, as all skunks are wont to go into action.
Seeing this maneuver on the part of the enemy, we
planted the battery and I immediately sighted the
gun and sprang behind the gunner who, on the spur
of the moment, thrust his pole forward to apply the
fire-coal to the touchhole. However, the enemy had
already discharged his battery with total victory,
extinguishing the fire-coal and causing us to flee.

The gun, of course, fell into enemy hands and we made no attempt to recover it that night. The loss of the battle was easily accounted for; we had too much tactics. We had to plant our gun, sight, and apply the fire-coal, while all the skunk had to do was to plant himself and fire.

Now, what was the first thing to be done after the battle? Bury the dead? No! There was no dead except the dead fire-coal and that was left on the field where it fell. The next thing was to bury our clothes. We went to the garden and stripped off our clothes, and buried them, then went to the house and to bed. Just before I fell asleep I heard the gunner say, "By George, warn't that skunk sure loaded for bear?"

A boy in those days always wore his best clothes, not because he was vain, but because he had only one suit; so when we got out of bed in the morning, we did not have to dress before breakfast, and we enjoyed this change; for we had been required to dress before breakfast so long that it had become monotonous. Our appearance at the table the first time attracted some attention and was the subject of several remarks, but they do not belong to this story. After breakfast, we skipped out to the garden, dug up our clothes and dressed. Then we visited the battlefield; the cannon was there but the skunk had gone. We removed the gun to the garden and left it to deodorize at leisure. There was no danger of anything with a nose disturbing it. About noon, becoming ahungered, we approached the house and had reached the porch when we were warned away with threats of violence and told to go to the kitchen window. There our dinner was handed out to us in a squaw-cap on the end of a pole.

The full text of the law in our case was now promulgated: Our garments must be buried in the earth three days and three nights. If the clothes were in the ground only of nights, then the program to be carried out would take nearly a week— we chose the longer horn of the dilemma. In the course of three or four days, being confined from day to day to our own society, we began to feel lonesome and made several attempts to add to our circle. We tried to approach the dogs, but they declined our advances. We discovered Jake passing by one day and tried to engage him in social chat, but before we got very near him a zephyr passed by and gave him our wind and he began to make off talking back in Chinook, saying among other things, "Uh! Hya humm, skukum humm now witka; clonas mika muckamuck humm-ena. Uh! Big, strong smell you bet; maybe you eat skunk." He also made several warlike signs, such as taking hold of his hair at the crown with his left hand and putting an arrow in his teeth with his right. The cannon stood there heavily charged and we would have aimed and fired at the impudent and ungrateful savage if we'd had a live coal, but we hadn't and we didn't have time to disrobe and hurry into the house after one. I think I might have been justified in shooting him on the spot, for you know it hadn't been long since I had given him a whole plug of tobacco I had manufactured myself. However, on the fifth day in the evening a committee visited us and we were allowed to enter the house in full dress.

The reader must not infer from the foregoing that we were always idle and bent on amusing ourselves. We were each required to do our share of work of whatever kind we were capable of doing. Every boy had to put his hands to the plow as soon as he became old enough to guide a yoke of oxen or plow a straight furrow. Rails had to be cut and split for all the fences were built of rails. There were the hundred and one chores to be done on a farm, and so we truly earned our hours of leisure. We were also required to attend school throughout the winter season, and we had some very excellent teachers during the time we lived in the Willamette Valley.

In the year 1846 my Father, along with several other pioneers, agreed to go on an exploring expedition, the object being to find a more direct route for emigrants coming to Oregon. They hoped to find a route by which others might reach the new country without having to suffer the hardships they had endured and could never forget. Another reason which had great importance in prompting the pioneers to undertake the expedition was the continuing question as to which country, Great Britain or the United States, would eventually secure a title to the

Oregon Territory. Therefore, in case war should occur, and Great Britain be successful, it was important that we should have a way by which to leave the country without running the gauntlet of the Hudson's Bay Company forts, or falling prey to the Indian tribes which were under British influence. Fifteen men were found who were willing to undertake the hazardous enterprise, Father and Uncle Jesse making two of the party. Each man had a saddlehorse and a packhorse. After making arrangements for the subsistence of their families, this little party started out into the unexplored wilderness among tribes of hostile Indians. They left their homes in the Willamette Valley on the 20th day of June, 1846. The route they followed led them across the Kalapooya Mountains into the valley of the Umpqua, thence south through the mountains into the Rogue River Valley to the base of the Siskiyou Mountain chain, thence east over the mountains into the Klamath Country between the upper and lower Klamath lakes, across Lost River and along the shore of Tule Lake, and thence around the south end of Goose Lake and over the mountains in a southeasterly direction to the Humboldt River. After more than three months of perils, privations, and hardships, they arrived back home in October having blazed a route upon which emigrants could reach the Willamette Country.

I give here a short extract from Father's account of this road expedition, written in 1878, thirty-one years after the event. This sketch takes up the narrative of the experiences of the party when on the return trip:

"No circumstances worthy of mention occurred on the monotonous march from Black Rock to the timbered regions of the Cascade chain; then our labors became quite arduous. Everyday we kept guard over the horses while we worked the road, and at night we dared not cease our vigilance, for the Indians continually hovered about us, seeking for advantage. By the time we had worked our way through the mountains to the Rogue River Valley, and then through the Grave Creek Hills and Umpqua chain, we were pretty thoroughly worn out. Our stock of provisions had grown very short, and we had to depend, to a great extent, for sustenance, upon game. Road working, hunting, and guard duty had taxed our strength greatly, and on our arrival in the Umpqua Valley, knowing that the greatest difficulties in the way of the immigrants had been removed, we decided to proceed at once to our homes in the Willamette. There we arrived on the third day of October, 1846, having been absent three months and thirteen days. During this entire time our friends had heard nothing from us, and realizing the dangerous character of our expedition, many believed in the rumor which sometime before reached them, that we had all been murdered by the Indians. As soon as we could possibly make the arrangements, we sent out a party, with oxen and horses, to meet the immigrants and aid them in reaching the Willamette settlements. For this assistance we made no demand; nor did we tax them for the use of the road, as was alleged by parties inimical to our enterprise. It had been the distinct understanding that the road should be free, and the consciousness of having opened up better means of access to the country than was afforded by the expensive and dangerous route down the

Columbia, which we had tried to our sorrow, would be ample compensation for all our labors and hardships in opening the south road. Of course, our undertaking was opposed by that mighty monopoly, the Hudson's Bay Company, whose line of forts and trading posts on the Columbia gave them rare opportunities for trade with the immigrants. Many of the immigrants who followed us during the fall of 1846, had a hard time, though not so hard as they would probably have experienced on the other route; and some of them, not understanding the situation fully, became infected with the spirit of persecution which originated with the Hudson's Bay Company, and joined in charging us with leading the travel away from the northern route for purposes of personal speculation. Certain members of the party were singled out to bear the burden of persecution, whereas, if any member of the party was animated by improper motives in seeking to open the road, all were equally guilty, as the party was governed by a majority vote of its members.

"The efforts of the Hudson's Bay Company to minimize the road proved an eminent failure. Its superior advantages were better and better known and appreciated every year. It never ceased to be an important route of travel, and a large portion of the population of our state entered by this channel. It is a very significant fact that the great thoroughfare in use today, from the Willamette to the Siskiyou chain, and thence out through the Lake country and on to the Humboldt, departs rarely from the route blazed out by the road company 31 years ago."

The tragedy of the Whitman Massacre occurred in 1847 and the Cayuse Indian War followed. A number of young men who had come to Oregon in our train in 1843 answered the call for volunteers. These young men had followed the fortunes of the

Applegate families and had been faithful and loyal friends and helpers, and I recall with pride their ready answer to the call for volunteers to follow the treacherous Indians who had murdered the whites at the Whitman Mission.[1] Whatever was lacking to complete the equipment of these young men, Father and my uncles supplied. We boys were too young to go to war, but we turned over our little lead cannon to Billy Doke so it could be melted and moulded into bullets.

I believe it is well understood that the discovery of gold in California took place on January 24th, 1848, in a millrace that General Sutter was having excavated on the Sacramento River. Means of communication were poor, and it was sometime before the news reached our straggling settlement in the Willamette Valley. When it did, it caused great excitement and an exodus for the mines. Father, with a large percentage of the male population, left for the gold fields. The party prospected a little on the Rogue River in the Rogue River Valley, then on a smaller stream now known as the Applegate before pushing on to California. After spending a number of months in the mines of California, the Oregon party, numbering about 40 men, chartered a small

[1] After the Whitman Massacre, settlers in the Willamette raised a force that harried the Cayuse until half a dozen Indians surrendered to save the tribe from extermination. The six Indians were later taken to Oregon City and hanged. After peace was established, the Cayuse virtually disappeared as a tribe.

sailing vessel at San Francisco, intending to return by water to the Columbia. We often heard Father tell the thrilling story of the dreary voyage in winter weather, of how for weeks the little craft was buffeted by chilling winds until the sails and ropes were covered with ice, and the passengers were half-starved and half-frozen. Of how they were tyrannized over by a heartless captain and crew until they surely thought they were in the hands of pirates whose purpose was to starve them to death and throw them overboard in order to gain possession of the gold they had accumulated in the mines. Of course, the Oregon men would not stand this. They organized a rebellion and took the ship. The captain and crew were put on short rations, along with the other men, and were required to make the mouth of the Columbia River in as short a time as possible. This they did, landing the Oregon party at the old pioneer town of Astoria.

V

We Move to the Valley of the Umpqua

WE HAD lived in the Willamette Valley seven years when Father and my uncles decided to move to the Umpqua country. Father and Uncle Jesse had admired this part of Oregon very much when they passed through it while on the southern road expedition in 1846. Uncle Jesse settled there first and built the first cabin. When we had crossed the Kalapooya Mountains, he came to meet us and escorted us to his new home. We camped near his house for about ten days while Father and Uncle Charles located their claims. They chose two sections lying directly east of Uncle Jesse's section. Father's section was the easternmost while the home of Uncle Charles was midway between the two, and was the gathering place of the young people of the three families. Looking back across the years, I still can see that gathering of happy young people. Days of toil were nothing for we had that greatest of life's possessions, youth, with its hopes and dreams. Our first dwelling was built of logs, but in about two years after we settled in the valley, a frame house was built, Brother Elisha doing the greater part of the carpenter work. After we were comfortably located, Father built a flouring mill on a small stream not far from our dwelling. With the knowledge acquired from his old book on mechanics, Elisha was able to do all of the reckoning necessary in laying out the work to be done in making the machinery for the mill. This was the first mill for grinding grain built south of the Kalapooya Mountains.

A half mile from our house was an Indian village. Here lived a lesser tribe called the Yangoler or Yoncalla Indians. They belonged to the Kalapooya tribe and spoke the same language. Our gristmill was only a few paces from this village and the footpath used by the Indians passed near the door of the mill. They were frequently in and about the mill and looked upon it as a marvelous thing. We gathered many interesting stories and traditions from these neighbors of ours. The Indian's theory of the origin of the red man is interesting. I first heard this tradition from the lips of a venerable Chemomochot priest or doctor, sixty or more years ago, and I have never found an Indian who was able to add a word to it. All the priests or "medicine men," and, I believe, all the people knew this much of their origin. This is the tradition: "In the beginning was a mountain, and on the mountaintop was a table of stone. On this table was a deposit of some sort of matter, jelly-like in consistency—we would call it protoplasm—and out from this protoplasmic mass grew a living being in the shape of, and was, a woman. She held in her arms a male child, and when she was fully grown she descended, carrying the child on her bosom, to the base of the mountain, where the two were joined by a wolf. The woman placed the boy astride on the wolf's back and passed a strap around the child and over the wolf's head above his eyes." This closes the story of the origin of the red man. It ends abruptly with the group of three persons: Snowats, Iswukaw and Quartux (woman, boy, and wolf). Some of the Indians believed that when a man died he became the same as a clod of earth or kahte (a stone). Others seemed to believe in the transmigration of souls. I recall a number of times when an Indian, pointing to a wolf which was often seen near the village, suggested that the Quartux was some person, naming someone who had recently died. They regarded the wolf as a sacred animal.

Indians from the village were frequent visitors at our home. One day when a number were there, I was reading in a small book which was illustrated. I read from the book and showed some of the pictures to the Indians, expecting them to be greatly surprised, but they were not, and it appeared from what they said to me and to one another that they had seen "paper that talked," as they expressed it, or had some information in regard to books. This discovery aroused my curiosity and led to the following tradition which I gathered after much labor and many interviews with the Indians. Squiyowhiynoof was a man, a foreigner, of what nationality I could not learn, who came to the tribe from they

knew not where. He was a doctor or priest and
healed the sick, but I could not learn anything
about his methods. He had a book or books which
he read and he showed the Indians pictures of a
good country up in the heavens. He told them good
people would go to this country after death. Another picture was of a place down below where the
wicked would go for punishment after death. This
priest must have gained considerable influence over
the tribe for he undertook the punishment of those
who did not obey his teachings. He had those who
took what did not belong to them severely whipped
with hazel sprouts. This was a fatal mistake on the
part of the priest or doctor, and eventually led to
his death. The Indians feared their own native doctors and sometimes put them to death when they
failed to restore some patient to health. It seems
that a number of Indians came across the hills to
the priest's abode intending to kill him, and did kill
him. They left his body filled with arrows and fled
back across the hills in the direction from whence
they had come. When they had reached the hilltop
they were overtaken by a storm and sought shelter
under a large spruce or pine tree whose drooping
boughs protected them from the rain. An immense
black cloud was seen to hang directly over the tree,
and a great flash of lightning was seen to drop from
it onto the tree; there was a crash that made the very
earth tremble, and a column of white smoke shot
up to the very heavens. Then the cloud and smoke

passed away and the sky was clear. But the towering tree was gone. When the frightened people came near they saw the broken and shattered tree and all around were the scorched and blackened bodies of the half score of assassins who had sought shelter under the branches and had been punished for their sin by a bolt of fire from the heavens. We children were frequently at this place where a broken and shattered stump still stood. I finally found the grave of the murdered shaman; doctor or missionary, he must have been. This lonely grave was in the valley, a sunken place six or seven feet long, overgrown with the heavy sod, and at one end a slab of wood probably five feet high.

Lolokes-psis was the name of a native doctor of the Yangolers. His name is literally "nose-on-fire" (Lolokes, fire and psis, nose). This shaman had a nose almost as red as fire. He was a very interesting man and I frequently whiled away my leisure hours in his company. One day I went with him to visit a fish trap some of his people had in a small stream. As we were walking along a footpath, I saw a large rattlesnake crawling slowly across the path directly before us. I immediately began to search for a stick or stone intending to kill the snake, but Lolokes-psis objected, assuring me the snake was friendly as he would quickly prove. He gathered a reed stalk about two feet long, then began chanting or singing a most peculiar song, at the same time stroking the back of the snake with the wand. Back and forward, very gently, went the wand and more weird became the song until the snake ceased to move and lay at full length as straight as a rod. The doctor then sank slowly to his knees near it, placing his right hand, palm upward in front of the snake. Incredible as this may seem, it is nevertheless a fact that the snake began moving slowly up the Indian's arm to his shoulder, then doubling back, lay along this arm with its head in the palm of his hand. He carried it this way a few paces. When I ventured near, the snake shot out its forked tongue in a threatening manner and Lolokes-psis said to me, "Wake tenas siah," that is, "not so near." He then dropped on one knee and slowly lowered his arm until his hand rested on the ground when the snake slid down without showing any signs of anger or fear, and crawled away into the grass. Unreasonable as this account may appear, it is faithfully and truly told. Like the Moqui Indians, and some other tribes in New Mexico and Arizona, Lolokes-psis seemed to have had power to charm and render harmless the rattlesnake.

In the village near to us lived the proud chief of the Yangolers. He was universally known as Chief Halo. His was a noble character; he awoke early to an appreciation of the great advantages enjoyed by the white man. The food afforded by the cultivation of the soil, the growing of grain and vegetables, were to him a revelation. He often expressed his gratitude for the rich gleaning the settlers' grain

Chief Halo of the Yoncalla Tribe
from a newspaper engraving about 1890
Courtesy Douglas County (Oregon) Museum

fields afforded his people, and for the abundant supply of vegetables given them. He was pleased when he saw us plowing up the soil of his beautiful valley. No effort had been made to treat with the natives for their land at the time we settled in the Umpqua Valley, and nothing was done for a number of years afterward, but the chief never complained that we came and established homes. Five or six years after we settled in the country Chief Halo built a new house. We furnished him with rails to fence a few acres and were always ready to assist and encourage him in his ambition to become a "Boston," the Indian name for the white people. When we were helping him to harvest his first crop of wheat, he was very proud. He tried three languages in his efforts to express his appreciation and his idea of the evolution accomplished by him since the coming of the white man. Finally, an agent appeared to treat with the Indians and purchase the land from them. There had been peace between the settlers and these natives from the first, and our title to the country was good as far as they were concerned. However, the Indians were invited to assemble, a fat ox was slaughtered, and a great feast prepared. The Indians responded with alacrity. Of course, they were not much enlightened as to the important business to come before the assembly. The promise of houses, farms, and agricultural implements, plus a yearly food supply to be given them on the reservation appealed strongly to the majority of the Indians. Of course the agent spoke to the Indians through an interpreter, and the Indians responded through the identical medium. Chief Halo said, "I will not go to a strange land." This was not reported to the agent. When the tribe arrived on the reservation without the chief, the agent was troubled and came to our house to get Father to go with him to visit the chief. We boys went with them. When Halo saw us coming he came out of his house and stood with his back against a large oak tree which grew near the door. We approached in our usual friendly fashion, but the chief was sullen and silent. He had lost faith in the white man. The agent said, "Tell the old Indian he must go to the reservation with the other people, that I have come for him." The chief understood and answered defiantly, "Wake nika klatawa," that is, "I will not go." The agent drew his revolver and pointed it at the Indian when the chief bared his breast, crying in his native tongue as he did so, "Shoot! It is good I die here at home. My father died here, his grave is here. 'Tis good I die here and am buried here. Halo is not a coward, I will not go." "Shall I shoot him?" said the agent. "No!" cried Father, his voice hoarse with indignation. The old chief, standing with his back against the giant oak, had defied the United States.

We returned home leaving the brave old man in peace. Father and my uncles protected the old chieftain and his family, and they were allowed to remain in their old home. I have read histories of

Oregon, volumes of memoirs, and many tales of the early days, but have never found anything relating to Chief Halo. He was a character worthy to be remembered. Should the coming generations learn to know him as he was, they will see a noble figure standing with face uplifted and eyes wide with wonder and delight to behold the coming of civilization. This noblest and last sachem of the natives of the Umpqua Valley has slept with his fathers "Lo these many years." And his people; where are they? Their war songs, and their songs of exultation and lamentation will no longer be heard in these beautiful hills and valleys.

In the summer of 1853 the Rogue River Indians swept down upon the unprotected settlements in Southern Oregon, murdering the inhabitants, burning homes and carrying away captives. There was a call for volunteers and Father organized a company or detachment known as "Captain Lindsay Applegate's Company of Mounted Volunteers." Brother Elisha was then twenty-one years of age, I was seventeen, and we both enlisted for the war. The tribe inhabiting the Rogue River Valley was small and has been estimated at eight hundred people; less than half were warriors. This tribe was divided into small bands or tribes under sub-chiefs. Chief John, as he was called by the whites, was head chief of all these tribes, their great war chief. A treaty was made with these Indians in September of 1853, at our encampment, which was between the upper Table

Rock and Rogue River. After the treaty had been made Chief John and his son visited our camp. The son was about my age, a mere boy. We had many interesting talks together, and I liked and admired the young chief.

But here my little story must end. Of those courageous men and women who made that half year's journey to Oregon in 1843, only a little handful are left, like the last leaves on a tree. But those who have gone on their last, long journey lived to see the wilderness bloom, and lived to realize that railroad trains were flashing across the plains and mountains over which they had toiled with their weary ox teams in the long ago. May their sleep be sweet in the bosom of the land they struggled so hard to gain and loved so well!

2

By Ox Team to
California

by
Lavinia Honeyman Porter

Lavinia Honeyman Porter
Courtesy The Newberry Library

Editor's Comments

THE original printing of Lavinia Honeyman Porter's *By Ox Team to California* consisted of only fifty copies, yet it has always been a popular book for those studying the Overland Trail. Recently it has received renewed attention because of the current interest in women studies, and her memoirs have been used as ammunition by scholars debating women's attitudes toward westward migration. John Mack Faraghar in *Women and Men on the Overland Trail* quotes from Porter extensively to emphasize that women found the westering experience distasteful—their sad parting with sisters and home, their unpleasant contact with the crudest aspects of male society, and their own gradual loss of dignity as their appearances deteriorated under the exigencies of overland travel. Sandra L. Myres *Westering Women and the Frontier Experience, 1800–1915* argues to the contrary and relies on Lavinia Porter to show how women were fascinated by the grandeur of the western landscape, courageous to the point of foolhardiness in the face of the Sioux Indian threat, innocently amused at their determination to travel in stylish clothing, and independently-minded enough to tell a husband where to camp, even if it meant defying the male captains of a wagon train. Certainly, Lavinia Porter would never have guessed that her memoirs, intended for her grandchildren, would be put to such scholarly use.

It is safe to say that Lavinia Porter does not rival Jesse A. Applegate's position in history. She was not part of a distinguished family but rather lived a more private life. She would probably be unknown today except for her published remembrances. What we know about her comes from a few city records, a biographical entry in the California State Library that lists her as an author, and her obituary.

She was born on November 13, 1836, in Charleston, West Virginia, which prior to the start of the Civil War was part of Virginia. Information regarding her family is quite sketchy. Her parents were Robert D. Honeyman and Amanda Launders. When Lavinia was a child, her family moved from Charleston to Missouri. It appears she must have received an adequate education because her memoir, although perhaps somewhat overwritten, is a well-constructed and interesting story.

On May 23, 1854, when Lavinia was seventeen years old, she married James J. Porter of Hannibal, Missouri. As she explains, James was educated for a white collar job and had little or no experience as an outdoorsman or farmer, yet he seems to be quite knowledgeable about the care and handling of livestock—an important criteria necessary to complete the long westward journey.

There are several missing segments in the Porter family history. Their move to California was made in 1860, and her narrative ends with their arrival in Folsom, a neighboring community to Sacramento. Nothing is known about them until an 1870 entry in the Alameda County directory which lists James as a bookkeeper. In 1880 he is listed as a cashier in the Capital Savings Bank and in 1883 a teller in the California State Bank. The place and date of his death is unknown.

There is some ambiguity in the historical record regarding Lavinia's children. Her book includes a continuing reference to a son who was five years old when the family made the trek to the West, yet her obituary in the Oakland (California) *Tribune* of May 4, 1910, mentions only two daughters, one recently deceased. One may conclude that Lavinia probably had three children, one, a son, who was either long deceased or out of the region and forgotten or ignored by whoever prepared her obituary.

In the year of her death, Lavinia is listed in the Oakland City Directory as a renter in a boarding house, not an unusual place for an aging widow to reside in the pre-World War I era. Her obituary states that she had previously lived in Folsom and San Pablo before moving to Oakland. She may have taken up residence in Oakland to be near her surviving daughter or grandchildren. She refers to them in her introduction and to a sister, Charlotte Dunning Baker, to whom she dedicates her story.

The concluding statement on the California State Library biographical card is both sad and possibly apocryphal. It notes tersely that Lavinia Honeyman Porter died "just two days after completing *By Ox Team to California.*" Whether true or false it provides a rather dramatic finale as well as a unique way to remember her achievement as an overlander and a good story writer.

Author's Introduction

WHEN my two great, stalwart grandsons were little shavers, it was their favorite habit in the early hours of the morning to come creeping into bed with grandmother. Their soft little arms would twine lovingly about my neck and kisses from their dewy lips were pressed upon my cheek and brow. And were I ever so far away in slumberland their sweet voices clamoring for a story would banish all sleep from my drowsy eyelids. Usually they selected their own stories from the numbers I had so often repeated, but invariably wound up, when I had exhausted my lot, by saying, "Now, Grandmother, tell us about crossing the plains."

The true stories appealed more strongly to them than all the illusory conceptions of fancy, from the fact, perhaps, that I could tell them what really had occurred better than I could take from my imagination. Be that as it may, they never wearied of hearing how I crossed the plains, climbed the Rocky Mountains, and traveled many months on my way to California. To gratify them and their dear mother I have consented to write for them the history of my overland journey.

Those who may favor the succeeding pages with

their perusal must not expect any attempt at fine writing or glowing descriptions. The author's intention is to furnish a plain, unvarnished tale of actual occurrences and facts relating to her long journey. Nothing not strictly true will be admitted into its pages, and if some of the incidents related be found of a thrilling character, the reader will experience satisfaction in knowing that they are not the results of imaginary picturing. Whenever a personal adventure is narrated, it will be found to illustrate some particular phase of character, and none are recounted which do not convey information.

As I recall those years, they are as vivid as the memory of yesterday's events. It has been a positive delight in the midst of this modern life to live over some of those scenes. Those peculiar conditions no longer exist because the advent of the overland railway and the customs and usages of more civilized life have done away with much of the fascinations of romance and adventure.

If I have not laid sufficient emphasis on the difficulties and discouragement which we encountered, it is not because there were a good many obstacles to overcome, but in focusing the mind upon the past, the more pleasant memories stand out in bolder relief. Even when the cares and responsibilities weighed most heavily upon us, we had that saving grace of humor which enabled us to meet situations otherwise insuperable, and to gather courage whereby we might endure them all.

Necessarily in recounting these events so closely identified with our life on the plains, this narrative has assumed an autobiographical character to a larger extent than the author could wish, and I humbly beg pardon of the reader if I have exceeded the canons of good taste.

All through that tedious and extended time, I kept a journal of everyday's happenings as they occurred, but after our arrival in California, we settled on a remote ranch, and in those early and primitive days, books, magazines, or literature of any kind were rare among the farming community where we were located. My journal proving interesting to our neighbors, was loaned and re-loaned from one family to another until, at last, it fell into the hands of some careless persons who allowed it to be partially destroyed, particularly that part relating to the first months of our journey. The names of many different rivers, streams, and points and places have slipped from my fading memory, but the principal places and events of our journey were so strongly impressed upon my then young mind, that they have become indelible and time can not efface them. Perhaps the repetition of them over and over to my little grandsons and their young playmates served to strengthen them in my memory, and, while I may be lacking in ability to embellish this humble history I can still give the plain facts and incidents of that never to be forgotten journey.

I

Preparations and Farewells

IT WAS in the fall and winter of 1859 that my husband and I decided to emigrate to the Far West. Imprudent speculations and other misfortunes had embarrassed us financially to such an extent that our prospects for the future looked dark and forbidding. Accordingly, we then determined to use the small remnant of our fortune to provide a suitable outfit for a lengthy journey toward the setting sun. We were both young and inexperienced, my husband still in his twenties, and I, only a young and immature girl scarce twenty years old. I had been raised south of "Mason's and Dixon's line." My parents were well-to-do Southern people, and I was being reared in the indolent life of the ordinary Southern girl. My husband, educated for a profession, knew nothing of manual labor, and had no idea of any other vocation outside of his profession; nor had he the training to make a living on the plains of the West, or the crossing of the continent with an ox team a successful venture. However, we had youth in our favor, and an indomitable will to succeed, and I have since learned by experience that a kind providence watches over fools and children. Since that long ago time when I look back at the temerity of our undertaking, I have wondered why, and how, our older and wiser friends permitted us to be turned loose upon the wilds of the West without a guardian. We were two such precious dunces, but with a most exalted ego, and the utmost confidence in our ability to brave the dangers of the undertaking.

A journey across the plains of the West was considered a great event in those early days. It was long thought of and planned seriously with and among the various members of the family into which the would-be traveler belonged. Whoever had the temerity to propose turning their backs on civilized life and their faces toward the far-off Rocky Mountains were supposed to be daring with a boldness bordering on recklessness. Emigration then meant a long trek and the facing of unknown dangers in a half-savage country.

After many lengthy debates over the manner of transportation, and a diversified quantity of advice from our numerous friends as to the merits of horses, mules, or oxen, we at last decided (and it proved to be a wise decision) to purchase three yoke of strong, sturdy oxen and a large well built emigrant wagon, roomy enough to hold all we wanted to take with us, and in which we might travel with some degree of comfort. In a short time the oxen were bought. The six animals were young and had never been broken to the yoke. When they were driven to our home and turned loose in our barnyard, they

were as formidable a lot of wild brutes as the eye
ever gazed upon, as agile as deer, and as handy with
their heels as with their horns. Not one of us was
brave enough to venture into the corral with them,
and we soon concluded that we had six white ele-
phants on our hands. Finally, my husband found a
Negro man who agreed to break them to yoke and
chain. It proved to be rare sport to our neighbors
who watched him in the somewhat difficult task of
training that bunch of young steers. But with time
and patience they became more amenable to yoke
and chain, and sullenly submitted to be harness-
ed to draw the wagon. I shall never forget the first
time I ventured to ride behind them. We had invited some of our neighbors who were brave enough
to risk their necks to ride with us. There were several ladies and children and a man or two included. It
was our intention to drive our new ox team a short
distance into the country and allow our friends a
taste of what a journey would be behind the slow-
moving cattle, but before we had driven a block our
skittish and newly-broken team took it into their
heads to run away down the hilly streets of our village, pell-mell, first on one side of the street then
the other. In vain my husband called "Whoa, Buck,
whoa, Jill" to the leaders. It only seemed to add to
their fury, and as they recklessly sped along in their
blind rage, the way proper matrons and prudish
maids climbed and scrambled out of the rear end of
that wagon was a sight to behold if not to describe.

After continued trials and much patience on our part, our wild oxen became tractable, and long before the end of our journey we had become very much attached to them. They, in turn, had learned to love us, becoming docile and kind as kittens; any one of them would follow me wherever I went, eat out of our hands, or allow me or our little son to ride on his back.

The strong wagon with which we had provided ourselves had a staunch canvas covering, made watertight and firm enough to defy the ravages of wind and storm. Then came the loading and packing of provisions, raiment, and all the other paraphernalia necessary for a long trip. What to take and what to leave behind us was the problem that confronted us everyday. Many times the wagon was loaded and unloaded before the right order was found. Many of our most cherished treasures had to be left behind to give place to the more necessary articles.

The report of fabulous mines just discovered in the Rocky Mountains had extended far and near, and the Pike's Peak excitement was then at fever heat. It was at this time that thousands of people had set their faces westward towards that mecca of their hopes. While our friends imagined that we, too, would make that point the end of our pilgrimage, yet we had decided and promised each other that if Pike's Peak and its environments did not come up to our expectations, we would push on to California. With that final objective point in view we provided ourselves with provisions sufficient to last us for six months or even longer.

Young as I was at that time, we had been married nearly five years. We had a dear little, fair-haired son, Robert, who was both the pride and joy of our hearts. I began at once to prepare an outfit for both him and myself which I thought suitable to wear on the plains. In this I showed the callow ideas of an immature mind which would not be guided by older and wiser heads—proving also that my conception of roughing it for six months was incredibly primitive. Among the necessary garments in my outfit, I had made two blue cloth traveling dresses with an array of white collars and cuffs. When a sensible elderly neighbor suggested homespun or linsey woolsey as being much more appropriate, I scorned her advice. These fabrics were worn only by destitute people, and I was quick to assure her that I intended to look as neatly and well dressed on the plains as at home. However, I soon discarded my cloth gowns and my collars and cuffs, as I will relate farther on.

When our plans were fully matured and all our arrangements nearly completed for an early departure, there was revealed to me a most startling discovery that in the course of a few months the stork was planning to make us another visit. Welcome as he might have been under more favorable circumstances, his promised arrival in the near future brought consternation to our hearts, and we became afraid our plans would all have to be changed. We feared the perils of our journey might prove to be too hard for me to endure under these new circumstances. But I was well, young, and strong; and had the courage and bravery of ignorance. Besides, we were hoping to reach our final destination and be settled down into a homestead before the advent of the stork's promised visit, which I was careful to conceal from my friends. I did not wish to give my dear parents any unnecessary worry since they were already filled with dread and anxiety at the undertaking we had so lightly assumed. We concluded to make the best we could of the situation, and with stout hearts continued our final preparations.

Everything being now in readiness, we waited impatiently for the warm days of spring, as we were to depend mostly on the wild grass of the prairie for food for our stock which now consisted of the aforesaid three yoke of oxen, a full-blooded Arabian saddle horse and a milch cow.

It was the third day of April, 1860, that my husband and eldest brother, Sam, who accompanied us as far as Pike's Peak, left the little town of Hannibal, on the Mississippi River, and started overland across the state of Missouri for St. Joseph. My little son and I took the train and joined them in St. Joseph. There I made my farewell visit to my dear sister who resided there.

On the fourteenth day of April we left St. Joseph, driving aboard the ferry for the farther shore of the

Hannibal, Missouri
from a sketch by Edwin Whitefield in 1857

St. Joseph, Missouri
from a lithograph by Herman Meyer in 1853
Courtesy Missouri Historical Society

199

muddy Missouri River, accompanied by my sister, her husband, and a few other friends. We landed in a little village on the Kansas shore, and drove our friends out a few miles onto the prairie, where we made our first halt for our noonday meal at which our friends would join us for the last time. It was a most sorrowful picnic for the hour of our parting was near at hand.

Forty-seven years ago it was a serious thing to say good-bye to all that was nearest and dearest, to uproot ourselves from home and go forth into the wilderness, and into many and unknown dangers.

My sister and friends were to return by the ferry to St. Joseph. My husband and brother were too tenderhearted to remain and witness our sad parting. They hurriedly gathered the cattle from where they were feeding on the short grass, yoked them to the wagon, put my little son into the wagon beside them and drove slowly away, leaving me to bid my friends a long and last farewell.

I never recall that sad parting from my dear sister on the plains of Kansas without the tears flowing fast and free. Even now as I write, although so many long years have passed since then, I cannot restrain them. We were the eldest of a large family, and the bond of affection and love that existed between us was strong indeed. It was like tearing our heartstrings asunder. But such sorrows are to be endured not described. As she with the other friends turned to leave me for the ferry which was to take them back to home and civilization, I stood alone on that wild prairie. Looking westward I saw my husband driving slowly over the plain; turning my face once more to the east, my dear sister's footsteps were fast widening the distance between us. For the time I knew not which way to go, nor whom to follow. But in a few moments I rallied my forces, and waving a last adieu to my beloved sister, turned my dim and tear-stained eyes westward and soon overtook the slowly moving oxen, who were bearing my husband and child over the green prairie. Climbing into the wagon beside them, with everything we possessed piled high behind us, we turned our faces toward the land of golden promise that lay far beyond the Rocky Mountains. Little idea had I of the hardships, the perils, the deprivation that awaited me. When the reality proved to be more than my most vivid imagination had pictured it, I was still able to endure it with a staunch heart, but often as I walked ahead of the team and alone, thoughts of home and my dear Father and Mother would almost overwhelm me with grief. As each step bore me farther from them, the unbidden tears would flow in spite of my brave resolve to be the courageous and valiant frontierswoman. I had been taught that a wife owed her first duty to her husband, and hard as it seemed, I had the courage to do what I had promised under the highest and most solemn sanction.

We had been several days on our journey before I began to realize the immolation and sacrifice I was

to endure; giving up my comfortable home and all
my dear ones, cut off from the congenial society of
my associates and personal friends, the ease, luxuries, and comforts of civilized life. Enduring the disagreeable drudgery of campwork, the everlasting
exposure to the elements, the glare of the scorching sun, the furious and fearful thunderstorms that
often overtook us, the high winds, and blinding
sandstorms that blew for days without hesitation,
the dread that settled down upon us at nightfall
for fear of wild beasts and the many other dangers
that so often menaced us in our utter loneliness, the
necessity of still moving onward, each day, whether
we were in the humor for traveling or not. At first,
the novelty attending the starting out on such a trip
and the continuous change of our environment kept
up our interest. But as the days wore on, the irk-
some monotony of the journey began to pall upon
me, and I spent many unhappy hours which I tried
to conceal within my own breast, sometimes confid-
ing to my journal my woes and disappointments,
but managed to keep up a cheerful exterior before
my husband and brother. Gradually, however, I became used to the peculiar situations by which I was
surrounded and learned by daily experience how to
surmount the trials and difficulties, and with a naturally cheerful and optimistic temperament soon became philosophical enough to take things as I found
them and make the best of the situation.

II

Novice Ways

OUR FIRST night in camp was near a small stream.
On the banks were a few stunted and wind-
blown trees. The forage for our stock was not good.
During the night the cattle strayed from camp in
search of better grazing or the inclination for the
old pastures, and turned backwards toward home.
When morning dawned we had nothing left but our
"Arabian steed," which, fortunately, we had securely
picketed or he, too, might have deserted us. James,
my husband, took the horse and went back rapidly
over the road we had traveled the day before. My
brother, taking the field glasses, went on foot in another direction to find traces of our wandering
herd. With my little son I was left alone in camp to
wrestle with the campfire and breakfast.

I must admit that my first experience with real
cooking occurred on this journey. Like many other
Southern girls, I had learned how to make a delicate
torte or a fancy pudding, but never before had I
tried to cook a meal. You can well imagine what a
difficult task it was for me to build a campfire, then
get two kettles to stand upright upon the rolling
wood, keep the smoke from my eyes and ashes out
of the food, hampered as I was with my blue cloth

traveling dress and the constant effort needed to keep my white cuffs clean. Quite near to our camp an old man and his two sons had set up their tent. I learned that they also were enroute to Pike's Peak, traveling from their thrice remote New England home. I was conscious that they were watching my poor efforts very closely, and after I had upset my coffee pot, and the camp kettle had turned over and put out the little fire I had at last got started, the elderly man came to my assistance, rebuilt my fire, adjusted my kettle in the proper way, expressed his kindly sympathy in our dilemma, and then bidding me a polite good day returned to his own camp. As the morning advanced, my Yankee neighbors soon completed their campwork, folded their tent, and moved along on their way, leaving me alone on that forlorn prairie with not a soul in sight anywhere. Had I been a timid creature I might have wailed my lonely plight. My little son and I ate our poorly cooked and joyless breakfast alone after waiting long for the return of my husband and brother. Not until the noonday sun was high in the heavens were my tired and strained eyes gladdened by the sight of them afar off driving the lost cattle before them. After that experience, the stock was herded until bedtime, and then securely staked to prevent another occurrence of that kind.

I very soon discarded the blue cloth dress and white collars and cuffs, after finally realizing that they were just not the proper thing for camplife.

Fortunately, I had with me some short washdresses which I immediately donned, then tied my much-bedecked straw hat up in the wagon, put on my big Shaker sunbonnet and my heavy buckskin gloves, and looked the ideal emigrant woman. The initial days of such a long trek, however commonplace, were interesting to us. Every faculty was on the alert. Even so trivial a thing as a jackrabbit rising out of the grass, scared, and scampering with long leaps, striving to widen the distance between us, was able to hold our attention. Or we watched the misfortunes of a fellow traveler by the wayside, who, in his great haste, had neglected to lubricate his running gear properly; hence a hotbox which he was vainly trying to cool down with a wet blanket. Crossing a deep stream on whose opposite side were a few rough houses and the usual saloon, the entire population turned out to watch us go through their village. As we passed the last house, an old crone was bending over her tub busily washing, but she stopped her labors long enough to ask us in drawling tones, "be you gwine to Pike's Peak?" Answering her in the affirmative, we inquired the name of the village we were just leaving. "Oh," she replied, "this is Mason City." Anywhere through Kansas, three or four log huts constituted a city.

My young brother who came along with us was a youth of susceptible proclivities, fresh from the restraints of college life, and with the exhilaration of his new found freedom unusually elated. For was not his face turned towards the wonderful land of the Golden West? While we were only children around the home fireside, we had planned a life of travel and adventure, and now our childish longings were to be realized. He had an absorbing passion for nature, for every curious formation of rock or stone, a quick eye for all the beauties of the unfolding landscape, a ready ear, too, for every touch of humor, and was hilarious over the interminable picnic that he imagined we had begun. Nature had also endowed him with a nimble tongue, and he was constantly telling us funny stories of college life. Often we would laughingly accuse him of drawing the long bow, on relating some very unusual experience. In vain we would try to outwit him and play our own jokes upon him, but his lively retorts were nearly always to our complete discomfiture. Generous hearted boy was he, and round the campfires and over many of the wearisome stretches of our journey he made the hours seem shorter with his cheerful badinage.

Part of my work when in camp was cooking. I have already acknowledged my great deficiency in that accomplishment. The breadmaking at first was a total failure. When I attempted to make light rolls for breakfast, they were leaden. My husband, wise man that he was, ate them in silence, but my humorous brother, less polite, called them sinkers. I felt chagrined at my failure, but persisting in my efforts I soon overcame the mysteries of the dried yeast cakes with which I had been supplied, and in a short time learned to make sweet and wholesome light bread.

As we had no tent, we slept in the wagon, my brother taking the rear part to be his "Pullman," spreading his blankets above the bales and boxes, not seeming to mind the bumps, ridges, and uneven surface of his couch. James, myself, and our little son, used the front of the wagon. We had a huge, old-fashioned featherbed that made sleeping on top of the boxes and barrels a trifle more comfortable. During the day it was necessary to stow away the beds more compactly to enable us to get at the stores beneath them. This also was my work while the men brushed and curried the stock, lubricated the wheels of the wagon, and reloaded the various camp equipage. James was kindly solicitous for the welfare of his cattle, giving the oxen the same careful grooming that our horse received, and they fared much better for this attention, looking sleek and fine for the extra care.

When I had finished my part of the campwork, I would wrap myself in a warm shawl and start down the road ahead of the team. The early spring mornings were keen and cold, and I felt the need of brisk exercise. I had always been an enthusiastic pedestrian and greatly enjoyed walking over the gently undulating plains of Kansas. It was our endeavor to make from twenty to thirty-five miles of westward progress every day. If the weather permitted and the roads were not too heavy from the incessant rains, it became my habit to walk the entire distance. As I grew accustomed to the continued exercise, I could accomplish the long walk with ease. At other times, mounting my horse, I would enjoy a gallop over the prairies, occasionally getting a bad fall. My horse was a kind and gentle animal; but I soon discovered that he was possessed of one most treacherous fault, namely, that when frightened instead of swaying or shying sidewise, he would quickly squat, and the best rider would become unseated. I had been thrown from his back once or twice in this manner, luckily without injury, and Sam, my brother, made great sport of my failure to stay seated in the saddle on these occasions. This mortified me exceedingly, as from my early childhood I had ridden horseback. There were few horses that I dared not mount, and I was extremely vain of my skill as an equestrienne. However, one fine day, he too, came to grief. I had been riding for several hours and becoming tired, I had dismounted. My brother vaulted lightly onto my horse and rode swiftly away. While I stood admiring his graceful posture and the undaunted manner in which he rode, suddenly I saw him go flying out of the saddle and quickly strike the ground, and not on his feet either. After his own failure, he completely stopped vexing me with his jests and raillery.

We had only been a few days out on our journey when we witnessed an electrical storm, something unusual at this time of the year. This storm was frightful in the extreme for us as we were so unprotected from its fury. The sky was overcast with dark and threatening clouds, a low, sullen murmur as a distant wind filled the air. The lightning blazed incessantly as it lit up the darkening horizon. The thunder burst forth in peal after peal of deafening reverberation. We hurriedly drove our frightened team into camp as this storm continued. By midnight a furious gale swept over the bare prairie. Our wagon, exposed to the fury of the wind, shook and rocked in such a manner that every moment we feared it would be overturned. Yet with all this flurry of the elements scarcely a drop of rain fell in our vicinity. Farther on we discovered next day by the condition of the roads there must have been heavy showers. For the first two or three weeks it rained almost daily which made the conditions very uncomfortable, and with difficulty we made our fires from the water-soaked wood and cooked our meals under the falling rain.

When the days were bright and clear, the travel through Kansas was delightful. The aspect of the prairies in the early morning sunshine was most alluring. The air was fresh and bracing, filled with the fragrance of countless spring flowers, and every little blade of grass hung with drops of dew that scintillated like jewels as they swayed in the gentle breeze of morning. The sweet note of the meadowlark was music to the listening ear. On every side was high, rippling grass that covered these vast stretches of undulating land. I rode or walked over the tufted plain, seeing, unvexed by sound of wheel or human voice, the pleasant sights along the way. The solitude upon this wide expanse of open plain was absolute. No smoke arose in the clear air from any habitation. No cattle browsed upon the succulent grasses. No whistling plowboy tore the sod-grown turf with his shining plow, nor uprooted the tinted blue star flower that sprang up everywhere. There were numerous winding streams fringed here and there with miniature forests. Our cattle grew sleek and fat with the nourishing food that nature so lavishly provided. And just within the woodland that fringed the banks of some small stream, we would halt for the night, and be happy to find both wood and water, the two great essentials for a comfortable camp.

When we had been about two weeks on the road, we came to one of the larger streams in Kansas, the Big Blue River, timbered with sycamores, cottonwood, oaks, and occasional elms. After breakfast one morning, my brother loaded his gun and took a short excursion in search of prairie hens. We had seen numbers of them along the road. Much to his great disappointment and ours also, he was unable to startle a single one in the high grass. This we learned was the fate of most huntsmen at this hour of the morning and season of the year. These birds wait until the sun gets high and warm before they

come forth from their hiding places to strut and co-
quette with each other. This led Sam to take a much
longer detour than he had anticipated, and it was
nearly noon before he presented himself wet and
bedraggled, but triumphantly bearing one prairie
hen. Only wounded by his shot, it had weakly flown
just beyond his reach until it led him near the
shelving banks of the Big Blue, where, in a last successful effort to reach his fluttering victim, he had
stepped too near the edge of the crumbling banks
of the river, and huntsman and bird disappeared
beneath the waters of the stream. Luckily, grasping
a willow sapling as he went down and still holding
onto his feathered victim, he pulled himself back
on shore and came back to camp elated with his adventure. We enjoyed the flavor of the wild bird, as
our appetites had palled on salt meat. Up to this
time wild game had been scarce near the road. As
we proceeded, prairie chickens, quail, and the ring-
dove became more plentiful and proved a grateful
addition to our larder.

Here and there along our way we saw numerous
dugouts which we were told had been occupied by
herdsmen. These were supposed to be a secure shelter from the cyclones that came so suddenly upon
these vast plains which were treeless; and as lumber
was scarce they also afforded cheap homes for the
pioneer emigrants who occasionally settled here.
Anything that looked like a home attracted us and
brought to our minds the association of home life

from which we were going farther and farther away.

While we were camping near the Big Blue, we were in the midst of a large company, who, like ourselves, were bound for Pike's Peak. The beautiful undulating meadowlands were dotted here and there with tents. The blue smoke from numerous campfires rose up all around us, while huge prairie schooners were anchored within hailing distance; in many instances, like our own, serving for tent and shelter. Cattle were leisurely feeding on the luxuriant grass, campers were fishing or hunting along the stream, while the women were on duties bent or sitting near their campfires. The children of the emigrants, released from the confines of travel, were romping over bush and briar, and their shouts of glee resounded as some unfortunate one stubbed his brown, uncovered toes and fell face forward on the soft earth.

As we approached Nebraska, the country became wild and somewhat more sterile. All signs of human habitation disappeared entirely, and the wild game became less abundant. No longer the prairie hen nor the quail flew from the grass as we approached, though plovers and doves still seemed plentiful.

Between the Big Sandy and the Little Blue River was a monotonous trail, hot and uncomfortable with only a few cottonwoods to enliven the landscape. Here we came upon a settler whose humble, but comfortable cabin was filled with children of all ages. They seemed to flow from doors and windows;

their brown and sunburned faces forming a strange contrast to their tow-white hair. We were invited to visit them in their humble home and were surprised to find so much culture and marks of refinement in this faraway land. The mother was an educated, eastern woman, and in spite of the hard work necessary on a new farm and the encumbrance of a large and growing family, she, without the assistance of either maid or servant performed all the labors of her household, and still found time to instruct her children in the rudiments of a good education. Her courtesy and good manners I never saw excelled in the best society. While the cabin was very meagerly furnished, yet on the cheap wooden shelves that adorned the walls were many good books of standard authors, which bore the marks of being well read. The children were clean and well clad although their clothing did not need the services of a French laundry; neither did the mother have time to dawdle away her time at bridge or go to card clubs, even if these things had existed or been thought of in that isolated home on the plains of Nebraska. The father was a typical sturdy rancher, both horseman and herdsman, with a rich vein of humor combined with strong common sense. He proved to be most interesting and amusing as well as instructive. His fund of backwoods stories and his inexhaustible humor kept us in a constant roar of laughter. We left these delightful people with feelings of regret.

III

Kansas and Nebraska

To the inexperienced traveler the approach of
nightfall is hailed with joy, for the campfire is
among the chief pleasures of outdoor life. We vied
with each other in replenishing its cheerful blaze.
There was always a fascination in watching it kindle
from its little glimmering light into the roaring
flame. The flicker and glow illuminating the countenance of those nearest the fire for a brief moment,
bringing out each and every feature with a peculiar
distinctness, then suddenly masking them with an
intense shadow. Then, too, if the night was bleak
and the wind blew its frosty breath, you were reminded by your freezing back that picturesqueness
and comfort did not always go together. The brilliant tongues of flame and the innumerable sparks
floating off into the air had no charms for those who
were roasted on one side and frozen on the other.
The flying sparks on windy nights would blister
any exposed surface of the skin, while the smoke
with every change of the breeze was whirled into
your eyes. For all that, in many of our lonely stopping places, the bright and cheerful glow of the
campfire served to drive away the gloom that surrounded us, and keep the wolf and howling coyote

at a respectful distance. When we were far out on the great plains, with no wood or tree in sight, our main dependence for any sort of fire was on the despised buffalo chips. These emitted scarcely any flame, and we hurriedly cooked our evening meal before its unsatisfactory glow dissolved into a few light ashes. Then we appreciated fully, in spite of its minor drawbacks, our bright wood campfire.

In the early stages of our journey before we had grown wise by experience, it had been our custom when we came to a stream at evening to camp before crossing it. Storms that occurred so frequently at night caused these streams to then rise suddenly and overflow their banks. These shallow brooklets which we could wade easily at night, would become angry, rushing torrents before morning, filled with driftwood and debris. While these floods were raging, we had no alternative but to swim our cattle across or wait for the stream to subside. We had made this mistake once too often and at last found ourselves, as the rain continued, waiting in camp for several days for the waters to fall. But we were not alone. Each day brought us more company and before the water had subsided there were fifty or sixty other emigrant wagons in view, their tents dotting the landscape on all sides while their stock was grazing on the rolling prairie around us. The emigrants worked about their camps, the women busily employed in cooking or in trying to dry their clothing that had been drenched by the continual rain.

Sitting around their wagons were other unkempt, soiled, and bedraggled women, most of them lean, angular, and homely; and nearly every one of them chewing on a short stick, which they occasionally withdrew and swabbed around in a box containing some black powder, while a muddy stream oozed from the corners of their polluted mouths. It was evident to the most casual observer that they were snuff dippers from Arkansas or Tennessee.

A number of ragged and half-clothed children of both sexes swarmed around their camp, barefooted and barelegged. One of the women, to whom my attention was particularly called, sat disconsolately apart from all the remaining who were pottering around their regular chores or gossiping in little groups. Her thin knees were clasped by her bonier hands, and her disheveled head drooped forward. There was a most tragic expression on her care-worn countenance and she looked as if she cared for nothing on earth. A strong measure of human suffering was depicted on her hopeless face, and it seemed as if nothing would rouse her. But in this I was much mistaken. Two of her barefooted boys had committed some childish prank which roused the fierce anger of one of the men who stood idly by smoking his short pipe. In a voice thick with sudden rage he called the boys to him. The terror as well as panic displayed on their faces plainly showed their great fear, and instead of obeying the surly call they started to run. The man, seizing an ox goad, soon overtook them, and quickly applying it to their naked legs caused them to emit screams of anguish due to the severity of the blows. Then, in but an instant, I saw that mother aroused from her seeming apathy. With one bound, like an enraged tigress, she cleared the wagon, catching up a horse-whip as she ran, and soon reached the man, who was so unmercifully beating her children. Her attack was so sudden that he was unprepared for the onslaught. She rained quick and sturdy blows on his head, face, arms, anywhere in her blind fury. It required the combined efforts of two men of the company to make her desist. The man whom she had beaten was wild to chastise her in return, but those who had separated the angry couple protected the woman. The boys in the meantime had scampered out of sight. After many hot words, a truce was declared and the commotion soon died down. I comforted myself with the thought that we were not part of such an inharmonious company.

This was a time when we were being continually overtaken by trains pulled by fast horse and mule teams. Many of them painted on their wagon covers such fanciful legends as "Pike's Peak or Bust," and "Root Hog or Die." However, before our slower moving oxen reached Denver, we met these teams coming back, and underneath their legends was the scrawled term "Busted" or "The Hog's Dead." The wild rush was not confined to wagons alone. Hundreds of men had pack animals which were loaded with blankets, provisions, coffeepots and cooking utensils. A few even had pushcarts which they had loaded with all their possessions. Traveling alone with our one wagon, independent of the numerous caravans that overtook us, we were passed by most of them for our oxen were much slower than the horse and mule teams which seemed to predominate. Yet the days were full of excitement as we came into contact with such a diversified lot of human nature. Nearly every state in the Union was represented, and all had the common goal of finding their fortune in the rich mines scattered through the Rocky Mountains.

These vast prairies of Kansas and Nebraska were sadly deficient in bridges. While at low water many of the streams were not difficult to cross, yet often we found ourselves at the brink of others whose steep and slippery banks looked very formidable. Down the precipitous incline our wagon-home would seem almost to topple over on the oxen, then into the moving stream and up the difficult pull on the opposite side. We had been on the road nearly a month, owing to the delays of wet weather and to the high water we encountered, when we came to a large stream too deep and treacherous to ford, called the Republican River, where arrangement was provided to cross by a rope ferry. At this place we found a large number of families, with an immense herd of horses and cattle, migrating from Illinois and Missouri to California by the way of Fort

Kearney,[1] where they would strike the old military road. They had been trying to swim their stock over this stream. This was slow and difficult and their patience was well nigh exhausted. It was impossible to get such a large number of animals ferried over in a hurry. Consequently, we had to wait our turn and nearly two days went by before we could take this primitive ferry across the deep stream.

One often hears the plains of the West spoken of as monotonous levels. But here and there they rise and fall in gentle undulations, sometimes crossed by narrow streams fringed by the homely and ragged cottonwood. One morning, while climbing a rather high divide, we caught sight of our first antelope, and my impulsive brother was ready to give them a chase at once; but they soon showed us by their swift flight that they had no desire for a closer acquaintance with us. We were sadly disappointed, for by this time we were beginning to grow tired of bacon and salt pork and longed for a taste of fresh meat. In a day or two they became more frequent and less wary, and one afternoon we sighted several in a group so intently feeding that my brother laid one of the beautiful creatures low with his rifle. The others soon sped out of range. They were beautiful, graceful creatures; in color a yellowish brown on

[1] Fort Kearney, located in south central Nebraska, was established in 1848. The soldiers at the post provided assistance and protection for travelers on the Oregon-California Trail. It became obsolete with the completion of the Union Pacific Railway and the suppression of the plains Indians.

Fort Kearney

Courtesy Nebraska State Historical Society

the upper portions of the body and almost white on the underparts. The nose, horns, and hoofs were black, with eyes bright and most beautifully expressive. We afterwards saw numbers of them in the distance, but this was the only one we ever came near enough to shoot. I could not forget the startled look in the beautiful eyes of the timid creature as it fell dying to the ground, and I did not enjoy the meat prepared from it as I had anticipated.

One Sunday while resting in camp, my husband accompanied me and our son to a lovely stream some distance from our wagon, where we could take a refreshing dip in the clear water. We had enjoyed our bath greatly. Leaving the middle of the stream I seated myself on its banks and as I was drawing forth my foot from its depths, a huge snake came gliding out of the water close by my side. With true feminine instinct I uttered a shrill scream and started on a swift run toward camp in my scanty bathing attire. Before my husband could overtake me, however, I had recovered from my fright and went back for the remainder of my clothing. Frequently, when walking, the sight of a huge rattler would cause me to make a sudden jump into the air to avoid coming in contact with the repulsive creature. James, who ever kept a watchful eye on me as I walked ahead of the team, would jokingly ask, "Why did you jump so high and run so swiftly at intervals?" A variety of reptiles were quite numerous along our route, rattlesnakes predominating.

IV

Buffalo Country

BY THE frequency of the trails that continually crossed our road, we found we were nearing the land of the buffalo. Now and then the heads and skeletons of buffaloes dotted the plains, and in certain localities the ground was fairly white with the bleached bones. We never imagined that any use could be made of them, but many years after that time I was informed that a regular trade had sprung up for these bones, and that a number of eastern firms did a large business in shipping them to their markets, where they were used in manufacturing buttons or ground into a fertilizer. As yet we had not seen a herd of buffaloes. We had listened to many tales of how they loped over the plains, coming swiftly with bended heads, tearing the turf in their mad rush, which no obstacle could oppose. They had been known to run directly through and over trains of emigrant wagons leaving scarcely a vestige, and while we were now constantly on the lookout for a sight of these animals, it was with fear and trembling.

One morning we had just finished our breakfast of salt pork, fried mush, and coffee, of which I had partaken with little relish. My hitherto pampered

appetite had begun to rebel at the coarse and homely fare. I was hungry for some fresh meat. Nearly a
quarter of a mile beyond us was another camp of
emigrants—men, women, and children—with their
full complement of tents and wagons. All at once
from this camp, I saw a man come running toward
us, and as he came nearer, pointing and gesticulat-
ing madly, I heard him shouting "buffaloes." Looking quickly in the direction he was pointing, I saw a
large herd of a hundred or more. They seemed to
be making a wild dash for our camp, bellowing as
they ran with lowered heads in a long awkward gallop. Several of the men were running on foot to get
a shot at them. My brother leveled his Sharp's rifle
and fired, but it seemed rather to hasten than arrest
their flight. On they came with rapid strides, and
crossed the stream almost beside our camp. One
shaggy-headed old fellow, shambling up the bank,
was fired at several times by a number of the men
just as he entered the water. Falling to the ground
as he emerged on the bank near our side, he caused
the rest of the shaggy herd to veer suddenly in their
course, making their way between the two camps,
and quickly disappeared around a group of low
rolling mounds just beyond us.

My little boy and I had taken refuge in the wagon, expecting at any moment to feel the trampling
of their hoofs, for we had heard much of their rushing through and over trains in their mad flight, leaving them destroyed and their occupants mangled

Stampeding Buffaloes
Courtesy Nebraska State Historical Society

beyond recognition. The buffalo the marksmen had wounded so that he could no longer follow the herd was quickly dispatched. The men dressed the carcass, and each one of the campers took a portion of the animal. When we received our share, I immediately raked together the coals and embers of my breakfast fire, and broiled thereon a piece of the fresh meat to satisfy my craving appetite. It proved a great disappointment for it was tough, strong, and dry. I had heard that no meat could equal or excel that of the buffalo, but the piece I had cooked was not relished. I also learned that this was the meat of an old bull, and we had not even taken the best part of the animal, which was the hump on the shoulders and was considered a very choice morsel. After this, we saw many large droves of buffaloes in the distance. There must have been thousands, but they had grown wary. The overland traffic in 1860 was so enormous that the buffaloes kept too far from the main traveled road to give much sport to the skillful hunters. We never again fired a shot at one. Occasionally, we were able to buy from the Indians a few pounds of what was then termed "jerked buffalo." This was strips of the wild meat dried in the sun and wind without salt. The tongues of the animals dried in this manner were fairly palatable, but one could chew for hours on one small piece of the dried meat, and the longer you chewed the bigger it grew. However, it was a decided change from salt pork and bacon.

We passed hundreds of new-made graves on this part of our route. One would imagine that an epidemic had broken out among those preceding us, so frequent were these telltale mounds of earth. One day we overtook a belated team on its way to one of the distant forts with only a man and his wife. The wife was quite ill and was resting in their little tent. She had given birth to a child a day or two before and it had lived only a day. The father had put it in a rude box and laid it away in its tiny grave by the side of the trail. The grieving mother was sobbing her heart out at the thought of leaving it behind on the lonely plain with only a rude stone to mark its resting place.

I think it must have been near the middle or last of May when we met our first Indians, a band of thirty or forty Cheyennes. They did not trouble us to any great extent, although we felt rather annoyed at their proximity. The first Saturday after we came into the neighborhood of this tribe, we called an early halt in the afternoon. For several days the grazing for our stock had been very poor, but in this Indian country the buffalo grass was more plentiful, and although it was short, it grew very thickly over all the ground. The roots of this buffalo grass were long and sweet, and the cattle devoured them with as much relish as the tops of the grass. In any stage of ripeness it was highly nutritious, and the stock throve upon it. Taking advantage of this good pasturage we concluded to wait over a day or two and

let our cattle recruit, while James made some needed repairs to the wagon. It gave me a convenient
time to do my necessary washing and baking. Continual moving on did not give much extra time for
cooking, and bacon, beans, and bread, day after
day, became monotonous; so I gladly embraced this
opportunity to have a change of diet. I made dried-
apple pies with bacon drippings for shortening; and
some ginger cookies, with the same ingredient entering largely into their composition in place of
butter. The latter was a scarce commodity, as all
that we had was from the milk of our one little cow.
We soon discovered that by pouring our morning's
milk into a covered can in the wagon, the constant
jolting would churn it as we slowly moved along,
and at night we would have butter enough for our
evening supper if we used it very sparingly. For
breakfast our bread was dipped in gravy as usual.
These two days in camp near a stream gave us an
opportunity for a bath, and me a chance to wash the
alkali dust from my hair, and to do the necessary
mending of our clothing.

We were now in the midst of numerous bands of
roving Indians, not hostile to us, but intent on begging or stealing. Whenever or wherever we made
our camp they soon found us and never left us
throughout the day. This Sunday I had discarded a
worn-out hoopskirt that I had worn thus far on my
journey, and much to my amusement and amazement as well, it was almost at once donned by a

huge Indian brave, who strutted proudly among the group of Indians who were squatting around our camp. As the skeleton hoop composed the larger part of his attire, he was a sight to behold. Even the stolid squaws were provoked to mirth at the ludicrous spectacle.

The following Monday found us ready to move on, and we began very soon to meet team after team of disappointed "Pike's Peakers" returning east. We talked with a number of them who had not even gone so far, but had been assured by the many returning that the whole country was a vast humbug. They, too, had lost courage and faith and decided to return to their homes. They told us of hundreds in Denver who would gladly work for their board, that men who were in the mines could not average a dollar a day, and all who could get away were leaving, urging us to go no farther. But we were not to be intimidated by their doleful tales. We would see for ourselves and continued on our way.

On the level lands and river bottoms of Kansas and Colorado were countless numbers of prairie dogs. These harmless little animals lived in villages, which we traveled through for weeks. These pert creatures filled the air with their chattering, a peculiar short, shrill squeak, rather than a bark, and the honeycombed soil was in motion with their antics. Sitting on their haunches on top of their pinnacled earth-burrows, they would peer curiously at us with their shining, beady eyes, until our approach jarred on their nerves, when they would suddenly disappear into the depths of their burrows. In many places there would be hundreds of them on an acre of ground. Beside the prairie dogs the coyote became familiar with us, never by day at close range, however, but at nightfall he could be heard prowling about our pans and kettles.

Occasionally we passed a small settlement where a hardy pioneer had built for himself a rude home, partly and sometimes wholly of sod, with a rude forge and a primitive blacksmith shop and the inevitable whiskey mill. As we went farther west, these little settlements were called cities, although consisting only of wretched little mud cabins, a few acres of land plowed but unfenced, and sometimes beside these cabins a wayside house from whose portals swung a wooden sign bearing the name "Tavern." They were odd structures, partly tent and partly cabin. A few rough posts would be driven into the ground, and these supported a ridgepole, across which some old pieces of canvas and ragged sailcloth formed a rude and primitive shelter, large enough, however, to hold several barrels of whiskey. On a dusty shelf above a counter made of boards resting on two empty barrels were a number of broken and cracked glasses, some half-emptied bottles, several cans of oysters and sardines, all of which constituted the goods of the so-called "Tavern." Probably the Boniface of this crude establishment knew his business much better than we did and had decided not to squander his capital in items that were not considered a prime necessity.

And here I found, as well as at other places on the road, that whiskey was considered a prime necessity of every outfit on the plains. This had been the subject of many spirited discussions between my husband, brother, and myself before and after starting on our trip. While laying in the supplies for our journey, everyone said we must take a barrel of that article with us. In spite of strenuous objections on my part, which were overruled, the whiskey was bought and duly stored with the rest of our provisions. At different points on our journey, I began to notice when we camped at night and also at our noon halt that our wagon had a drawing attraction for many of the other emigrants whose camps were in the vicinity, and it finally dawned on me that the barrel of whiskey was the alluring charm. While my husband was a temperate man, yet he was socially and hospitably inclined, and several of the emigrants, taking undue advantage of these qualities, would too frequently for their own good and my peace of mind visit our camp. I knew it was useless to complain or interfere. But I patiently bided my time, and one day when no one was around, I quietly loosened the bung of the barrel of whiskey and by nightfall there was nothing left of the precious stuff, save the empty barrel and the aroma of its spilled contents. Not even a bottle was saved for emergencies and we never needed it.

The continual walking day after day over the hot, dry roads; the wading through heavy sand and dust for much of the distance caused extreme suffering to the feet of many emigrants. My husband had not taken into consideration that he needed larger and roomier boots for this long tramp and continued to wear the same size he had been accustomed to wear at home. After a few weeks, he began to complain that his feet hurt him. Every morning it required greater effort to get on his boots. At length, finding his feet continued to enlarge, he tried splitting his boots open to give his feet added room. This, of course, let in sand and alkali dust, which irritated them still more. There was no store of any kind on the road where we could buy either boots or shoes or any other merchandise. Finally, his feet became so painful that he discarded boots altogether, and becoming too disabled to walk, was compelled to ride in the wagon for several days to allow the painful swelling to subside. My brother and I took turns in driving the oxen. Finally, we met a band of Indians from whom we were able to buy some moccasins made from deerskin, which were large, soft, and comfortable, and afforded great relief. They proved to be both strong and durable, and lasted until we reached Denver, where he was able to replenish his footgear in larger proportions.

V

Indians

W<small>E GRADUALLY</small> approached more desolate regions where we could look for miles over immense distances and see nothing but the long, dim perspective, and yet no sooner were we settled in our camp at evening and our fire lighted, when our Indian friends would appear. Fathers and mothers, and, judging from the appearance of advancing age, grandfathers and grandmothers, besides children of all ages, squatting, as was their custom, on the ground; watching silently though with greedy, hungry eyes every mouthful that was cooked or eaten; sitting so near my fire that I was compelled to step over their feet in getting to and from the messbox while I prepared my evening meal.

By many crude efforts in the sign language and an earnest use of a few Indian words that we had picked up among them, we attempted to carry on a sort of "Pidgin English" with those various tribes with whom we came in contact. There were two words we found that were thoroughly understood by them, and universally used wherever we chanced to meet, and they were "*bishkit*" and "coffee." It would have been impossible for us to have fed any number of them, but frequently I gave an old man or old woman a cup of coffee and a biscuit, which they greedily swallowed, or a lump of sugar to a child, which was seized with extreme avidity. After finishing our evening meal and scraping off the remnants of food, bones, and meat rinds from our plates to the ground, there would be a mad rush by every Indian for the refuse, and it was amusing to see the scramble that would ensue for the discarded scraps. After lingering a while and finding there was no prospect of getting anything more to eat, they would slip away, one by one, as silently as they came, but there was no sign of any habitation, unless they burrowed in the ground.

When camping one Sunday near the Platte River we were surrounded by Indians as usual whenever we stopped for any length of time, and their continual attendance left us little privacy. This Sunday I had washed my long hair to free it from the dust of travel and was engaged in brushing and combing out the tangles, having near me a small handmirror. One brave, who had been watching me very intently, was so hideous looking that I began to wonder if he knew how repulsive he looked.

Without a moment's hesitation I took the hand glass and held it before him. I never saw such a look of surprise and consternation as came over his stolid countenance. He took the mirror in his hand, looked intently into it for some time, then turned it over, examined it, and looked again. Then he took it over to the other Indians who were loitering in our camp and showed them the glass with their different reflections therein, and this brought about much curious amusement. I think this must have been their first experience in seeing themselves as others saw them. After a while, he brought the mirror back to me. I had given up all hopes of having it in my possession again. At length, this Indian with several of his tribe silently departed, but in a few hours returned with some new recruits, all decked in their paint, feathers, beads, and blankets. Approaching me he made signs for the mirror again. When I handed it to him, he burst forth in a guttural sort of laugh and immediately turned it on his new followers, who in turn expressed much amazement at this first view of themselves. The Indians generally were not voluble, but a wonderful flow of unintelligible sounds came to my ears as they discussed among themselves the merits or demerits of the strange little mirror.

A band of mounted Sioux met us one day. They seemed friendly in their advances and stopped to trade with us. It is my belief that the Sioux Indians were the finest looking warriors to come our way. Their ponies and horses were richly caparisoned, and their blankets, which were given them by the United States government, were gay with bright colors. The headdress of the men was unique and imposing. Sable braids of hair fell down each side of their painted faces, and the crowns of their heads were decorated with the colored feathers from the wild birds of the mountain and plain. Their buck-skin jackets were jeweled with beads and hung with the teeth of wild animals. Descending from their long braids of hair were graduating discs of bright silver made from the half-dollars that were paid them by the government. These were hammered out very thin, until the first was as large as a small saucer, and the others grew gradually smaller as they reached nearly to the ground. These discs were hung on strong but slender strips of buckskin and glittered gaily in the bright sunlight as the warriors, mounted on their fleet ponies, galloped over the hills and plains.

We found the Sioux tribe to be quite friendly, too friendly in fact for my peace of mind, for one brave, gayly bedecked and most grotesquely paint-ed, took a great fancy to me. Bringing a number of ponies to our camp, he, at length, made my husband understand that he wanted me in exchange. This was the first time I was really frightened at their ad-vances. Though I knew they were a friendly band and under the watch and protection of the govern-ment, yet I was filled with a fear that I could not wholly overcome, and urged my husband to move on as rapidly as possible, so we left our camp next morning before the break of day. About noon, as we ascended some low rolling hills, I looked back on the plain and saw a number of mounted Indians approaching us at a rapid pace and driving a large band of ponies before them. My heart almost ceased

Sioux Indians
Courtesy Nebraska State Historical Society

beating, as we were completely at their mercy if they meant us harm. Finally, they overtook us. We stopped our wagon and had a lengthy parley with them. They proved to be the brave and his followers of the day before. He had added more ponies to his band, thinking my husband had refused to trade because they had not offered a sufficient number. After numerous signs and shakes of the head, they at last understood there was no prospect of business. Very reluctantly they mounted their ponies and left us, to my great relief. Before they departed, however, I cooked a good dinner for them, and James treated them liberally to his best tobacco, so we parted good friends. However, for the next few days I stayed very close to the wagon.

Early in the forenoon of one eventful day we met the first warlike band of Indians. I was walking some distance ahead of the wagon, when in that clear, bright atmosphere, there appeared on the level plain a cloud of dust far off to the left of our road. I usually carried the field glasses with me and I quickly looked to see what I could discover. At first, the dust was so dense that the eye could not penetrate it, but soon there was revealed the forms of many moving animals. My first thoughts were "buffaloes," and I hurriedly retraced my steps to the wagon and the protection of my husband and brother. I had scarcely reached the wagon before my ears were filled with the din of most uncanny character, and out of the cloud of dust on numerous ponies rode a formidable looking band of Indians, many of them arrayed in the most whimsical and barbarous style that one could imagine.

There was not the slightest attempt at uniformity in costume. Some of them wore the discarded and ragged clothes of emigrants, from which dangled strings of buckskin knotted with gay beads and buttons, and interspersed here and there with a fork or tin spoon stolen from the emigrants. Their faces were painted in the most grotesque manner, and their coarse and matted hair, which grew long and scraggy, was ornamented with tufts of feathers from the wild birds of the plain and the tails of wild animals. Some were attired in the usual breechcloth, while many were wrapped in gaudy blankets of red and blue. Among this motley crowd were several that might have been devils let loose from the so-called infernal regions, for on their beetle brows were crowns made from buffalo horns, their limbs, naked to the knee, were covered with buckskin leggins and on their feet were moccasins. Others had made great effort to array themselves in fanciful attire of skins peculiarly painted and embroidered by their skillful squaws. And we discovered among the number some few who were not dressed at all!

As they bore down on us in their rapid approach, we became almost speechless with fright. Our first impression was that we would soon be annihilated. We saw at a glance that they were warriors ready for the fray, and had made elaborate preparations to go

forth on the warpath. They were armed with all
sorts of weapons, knives, and shields of various and
strange devices, but the bow and arrow, the natural
weapon of the red man was most in evidence. They
surrounded our wagon on all sides, making numerous signs and gestures and uttering words of Indian
jargon that were all Greek to us, for we could not
understand a syllable. Then, despairing of making
themselves understood, they pointed first east then
west, then to their ponies and held up their hands
with extended fingers. All in vain. We could only
shake our heads. At last, finding it was only a waste
of time to parley with us, their chieftain gave the
command, and re-mounting their ponies, they sped
away, giving voice again to their blood-curdling
yells and leaving us to recover slowly from our suspense. We drew a long breath of relief when we realized that we were still possessed of our usual
amount of hair. We afterwards learned that they
were in pursuit of some other marauding band of
Indians who had stolen and run off with a large
number of their ponies.

That night we camped near a few cottonwoods
on the banks of a small stream. The wind blew in
fitful gusts and the limbs of the cottonwoods rocked
restlessly, making mournful sounds. From each side
we were startled by noises that we could not place;
strange rustlings caused us to peer sharply into the
shadows, footsteps seemed to stealthily approach
and then skulk away; even the thin and scraggy

bushes appeared to suddenly close together as if someone were behind them. We feared that the Indians we had met earlier, knowing that we were all alone, might surround us in the hours of darkness, capture us unawares, and massacre us. None of us could sleep through the long hours of that night. We were afraid to close our eyes for fear of their stealthy return, but dawn found us unmolested.

I have said that neither the Indians nor ourselves could understand each other in conversation. Yet we found on several occasions that they had picked up and readily adopted a number of phrases from the emigrants, particularly the teamsters, whose vocabulary of profane words was extensive. The usual salutation of the Indians whom we first met was "How." But after hearing the irate teamsters from day to day cursing their overworked and often contrary cattle, the Indians very quickly adopted some of their pet phrases. Often when we met them, they saluted us in this manner, "Gee, Whoa, Haw. G-d d-n you," and did not appear to know that this was not the regular manner of saluting.

We saw but few Indian lodges. Those we did see were of the Sioux and Pawnee tribes. Usually their camps were remote from the traveled highway. We had been induced to take a shorter cut that took us in sight of one of their encampments. These lodges were built in circular form, a number of light poles forming the support, around which were stretched buffalo hides which the squaws had ingeniously

*A Deserted Pawnee Indian Village
as drawn by J. Goldsborough Bruff*
Courtesy The Huntington Library

sewed together. Some of these lodges were unique in their way, decorated and painted in accordance with the red man's idea of art, with grotesque faces and odd figures of animals, and strange hieroglyphics emblematic of something in their creed.

Many of these tribes did not bury their dead. Perceiving at some distance poles set upright on the ground and what appeared to us like a huge shelf above them, we saw on approaching nearer the form of a human body well wrapped in blankets and buffalo skins, and found that it was the Indian manner of burial.

A little familiarity with these aborigines will convince one that it needs a very poetic mind to make them even bearable. We found them to be not only lazy but covered with vermin, and while squatting around our camp, it was the principal relaxation of the squaws to spend their time overlooking the heads of their papooses and catching and killing the insects that inhabited them, very much to my disgust. The Indian brave abhors any work, and they looked on the white man with scorn and derision whenever they performed any duties to relieve the labors of their wives. The squaw accepted her life of toil as her just due for being born a woman. It was the squaw who dressed and tanned the skins and made the garments that the lazy Indian wore. It was she who manufactured the rough utensils in which the food was cooked. It was she who took down and pitched the rude wigwam then gathered the fuel, dressed and cooked the game, often walking for miles to bring it home, when her arrogant lord returned from the hunt. She made his rude tents after tanning and dressing the rough hides of which they were made. She also made his clothing and his moccasins. In some tribes the women were exceedingly skillful, and it was amazing what they could accomplish although they used the most primitive tools.

In addition to this, when she felt the pangs of approaching motherhood, the squaw would betake herself to the banks of some closeby stream and there all alone without any help from a nurse or *accoucheur* her babe would come into the world. After giving her newborn child a hasty dip in the cold stream, it was wrapped in a rough skin, strapped to a board and borne back to camp on the mother's shoulders. Then with all the stoicism for which the Indian character is noted, she resumed her interrupted duties.

VI

Trials of the Spirit

EVEN TO the most courageous there were hours of depression and discouragement. Our days were not always sunshine, nor our route through pleasant lands. The fertile soil covered but a small portion of our long trek between the Missouri River and Denver. After the first month or six weeks of our pilgrimage, the change of vegetation became very apparent. The sagebrush, that forerunner of sterile soil, began to crop out here and there. The farther we traveled the thicker it grew, particularly in the dry and sandy localities. Its only redeeming feature that I could discover was that it served for fuel in the absence of any other wood. We were amazed at the magnitude of these barren, unfenced plains. The occasional little hamlet was left behind and only at rare intervals did we come to the solitary cabin of some brave pre-emptor, who showed more courage than wisdom in settling on such a forlorn hope in Uncle Sam's domains. The wind had full sweep over these barren plains. Many times it was almost impossible for anyone to walk against it. Frequently, we staked our wagon down with ropes and also our stock to keep them from stampeding, for the wind and showers of blinding sand came with such force that neither man nor beast could face it. At such times, we could cook no food, but crawling into the wagon, tying down the covers on every side, were forced to content ourselves with dry crackers and molasses.

These winds sorely tried my patience and they seemed to act directly on the nerves. The chore of cooking around a campfire while the wind was screaming about required a greater amount of fortitude and self-control than I possessed. I tried to keep my hasty temper within bounds, but no matter on whatever side of the fire I stood when cooking, the ever shifting smoke blinded me, and the gale whisked my short skirts over the fire, until I found not only my clothes but my temper ablaze. I would make a brave effort to be cheerful and patient until the campwork was done. Then starting out ahead of the team and my menfolks, when I thought I had gone beyond hearing distance, I would throw myself down upon the unfriendly desert and give way like a child to sobs and tears, wishing myself back home with my friends and chiding myself for consenting to take this wild goose chase. But after a good cry, I would feel relieved, and long before I was again visible to husband or brother, I had assumed a more cheerful frame of mind, whether I felt it or not.

Besides wind and rainstorms, we would often encounter great swarms of gnats, which would annoy our stock almost to the verge of madness, stinging our own faces and hands, getting into our food and making it impossible to drink our coffee, without first skimming them off. These swarms of insects would last two or three days before we would leave them behind us.

As we proceeded on our journey, the streams of water grew smaller and farther apart and the great plains drier and dustier. There were days of travel with scarcely enough water for our stock, and that being so strongly impregnated with alkali only a small quantity would satisfy. Oh, how we longed for the sight of a cold, clear spring of water. We could sometimes see for miles ahead of us what appeared to our longing eyes a lake of limpid water, but on coming nearer, we found it to be only a thin alkali incrustation covering many acres of the smooth sands, and later on we were compelled to make a drive of nearly sixty miles without a drop of water for our stock. Our poor cattle were choked and dry with a great thirst. When, at last, they scented water, they were almost unmanageable and struck a beeline for it, paying not the slightest attention to the roadway, but speeding as fast as they could travel over hills and hummocks, caring naught for the safety or comfort of those riding in the wagon. While in this almost arid region, we endeavored to keep our small keg filled with water, but found it impossible to carry enough for our stock. Indeed, we had to use it very sparingly ourselves.

Through many parts of Kansas, Nebraska, and

Colorado the question of fuel was constantly before us. Days and days passed without seeing a piece of timber as big as one's little finger. Our only fuel was buffalo chips. This was the sun-dried excrement of that animal. It was my custom in the early hours of the afternoon as I walked, to carry a basket or sack, and fill it with buffalo chips, often wandering a distance from the road to locate a sufficient quantity with which to cook our evening meal and enough to bake our bread for the next day. This proved, at last, to be quite a laborious task for me because the numerous caravans ahead of us had gathered up all that lay near the roadway and I was compelled to cover considerable territory before finding a sufficient supply. The sack of buffalo chips became a heavy burden before I reached the wagon. I had been performing this task for days when one afternoon we passed some low hills on which grew a few dwarfed and stunted pine trees. They were only about a quarter of a mile from the road and I asked James and my brother to drive to them and cut me enough of the wood to last us for a day or two. But men on the plains, I had found, were not so accommodating nor so ready to serve or wait upon women as they were in more civilized communities. Driving a lot of wayward cattle all day in the hot sun over heavy roads of sand and dust was not conducive to one's politeness or accommodation. When the drivers were weary and footsore, they were none too ready to deviate a hand's breadth from the traveled road.

*Cooking on the Plains with Buffalo Chips
as drawn by J. Goldsborough Bruff*

257

Therefore, as it required almost half a mile of extra effort to get that wood for me, they thought it unnecessary trouble and refused.

I was feeling somewhat under the weather and unusually tired, and, crawling into the wagon, told them if they wanted fuel for the evening meal, they could get it themselves and cook the meal also, and laying my head down upon a pillow, I cried myself to sleep. When I awakened, I found that we had camped and they were taking me at my word. The only fuel in sight was across the deep and cold stream of the Platte, but they waded across the stream hatchet in hand, the water coming up to their hips. On the farther side grew some small willows which they cut and bore on their shoulders back to camp, and after many efforts, at last got the fire to burn and the supper cooked. James came to the wagon where I was lying and meekly asked how much baking powder to put in the biscuits. I replied shortly, "Oh, as much as you please." I will admit that his biscuits that night were as light and nice as any that I have ever eaten, and both he and my brother were quite elated with their success in getting the evening meal, and said it did not matter whether I cooked anymore for them as they could do just as well, if not better, than I did. The coffee also was fine, but the dried corn which they had tried to cook was not a complete success. This was a delicacy we did not indulge in everyday. It was usually saved for a special treat for our Sunday dinner, and I had always put it to soak for several hours to soften it before cooking, a precaution the new cooks had not taken.

I was hungry and ate too heartily of the under-done corn. The consequence was that I was very ill with a severe and painful attack of dysentery for several days. Finally becoming so weakened that I could no longer climb in or out of the wagon, I was compelled to keep my bed as we journeyed along. The jolting motion of the wagon soon became a perfect torture to me, and, at last, became so unendurable that I implored James to take me out, make my bed on the sand, and let me die in peace. He, poor man, was very much alarmed about my condition, and was at his wit's end to know what to do for me. Complying with my wish, he had halted the team in the middle of the forenoon and was preparing my bed on the ground. We were in the meantime overtaken by another emigrant wagon, whose sole occupant was a brusque, old Missourian. He stopped to inquire the cause of our delay so early in the day. James told him of my illness, describing my symptoms. The old man then said, "What your woman needs is a good, heavy dose of castor oil. That'll straighten her out all right."

Now, one of the most peculiar oversights in preparing for this journey was that we had not provided ourselves with any medicine. Not one of us had ever been ill, nor had we been accustomed to illness in our families, and our friends believing in the hydropathic treatment,[1] had not suggested such a need to us. We were also five hundred miles from a drug store, but after a moment's thought, I remembered that among the toilet articles in my trunk was a bottle containing castor oil, bergamot, and bay rum, put up specially for a hair tonic that was much in vogue at that time. This was sought for at once by my husband, and pouring out a tea cup full of the vile stuff in order to get enough of the oil, with grim determination I swallowed it down. Oh, the horror of that draught! To this day I never smell the odors of bay rum or bergamot without the vision of a poor, sick emigrant woman lying on the sands of the desert. Offensive and obnoxious as the dose was, it had the desired effect and acted like a charm. I have since recommended the remedy a number of times. In a few days I was quite recovered and ready to continue our interrupted journey. I noticed that my menfolks were only too willing to turn over the culinary department to me again, and really made quite a commendable effort to keep me supplied with fuel thereafter.

The United States government dispatched many trains of provisions to the different posts that were stationed far out on the plains, and these wagon

[1] This was a form of health practice that became popular in America after 1840. It involved the use of both hot and cold water for baths, bandages, compresses, and poultices. As a competing medical system, it lost out quickly with the rise of the germ theory and the development of more scientifically tested cures.

trains would often travel near each other for help and protection, their white canvas-covered wagons sometimes reaching as far as the eye could see. Many of these trains were composed entirely of ox teams, and their drivers used a profane vocabulary that sent cold chills over me. Never in my life had I heard such strings of oaths from the mouth of man. These immense caravans were called bull trains and their captains were known as bull train bosses. The men who drove the ox teams were called bull-whackers. All of these government teamsters in their moments of leisure were anxious for something to read. Before leaving home I had stowed away among my belongings a few favorite volumes to while away the hours of enforced leisure. My Shakespeare, Byron, and Burns and a few others that I could not part with I soon learned to hide very carefully and peruse with drawn curtains or they would have disappeared from my eye. The few novels and magazines that I possessed were loaned and re-loaned until they were so tattered and torn as to be scarcely legible. It was astonishing how great was the demand for something to read in that period of overland travel. The majority of those crossing the plains had taken no books with them, burdening themselves with nothing save the bare necessities of life. Anything in the shape of print was greedily devoured. Every scout, trapper, or other lone frontiersman with whom we came in contact would eagerly inquire for old magazines, novels,

or newspapers—anything to read. It was impossible
to buy reading matter on the road in those days. In
fact over a stretch of five hundred miles there were
only three or four post offices, and from the moment
we left St. Joseph on the Missouri River until we
reached Denver, three long months, we had had no
news from home and the dear ones we left behind.

At intervals, we were electrified with a passing
glimpse of the overland stage, bearing the mails and
sometimes passengers from the East, but they flew
by us with such breakneck speed, that it was impossible to even hail them. Yet, I still watched for them
day by day for they seemed to be a connecting link
between us and civilization. Occasionally, we would
pass an overland stage station, a low hut or cabin
constructed wholly of adobe or dried mud. These
huts were said to be very cool in summer and warm
in winter, their walls being from two to three feet in
thickness, and were considered proof against the severe blizzards that swept over the country, as well as
bulletproof in attacks from hostile Indians. I often
wished that I might look into one of those huts, but
never chanced to pass one when the host was at
home. I had not the temerity to invade one without
invitation, although the latchstring invariably hung
outside the door. We usually stopped only long
enough to take a drink from the rusty cup that hung
near a pail of water.

One of the most incredible wonderments on these
desolate plains was the mirage. The first time this

strange phenomenon appeared I was overcome with astonishment. One day while riding on the monotonously level road and gazing ahead at the wide expanse of sand and sagebrush, a peculiarly brilliant and dazzling light appeared like sunlight on the water. My first impression was that we were approaching a lake or some other large body of water. As I looked, this seemed to change, and a number of buildings came into view, but all upside down, and while still gazing at them they slowly faded from my vision, and the supposed water again came into view. I was so overcome with the fantastic vision that I could not wait for the others to overtake me, and turning my horse, rode rapidly back to the wagon to see if my husband and brother had witnessed the wonderful sight. They were as much surprised as myself and, though we had often read of the phenomena of mirages, this was our first sight of one.

From Cottonwood after a tediously long drive, we arrived one evening at a place called Fremont Springs, and here we found a fine spring of clear, cool, delicious water. For days we had climbed and descended hills and passed through a series of sand canyons. For many miles after leaving Cottonwood our road lay near the creeping, treacherous Platte. The Platte itself was not alkaline, but many times our trail was some distance from the river, and our cattle would become so thirsty before they could be driven to the river, that they would seek to satisfy their thirst in the various shallow lakelets that

Overland Stages at the Cottonwood Springs Station
Courtesy Nebraska State Historical Society

265

abounded near the stream, and these lakelets were in many instances almost saturated solutions of soda and potash. We, ourselves, as well as our poor cattle enjoyed the delicious draughts from Fremont Springs, which was considered the finest water between the Rocky Mountains and the Missouri River. We all felt like falling down and worshipping this fountain, cooling the parched lips of man and beast whose fate had led them beside the stagnant pool and dull, creeping, muddy waters of the Platte.

Much of our journey after leaving Cottonwood was near and in sight of the South Platte River, but its proximity failed to moisten the stretches of sand along our gloomy pathway. It crawled along between low banks, and one day I ventured to take a bath in its waters but, on descending its banks, the oozy loam glided too swiftly beneath my feet and in a moment I realized I was in its treacherous quicksands. I scrambled up the bank by main force, shuddering to realize how quickly I might have been snared in the muddy depths of its deceptive waters. On these desert wastes the wind blew at a rate of ten knots an hour and was so filled with sand that it seemed like earth in motion instead of air. Along this dreary route we walked day by day. Everything was gray. The few sickly weeds that grew upon its dry soil would crumble at the touch; here and there a single sunflower gave a touch of color; a few sickly cacti bloomed. Flowers that had enlivened the landscape farther back had now entirely disappeared. In their place the naked land swarmed with anthills, and myriads of grasshoppers and huge brown crickets abounded. At night, the wind blew even more violently, and the tempest of sand that came flying with it filled the air and everything that lay untouched for a time was powdered half an inch deep with it.

Through one of these storms the overland stage from the east overtook and passed us. It surged along with about a dozen wearied, dusty, dejected-looking passengers. I noticed that they appeared to be hanging onto life at the neck of sundry flat pocket flasks. As we came near Denver, the South Platte seemed to make its nearest approach to beauty, and in many places it was studded with beautiful islands, picturesque indeed, covered with emerald green foliage of graceful willows. When we neared Beaver Creek, a beautiful landscape began to unfold. The river seemed to widen itself into a huge lagoon. I recall the rosy hues of a beautiful sunrise that unfolded to our view. The mirrored water was filled with wild ducks, the river swarming with teal and mallard, their beautiful green and blue plumage looking gay in the early sunlight as they glided through the water with exquisite grace.

The journey toward Denver might have been divided into four stages—the prairies, the less fertile plains, the desert, and then the Rocky Mountains. At this late day, it is very easy to underrate the toilsome marches of many weeks—now that one can travel in forty-eight hours over an extent of country which forty or fifty years ago baffled the progress of the venturesome pioneer.[2] I remember how joyfully we greeted the first scrubby pine trees, giving us hope that the desert was nearly past and the mountains were not far off. Their soft and tender green was soothing to our sunburnt vision, and when we halted at nightfall we found a numerous band, who had made the tiresome journey through this woodless region, building huge fires with the dead pine branches, and taking solid comfort in the cheer and warmth of the ruddy, leaping blaze of which they had been so long deprived. Soon the foothills of the Rocky Mountains were in evidence.

Arriving at Bijou, Colorado, we encountered one of the severest storms I ever saw on the plains. We imagined we had seen severe storms in Kansas, but this one descended on us so suddenly, and the rain and sleet came down in such torrents, that we had scarcely time to stow away the provisions prepared for our evening meal. While James and my brother were hurriedly chaining our oxen to the wagon to prevent them from stampeding before the pelting rain and sleet, and staking the wagon to the ground to keep it from being overturned by the fierce wind, I and my little son climbed into the wagon for shelter. The noise of the rain and hail on our canvas

[2]The reader is reminded that this book originally appeared in 1910. Today's flying time from Kansas City to Denver is approximately 100 minutes.

cover was deafening and seemed as if it would tear our frail shelter into tatters. No warm supper for us on that night. We crawled into our blankets damp, tired, and hungry, wondering how long it would continue. Not until after midnight was the wild fury of the storm somewhat abated. A drizzling rain followed which made the roads almost impassable for days, while the heavy grades became so steep and slippery that we were compelled to wait for help to pull us up these steep inclines. As we came nearer the foothills, these high winds seemed to become more prevalent and swept over us at times with relentless force. Every night our wagon was securely staked to prevent an upset by the fury of the gale. These high winds no doubt accounted for the lack of timber, for the young trees were so rocked and wrenched that their roots were not firm enough to draw up what little nourishment that porous soil could give them.

But gradually a change was taking place. The pine trees which appeared at intervals, although stunted and dwarfed, gave variety and softness to the landscape which hitherto had been so monotonous and drear. The hills became more rolling and the valleys deeper with water courses more frequent in their depths, and our thirsty stock could drink their fill without robbing those who came after us. The timberless plain ceased to be desert and was once again fertile. Our progress now was one of gradual ascent. In many instances our pathway was unlovely and unsatisfactory. Here and there a shady ridge forcibly reminded us of the drift of the many terrible sandstorms we had so often passed through. When darkness appeared, we made our lonely camp near some little mountain stream, where our voices sounded singularly strong in the cool, clear air, and instinctively we drew nearer to each other with the knowledge of our loneliness. This loudness of our voices was the first thing we noticed that gave evidence of a change of air from the plains. We could distinctly hear the sound of a human voice two or three hundred rods away.[3]

Far out on the plains for miles before reaching Denver, we were told to keep a sharp lookout for a first view of Pike's Peak, and for many days we were straining our vision to the extreme limit. The first view I had of the mountain was in the form of a vaporous cloud. Gradually, this began to form a sharper and more distinct outline, until at last we could see clearly the glittering peak, covered with snow, rising to a height far above all other peaks, like a sentinel watching over the plain. As our gaze rested from time to time on this monarch of the mountains, so full of majesty and power, other less lofty peaks were presented to our view, until finally the whole majestic range of the Rocky Mountains was outlined before us. As our eyes were fixed upon

[3]There is no statistical evidence to indicate any meaningful change in the distance that sound travels on the high plains.

the towering mountains looming up so grandly, we easily fancied that an ordinary, swift pedestrian could reach them in a day's length. At any rate, our slow-moving team would bring us to them in a few short hours. But for days our course westward still lay along the plain and over additional rising foothills, while many weary miles intervened before we entered these mountain gorges and explored the strange and mysterious paths leading us up and down through those lofty ranges.

VII

Infant Denver

A<small>T LAST</small> in the latter part of June, after a three
month, wearisome journey, we made our way
down the mountains and over the lower range of
the foothills into the then primitive village of Denver. Picture if you can an almost level plain surrounded on all sides by towering mountains, whose
highest peaks were snow crowned even in midsum-
mer. In the center of this great plain stood Denver.
I shall never forget our advent into that "City of
Mountain and Plain." A few days previous we had
joined with several wagons which had their full complement of men, women, and children—a motley
crowd, the men unshaven and unshorn with long,
sunburnt whiskers, their weather-beaten and stained garments begrimed with the dust and dirt of the
plains—the women and children with their huge
sunbonnets pulled over sunburnt brows, unkempt,
ragged and dirty, their short, rough dresses in tatters from coming into too frequent contact with the
campfire, many of them barefooted from the rough
roads and long travel which had played sad havoc
with their only pair of shoes. I doubt whether any
one of us would have been recognized, so changed
was our exterior from the trim and nattily-attired

trio that left home in the early spring, now wearied from urging contrary and tired cattle over miles of treeless and waterless wastes, barren deserts and alkali plains.

I had pictured Denver as a thriving, bustling, busy city, but nearly fifty years ago it was an exceedingly primitive town, consisting of numerous tents and numbers of rude and illy-constructed cabins, with nearly as many rum shops and low saloons as cabins. Horses, cows, and hogs roamed at will over the greater part of the village. Very few of the humble homes were enclosed with a fence. These inferior shanties, built of logs and rough boards, were clustered together near the banks of Cherry Creek. In the lower part of the town the vacant places were occupied by the Indian huts of a band of the Arapahoe tribe, who were at war with the Utes, and who trusted that the presence of the white man in their vicinity would afford protection to their families against attack, while their own braves were off fighting or stealing in the mountains beyond. The relations of the Arapahoes and the Ute Indians were not of the most cordial character, for hereditary feuds and occasional warlike sallies had from time to time disturbed that perfect mutual concord so important for neighbors to maintain. Each tribe prided itself on its superiority to the other, and it would be deemed a great disgrace for an Arapahoe maiden to marry a Ute, and vice versa. The poor, overworked squaws were busily engaged

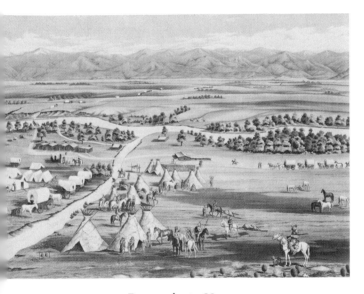

Denver about 1860
Courtesy Library of Congress

in the labors of the camp, cooking their vile com-
pounds and making the skins of wild animals into
the ungainly garments that they donned. Loafing
around in the sand and dirt were the indolent and
unemployed braves while their filthy and vermin-
covered offspring played naked in the sand. These
so-called braves wore nothing but a narrow strip of
cloth around their loins. While we were still camping in Denver, the warriors who had gone out to
give battle to the Utes returned, bringing with them
a number of horses captured from the enemy, and
making both night and day hideous with their pow-
wows and secret incantations. The dismal wailing
and howling of the squaws, bringing back from the
fight their dead and wounded, made the surroundings anything but cheerful.

Before our arrival, and imagining Denver to be a
center with some pretensions to civilization, I had
confided to my husband my intention of making a
more prepossessing toilet before appearing on its
streets. I carefully donned my best riding habit, and
made myself as comely as circumstances would allow. Mounting my horse sidewise in the saddle,
which I had hitherto ridden astride, I gaily rode
through the one street of the town until we crossed
a rude bridge spanning Cherry Creek. Here our
wayward cattle balked. A loud crack from the swirl-
ing whip urging them on brought fear to my "Rosi-
nante," who gave his accustomed squat, and I found
myself ingloriously dismounted and lying at full

length on the boards of the bridge. I was quickly lifted up by a chivalrous miner. After this ignominious debut, I was only too glad to retire from sight under the protection of our wagon until we located a place to settle down. We drove across the stream and camped on the banks of Cherry Creek opposite the village. We were very much discouraged by the outlook and the surroundings. The whole town seemed to be in a turmoil. In front of our camp on the other side of the creek we witnessed the hanging of two men by the Vigilance Committee. This filled me with horror and disgust, although doubtless they deserved it for the town was overflowing with vile characters.[1]

During our short stay in Denver we removed the bed of the wagon from off the running gear, to make some necessary repairs, and placed it upon the ground. One morning James had gone into the town to purchase some needed supplies, leaving me and my little son alone in camp, although other campers were in our vicinity. I had baked my day's supply of bread and placed it in the back of the wagon to cool. Seating myself in the front of the wagon bed, for more privacy I had drawn my curtains while I sat busily mending and conversing with my child. Suddenly, without sound or warn-

[1] The Vigilance Committee was so active in Denver during this period that nine lawyers published a notice stating: "Our professional business ceases until such time as regular and constitutional tribunals of justice are established in our midst." See *Rocky Mountain Herald*, 1860.

ing, my curtain was rudely pulled aside and there before me stood a huge, repulsive-looking Indian demanding bread. His tone and manner was so insolent and overbearing that it aroused my ire, and although frightened, I assumed a brave front and quickly told him I had no bread to give him. He said, "You heap lie. Plenty bread," at the same time pointing to my cooling loaves, but I shook my head and gave him to understand that he could not have it. My brother's gun stood within the wagon close beside me. The Indian reached in as if to take it, but I anticipated his thoughts, and seizing the gun, placed it beyond his reach. While his gaze was fixed upon me in open-eyed wonder, I also had time to look him over and saw hanging at his belt a number of bleeding scalps taken in the last fight with the Utes. These he loosened for my closer inspection and handing them to me, told or tried to tell in his broken jargon of English and Indian what a brave chieftain he was. Keeping up the show of courage I had assumed for the occasion but inwardly quaking, I took the bunch of bloody scalps in my hands and counted them, taking care, however, that my hands should not come in contact with the blood. The Indian looked amazed and surprised at my temerity, and with the startled exclamation, "Humph, white squaw no fear," left me as suddenly as he came.

The townfolk who inhabited the embryo city of Denver were a most diverse and varied lot. Every class of citizen was represented. Doctors, lawyers, merchants, stage drivers, gamblers, and preachers were all in evidence and from the general style of dress it was difficult to make a distinction. All alike wore the red flannel shirt of the miner and ox driver. The most prosperous lawyer or the most successful businessman or merchant was as roughly garbed as the commonest laborer. Low drinking saloons were to be seen on every hand and gambling dens of every kind abounded. Many of the squalid adventurers lived in the crudest manner, with no law save that enacted by the Vigilance Committee.

Miners and laborers were constantly coming into Denver from the various mining districts with conflicting reports. We hardly knew whom or what to believe. Many of them were out of money and out of heart. Others who had been more fortunate told of the rich strikes they had made.

We met and talked with a number of these more optimistic prospectors who had only recently come down for more supplies from a place that was then known as "Gregory's Diggings."[2] Their encouraging reports of gold discovered re-kindled the ardor of

[2]Gold was discovered by John H. Gregory on May 6, 1859, in a gulch on the north fork of Clear Creek about sixty miles north and west of Denver. This was the site of Central City, today only a tourist attraction, but a rival of Denver in the 1860s when it had almost 15,000 residents. The town faded when miners found that most of the gold was embedded in quartz, which meant that an expensive extractive process was necessary to make it profitable. What was once called the richest square mile in the world was exhausted before the First World War.

my brother, who thus far on our journey had been satisfied to stay with us, but who now decided that he was tired of travel, and was persuaded to go back with the prospectors to the mines. Taking with him a few tools and a stock of provisions and with high hopes that he was to make his fortune in a little while and return home a rich man, he started for the mines. He was as sanguine and eager as if none had ever failed. I dreaded to part with him and leave him in that wild country to battle with all the privations that must come to adventurous prospectors in their search for gold. All men were not fitted by nature to be gold diggers, and this brother of mine, hitherto a pampered and petted darling, just from college, unused to hardships, what dangers menaced his footsteps. What trials lay in wait for him! But no pleadings of mine were of any avail, so I bade him Godspeed and we parted in Denver on the banks of Cherry Creek. Long afterwards I heard that he had suffered untold privations and dangers. Finally, by weary stages of slow travel, sometimes on foot, he returned home, a sadder, poorer, but a wiser man.

I have mentioned our great disappointment in the village of Denver and its environment as we then found it in the summer of 1860. My husband said to me after we both bade my brother farewell, "What are we going to do now? Shall we remain here, return home, or push on to California?" My pride would not consent to turn my face homeward, although my heart yearned to do so, and I was so utterly disgusted with Denver and its squalid surroundings; with the Arapahoes who had made the last two or three nights indescribably hideous; with the combined drunkenness and rioting that existed everywhere in this society composed of the roughest classes of all states and nations; with this log city of maybe two hundred dwellings, not half of them completed, and the other half not fit to be inhabited by any self-respecting woman, that I felt life amid such surroundings would be to me unendurable. Without any argument or hesitation, I said, "We will go on to California."

By this time we had come nearly to the bottom of our very limited purse. We had our wagon loaded with plenty of provisions, enough and more to last us for a continued journey to California. Yet we could not think of going any farther without ready money to pay for the numerous ferries and other incidentals that were likely to occur on the road. So here we had to consider ways and means to replenish our scanty hoard, and to see what we could spare from our scanty belongings that could be disposed of to the best advantage. The weather was growing colder as we advanced farther into the mountains. Hitherto we had traveled without a tent. We now found that we could no longer dispense with that comfort, and we must provide a camp-stove for use in rainy weather. Among our stores we had packed two cases of thin, cutglass goblets and wine glasses, which were cumbersome and heavy, so we concluded to lighten our load of them and strengthen our purse. James approached one of the best saloons that infested the town and told the proprietor of his wish to dispose of them to the best advantage. As freight of all kinds had to be brought overland, articles of that variety were in great demand and expensive as well. The saloon man at once offered him a very satisfactory price for all the glassware, enough to warrant us to make the necessary purchases for the comfort of our extended journey, and money sufficient to last, as we hoped, until we arrived at our destination in California.

After re-packing and re-adjusting our load, we two alone with our little son took up the lonely march through seemingly endless mountain chains, and over desert lands for more hundreds of weary miles toward the land of the setting sun. Our road led over what was then known as the "Cherokee Trail" which we had learned formed the shortest practical route from Denver to Salt Lake City.[3]

[3]This route earned its name when a group of Cherokee Indians from Georgia traveled over it to reach the California gold fields. Later, most of the traffic on this route came down from the Oregon-California trail including the Cherokees who were returning to Georgia. The Porters were an exception when they traveled from south to north in 1860.

VIII

The Cherokee Trail to Laramie

WE CAMPED the first night out from Denver beside a small rippling stream, whose waters, as they flowed over the pebbly bottom, fell soothingly on the ear, while from its deeper pools, I caught the most delicious fish I ever ate. The night was cool and breezy, but within our now comfortable tent, we set up our little camp stove and built our fire. We soon crawled in under our blankets, said our prayers to the stars that brightly twinkled through the trees overhead, and thought of home and the comfortable beds we had left so far behind us.

For several days we pushed on through a reasonably level country, though we encountered many deep, steep-banked, dry gullies, and several very rough roads, until we arrived at last at the banks of the Cache-la-Poudre River, seventy or eighty miles from Denver and by far the most formidable stream we had met. We had been told that a rope ferry was stationed here that would enable us to cross this stream with safety. Unluckily, on our arrival we found that it had gone down the stream and nothing had since been heard of it. An old scout, whom we met here, assured us that there was no safe crossing for our team, as the current was very swift. If we were venturesome enough to try to ford it, our wagon and cattle would be carried downstream. Here was a dilemma. We dared to go no further without assistance, though anxious to pursue our journey with some degree of haste, prudence warned us that to cross an unknown stream alone was taking too many risks. We decided to wait and see what would turn up. A merciful providence had helped us before through many an obstacle. Why not trust once more? Here we prepared to camp for an indefinite period, as there were few people, if any, coming or going over this desolate road.

At the close of the second day of our waiting, there appeared, mounted on powerful horses, a white man and two Indians, trappers, coming from their isolated cabin in the center of the Rocky Mountains. They stayed with us an hour or more, sharing our evening meal. We begged their assistance in our perplexity, and they promised us if we would await their return the next day, they would help us ford the uncertain stream. Of course we waited for them, for we could not help ourselves, though we feared that they might not return for our relief. However, our breakfast was scarcely over the next morning when our eyes were gladdened by the sight of them returning with their horses loaded with pelts. These they hastily unloaded, and then after remounting their horses, plunged into the stream, swimming them up and down until they found a reasonably safe crossing and a secure landing place, where our team with their help could reach the opposite shore with safety. Upon tying a rope to the heads of our two lead oxen, a man on each side on their strong horses, we went boldly down into the deep and turbid stream. Anxiously we watched each move of the fearless horsemen as they measured the depths of the foaming stream. The current was strong and swift, and should any accident occur, a fatality seemed almost certain. Committing our all into the hands of our Heavenly Father, we rode down into what might have been the chasm of death, where the rapid current, yawning to receive us in its cold depths, seemed ready to bury us from sight. Owing to the steepness of the bank we came near upsetting the wagon as we entered the stream, but the second Indian rode by the wagon side and dexterously righted it. The water was deep for about fifty yards or more, the bottom broken and filled with huge boulders, and the current swift and strong. I crouched in the wagon with my little son trembling with fear, while my husband, riding the ox nearest the wheel, urged his swimming cattle on. Luckily our wagon bed was never afloat, although the water came up into it. When the brave oxen pulled us up the steep bank safe once more, I uttered a prayer of thanksgiving and gladly helped unload and dry out some of our goods that were dampened in the crossing. With many and heartfelt thanks to the obliging trio, who refused any further remuneration, we bade adieu to them, as they again mounted their horses, re-crossed the stream and went on their way. Another day's delay waiting for our goods and wagon to dry out, and we resumed our interrupted journey.

The Cherokee Trail, over which we were travel-ing, soon ran into the mountains near the Cache-la-Poudre, and henceforth for many weary miles we did not come across, neither were we overtaken by any emigrant or others moving westward. While in camp near this river, I could not help but wonder at the beauty of the grand scenery surrounding us on all sides. Above us was the bright dome of a heaven so free from all earthly smoke and vapor, so clear and transparent, that the stars seemed closer and shone with an incredible brilliancy. The air was filled with a balmy sweetness, and yet so limpid and clear that even in the starlight we could catch faint glimpses of the shimmering trees in the distant riv-er. Our campfire leaped high and roared in great flames, as if it, too, tasted the unlimited oxygen in the atmosphere. Beyond its bright light, purple, black, and gray bluffs towered up in the clear, dark sky. The silence was profound, broken only now and then by a yelp from a coyote as he sneaked war-ily beyond the gleam of our fire. The river flowed at our feet, hurrying on its way over rocks and boul-ders and bars of sandy debris, carrying its message of melody from Rocky Mountain snows to the Gulf and broad Atlantic. When, at last, our tired eyelids closed, we slept as if we were in our own bedroom.

On this portion of our journey we encountered many bad roads. In fact they were only trails, crossing high and rugged hills, deep ravines with rough and jagged sides, dark and dismal canyons between towering mountains. Many times we forced our way over the rocks that had fallen during the heavy rains from their steep slopes, and had to cross streams filled with boulders and choked with fallen timber and brush. Often we needed to chain and double-lock our wagon wheels to hold them back from crashing down some long and steep incline, and often a fallen tree lay across our path that had to be hewn and lifted by brute strength. For days our progress would not average eight or ten miles. At times, we came to a mountain up whose rugged slope it was almost impossible for our straining animals to pull the wagon. My husband would be at the oxen's heads urging and encouraging them in the fearful pull, while I followed closely behind the wagon carrying a big stone with which to block the wheels when the cattle stopped to blow and rest.

While traveling through the mountains between Denver and Laramie, we had determined on keeping the Fourth of July as a grand holiday. I had taught my little son all the patriotic songs that I knew, brought forth from my goods and chattels our American flag and decorated our wagon and tent with the red, white, and blue, regretting our lack of firecrackers or fireworks. From our limited larder I made preparations for a holiday dinner. We had camped the night before the Fourth in a little fertile valley, surrounded on every side by high mountains. Many of the higher peaks were covered with snow, but down in this little valley the air was balmy and mild as a Fourth of July day should be. Here we picked our first wild strawberries, a luxury indeed, to our appetites cloyed to satiety with salt bacon and beans. Our bill of fare was constructed on very simple lines, yet I do not think it would have been unacceptable even to a pampered epicure. A day or two previous we had bartered with an Indian: a pound of sugar for a leg of antelope. For our first course we had antelope soup, then roast antelope, and a piece of boiled ham with a curry of rice and our last can of tomatoes. I also made some very palatable cookies, even without the eggs which were considered so very necessary in their makeup. Stewed dried fruit and the fresh strawberries formed our dessert, and with an excellent cup of coffee completed a meal that anyone might enjoy, notwithstanding that the cups and dishes were of tin, and our table a board over a humble and empty soapbox.

We had hardly completed this bountiful repast when up the narrow defile that led into this little valley, we saw approaching us two white men on horseback, leading two horses. They informed us that they were prospectors on their way back to Denver, all they possessed being the few provisions and blankets that were packed on their extra horses.

They requested our hospitality for the night, which we gladly gave them. It was often our good fortune to meet with a trapper or scout or some wandering prospector from whom we could get some useful information. I was glad I had such a good dinner for them. When they had finished eating there was not enough left to feed the birds. They very feelingly remarked that it was the best meal they had eaten since they had left their homes back in the East. We knew not whether they were friends or foes, but treated them as royally as we could. Next morning after a hearty breakfast, they departed over the lonely road to Denver.

The next night brought a change of spirit for our camp was pitched near a little village of Indians whom we had been warned were very hostile to emigrants, and we were truly at their mercy for they were a warlike band. While I was preparing our evening meal, the chief and a number of his braves arrived and sat down in a semicircle around our campfire and asked in their broken means and by signs for coffee, sugar, and *bishkit*. I gave what I could from the quantity already cooked, and James gave them some tobacco to smoke. After sitting and smoking in silence, one got up and went away followed at intervals by another, then another, until finally we were left alone. How anxiously we spent that night none can ever know who have never been exposed to the dangers of savage life. Our fears proved groundless and the next morning we passed through their camp. They were making preparations to break up their own encampment. Having a large band of ponies they were compelled to move farther on for newer and more abundant pasturage.

This was our first sight of a moving Indian village and a more novel, curious, animated scene I never witnessed. I was quite indignant while I watched the indifferent braves lounging carelessly around, unmindful of the labor of their poor, overworked squaws—the former too proud and disdainful to assist the squaws in their burden of taking down their lodges, dismantling their camp, and loading their various trappings upon their primitive means of transportation, drawn by ponies and dogs. A number of lodge poles were fastened to the sides of the ponies, the ends of which trailed on the ground and on these poles, behind the animal, was fastened a light framework interlaced with slips of rawhide, which formed a sort of platform. Over this strong trellis of rawhide and framework were spread buffalo robes, the paraphernalia of their camp, and their most treasured clothing. On top of all were stowed their papooses and young puppies. The whole camp with the exception of the stolid and lazy braves was in motion. Squaws, dogs, and ponies were all on the alert and moving, ready to leave the old camp for the new. The women trudged patiently along by the litter that carried their offspring. These youngsters, strapped to their straight boards with their uncovered eyes blinking in the sun, looked anything but comfortable, yet I do not remember of ever hearing an Indian baby cry or murmur. Occasionally a squaw, becoming weary with her long walk after her arduous labor of loading up the animals, would mount the litter to rest or nurse her papoose. This method of riding was said to be very comfortable as the elasticity of the supporting poles made the motion easy. A number of these litters were prepared for the aged and infirm braves and others who had been crippled in their numerous combats, and this was their only mode of locomotion. They had to be assisted on and off by their faithful squaws, who drove the animals as well. The numerous dogs that seemed to infest all Indian encampments were put to duty on these occasions, and equipment similar to that of the horses, but on a smaller scale, was attached to them, on which were loaded the lighter articles of the camp.

We followed on in the wake of these moving aborigines until our noon halt, while they continued on their way to their further abiding place. The chief remained behind with us, waiting, no doubt, for an invitation to our midday meal, to which we felt compelled to invite him, very much to his satisfaction. After filling his capacious stomach to repletion and eating as much as three men would take at a meal, he arose and tried to express his gratification by rubbing his stomach with great gusto. It was characteristic of the Indians, whenever an opportunity offered, to lay in a supply of food against any future fasts. Evidently our hospitality and courteous treatment won their hearts for they showed no signs of hostility to us. In fact from their general demeanor they rather inspired us with a confidence which seemed to sanction our presence in their midst.

IX

Stress and Hardships

I CANNOT now remember how many times we crossed that wonderful river, the North Platte and its tributaries. It seemed to roam hither and thither at its own sweet will. It appeared quite a torrent as it rushed out of some deep canyon, clear as crystal and cold as ice, and again it was a wide stream filled with small islands, and except at the melting of the snows in the spring, one could almost wade across it. The Indian name for this river was "weeping water," but tradition said that the name had been changed to Platte for a woman missionary who was very much beloved by a tribe of Pawnee Indians. During high water the crossing of this river was very dangerous, owing to the quicksands and the continual changing of the channel. One could almost always find men stationed in the vicinity of the fords whose business it was to see emigrants and their cattle safely over, often at a tax of eight or ten dollars a wagon. Occasionally, we would arrive at the banks of the stream and find the ferryman away from his post, and much against our will were compelled to wait his return. We made the welkin ring with our shouts and halloas to bring back the missing guide.

At one of these crossings of the Platte, the ferry-man advised us to take the trail leading more to the north than west in order to more quickly reach the opening of Cheyenne Pass, thereby saving us several days' hard driving over a mountainous country. We arose at the dawning of day and with an early start hoped to reach the entrance of the Pass by nightfall. The drive, however, proved as usual to be longer than we expected, and the miles lengthened out until we found ourselves at night in a barren, inhospitable spot where the feed was not abundant. James tied two yoke of our oxen together in pairs and let them roam in order to get sufficient sustenance on the scanty feeding ground. The remaining two oxen he had picketed with long ropes, thinking that the loose cattle would not wander far away from them. Imagine our dismay when we woke the next morning to find no sign of the other stock. This was not an agreeable prospect as we could not expect to recover or replace our faithful animals. What were we to do? I was afraid to be left alone while my husband went in search of them, and I greatly feared for his safety in the uncertain chase. I watched him leave me with feelings of doubt and anguish, but we both knew there was no alternative as we could go no farther with only the one remaining yoke. So mounting the horse he ascended the range of mountains just beyond us, and there to his wonder saw an Indian driving the loose stock towards our camp. James halted until the Indian

*Ferriage of the Platte River
as drawn by J. Goldsborough Bruff*
Courtesy The Huntington Library

reached him, not knowing what was awaiting him. As the Indian neared, he began to make different signs and pointing backwards, implied that he had found the wandering cattle in the range beyond. James turned at once and came back to camp, the Indian following with the cattle. On reaching our camp the Indian, catching up the rope with which he had tied our cattle together, placed it in my husband's hands. We were overjoyed and surprised at the manner of their restoration and both wondered greatly that the Indian, who had us completely in his power, had returned them in that way.

It truly seemed to us in our long journey traveling alone that the Indians watched over us. Perhaps our simple loneliness and unprotected position, showing them that we had the most implicit confidence in them, awoke in their breasts a feeling of chivalrous protection. Our confidence and resolution in the face of overpowering numbers may have won their regard. Be that as it may, in our ignorant fearlessness we journeyed through the many hostile tribes unmolested and unhurt, while we heard details of various raids against emigrants who had preceded us. I was led to believe that the tribes with whom we came in contact had some secret sign whereby they communicated with one another, for we frequently noticed the smoke of fires on different heights as we traveled or stopped at our numerous camps. Sometimes the smoke would ascend straight up into the air in columns, at other times it would be diffused and wavering. By degrees learning then and long after that this was their method of communicating with each other at a distance, we at last came to the conclusion that in this or some other way the Indians had taken charge of us. With a feeling of gratitude for the kindly action of the Indian who brought our wandering stock back to us, I prepared a bountiful breakfast, for I had learned that the way to a red man's heart lay in the same direction as that of his more civilized brother, and I have never found an appeal to the stomach in vain. I even made extra efforts to whet his ever ready appetite. I made my lightest flapjacks, browned them with the lovely hue that made them most inviting, then sprinkled them with sugar so tempting to the Indians, and poured cup after cup of my aromatic coffee, which evidently from the number he drank, fully satisfied his critical taste, while many helpings of bacon and beans without stint entered his capacious stomach. I wondered if he had eaten anything for a month, so marvelous was the quantity that disappeared. He stayed with us until we left camp and started out on our day's travel. I gave him a loaf of the warm bread I had baked and a piece of bacon to take with him. He followed us for a while, then almost without notice took his departure down the canyon and was lost to view.

As we proceeded northward toward the main line of overland travel, our route lay over a badly gullied region, and we crossed many streams emerging from the mountains. By one of these our trail ran for more than forty miles, and in its tortuous windings we crossed it many times. The Red Buttes were conspicuous all along this river. The earth which gave them their peculiar color was said to be rich in iron. On the lower bottoms of this stream the grass was quite luxuriant, but the mosquitoes and gnats swarmed in such numbers that our stock could neither feed nor rest, while the annoyance to ourselves was more than tantalizing. Finding it impossible to sleep in this camp, we arose early and drove eight or ten miles before we could leave the persecuting horde of insects behind us. We drove until we came to a most excellent spring of clear, cold water, unimpregnated with any trace of alkali, and the best water we had drunk since leaving Clear Creek west of Denver. Nearly all of the many streams we had crossed were muddy and tasted more or less of the ever present alkali.

Finding it necessary to repair our wagon, we stayed at this spring for two or three days. It was a most picturesque spot, lying between rows of magnificent buttes, looking in the distance like ruined castles, some of them perpendicular and circular in form. They presented a variegated and fantastic appearance when viewed from a distance. In spots they were brilliant vermillion, but when broken by the water courses passing over them, they presented many uneven surfaces of white clay which gave them their peculiar appearance. After leaving these larger buttes, our road slipped slowly downhill until we reached the banks of a ravine, where we had great difficulty in getting down to the bed of the stream. Unyoking the forward oxen, leaving only the wheel oxen attached to the wagon, we chained and locked our wagon wheels, but even with all these precautions we came to grief, for the heavy wagon rushing down the steep incline caused the oxen to swerve in such a manner that the wheels cramped and the wagon was thrown against a mound of earth and loose rock that partly held it from a complete upset. Here we were in a deep ravine with no help near. We could neither get out nor go on. Not a spot of ground was level enough to stand upon in any comfort. The wagon had to be unloaded before it could be righted, and as the noon hour had passed there was a prospect of spending the night in this gloomy cavern. There was no other alternative but for both of us to go to work and unload as soon as possible. Even unloaded, the wagon was too much for one man to lift. James rigged up a sort of lever and with the help of the oxen, managed to right it again and pull the half empty wagon to a place less steep and more secure farther down the slope. By the time we had carried our goods down the hill to the wagon and reloaded it, it was near sundown. Hitching on all the oxen, we drove down into the narrow and deep stream. The opposite side was fully as steep and it required the combined strength of our cattle to pull us up the bank. This stream was called the

Chugwater, where we spent the night, expecting in a few days to arrive at Laramie.[1]

Before reaching Laramie we drove one night into a little park at the base of a mountain. It was almost in a semicircle, rimmed with dark and forbidding mountains. A small stream wended its way along its timbered banks. There seemed to be a strange witchery throughout this place. The wind moaned and wailed most sadly. During the night we imagined we heard strange sighs above and around us. We could hear stealthy trampings which seemed to come from other beasts than those that drew us on our journey. While we were stopping in Laramie, a soldier told us that this peculiar spot was called the "Haunted Hole of the Black Elk." Perhaps if we had known that this little park had such an uncanny reputation, we might have pushed farther on for our night's rest. However, nothing harmed us, and only the enormous mountains that surrounded us so closely overpowered us with their immensity.

The next morning, awhile before the sun's rays could penetrate this little dell, we were prepared to push onward, but not with great speed, for we were to climb another mountain, up whose steep ascent we were to lift ourselves over two thousand feet. In one place we wound around tall, ragged cliffs. The

[1] The Porters probably crossed Chugwater Creek, the south branch of the Laramie River, at what is now the town of Chugwater, which is north and west of Cheyenne, Wyoming.

soil was loose and unstable, composed of pulverized debris and shaly rock, which kept constantly slipping, so that the oxen had great difficulty in keeping their footing. It had been a steep and tiresome climb. For a time we had been riding in the wagon, but the way seemed so rough and dangerous that to assure our safety, we alighted, and very fortunately, for in less than twenty yards farther, the rear wheels of the wagon began to slip over the shelving embankment, and it was with almost miraculous effort that our brave cattle pulled the wagon beyond the danger point. Every moment I expected to see it topple over the precipice, pulling our valiant oxen with it. James plied his ox goad more furiously than our cattle had ever felt before, but it was the time for greater effort, and after the danger was past, he almost wept over the cruel blows he had given our gallant team. Now weary from the day's excitement, probably more than the fatigue, we went into camp. I made great effort to be cheerful and happy, and tried to laugh away the remembrance of the peril through which we had passed, but all through the night in my fitful slumbers I had visions of the towering cliff, and in my broken dreams felt the motion of the treacherous soil giving way over the sloping walls of the precipice.

While traversing this slope of the Rocky Mountains, we climbed numberless ridges and penetrated many passes, descending one lofty plateau only to encounter another. One morning we struck an almost level plain which appeared several miles in extent. There was only a dim trail to follow, growing fainter as we proceeded, until we finally lost it altogether. The grass on this plain, though coarse, grew thick and close. The way had been little traveled that season and the heavy growth had obliterated all signs of the trail. We wandered over this plateau for hours, trying to keep our northerly course, growing more fearful every moment that we were lost. At last, we discovered afar off a fringe of trees denoting a stream. On reaching it we drove up and down its timbered banks, and then to our great relief, we again struck our lost trail at the ford. We named this stream, "Lost Trail Creek," but it should have been "Box Elder," so thickly was the area covered with a growth of those trees.

After crossing this stream, we again ascended a high, rocky, barren plain, and for two or three days the trail led us over a most peculiar formation, composed of large pebbles, averaging the size of a goose egg. Our cattle became footsore traveling this rough roadway. Their hoofs became worn almost to the quick. They could no longer travel with any degree of haste, and it was truly pitiful to watch their limping efforts. We decided to stop at the first water we came to and give them a chance to rest. It was almost dark that night before we arrived at a little spring near the roadside, and as soon as the poor brutes were unyoked, they immediately lay down in their tracks, and for several hours neither ate nor drank, so exhausted and footsore had they become.

Next morning, on looking down from our lofty camp into the small valley below us, we discovered a tiny cabin and a wreath of smoke issuing from its wide chimney. This cabin, though rough and primitive, denoted the presence of the white man. Our curiosity soon grew beyond bounds and the next day we yoked up our lame team and drove down to investigate. We found two grizzled, old mountaineers located in this fertile valley. They had a small herd of cattle with which they supplied the nearest forts with beef. They informed us that they had lived in this lonely place for four or five years, seeing no one for months at a time, except the few emigrants who passed during the summer season or when driving their stock to the forts. They had built a rude forge, where they shod their own horses and those of passing emigrants. From them we learned that we could have our lame cattle shod with heavy leather shoes. This detained us, however, for two or three days as each ox had to be tied and thrown during the shoeing process. But it enabled them to travel in comfort for many miles before it had to be repeated.

Perhaps I have too tediously described this cross march from Denver before we reached the high road that led to California. This part of our journey was the only portion not traversed by mail, stage, or pony express. It lay through a region in which there were few white settlers, but the providence which had been with us from the beginning, safely guided us through all the perils that might have beset our path. After many days, we arrived at Fort Laramie from where we were to follow the regular overland road to California. We forded the swollen Laramie River in the early twilight and camped on its farther shore, feeling thankful that the loneliness which had hitherto oppressed us over the Cherokee Trail and through Cheyenne Pass was removed. Though young and inexperienced, I had learned to adapt myself to the rough life of an emigrant—crossing swollen streams, encountering terrific storms, and dreading constantly an attack from hostile Indians. But an American woman, well born and bred, is endowed with the courage of her brave pioneer ancestors, and no matter what the environment, she can adapt herself to all situations, even to the perilous trip across the western half of this great continent, always ready to wander over paths which women reared in other countries would fear to follow.

X

Back on the Overland Road

WHILE WE were camping near Fort Laramie, the soldiers warned us of danger. A detachment had been sent out from the fort on a reconnoitering expedition and reported an attack of Indians on an emigrant company of eight men, whom they had killed or taken prisoner, burned their wagons, and taken their mules and horses. These soldiers also informed us of the approach of a train of emigrants of about sixty men with a large number of horses and wagons. The officer at the fort insisted on our remaining in its vicinity until the arrival of that company, as we were running recklessly into danger traveling alone. Deciding that it would perhaps be wiser to heed his counsel, we waited and in due time the large caravan made its appearance and we joined their company.

This proved to be the most unhappy part of our journey. Hitherto we had proceeded at our own sweet will. Being accustomed to traveling alone, we stopped when and where we pleased, and started out in the same manner. Now all was changed. It was the custom for every large company of emigrants to select from their number a captain. His word was law. Everyone belonging to that company was supposed to do and act as he ordered. We were obliged to keep our place in the moving caravan, travel as long and as fast as he thought best, and camp when and where he chose. Previous to this time we had made shorter drives and stopped before dark. With this company we frequently drove until after nightfall. This was to me an unaccustomed hardship. Cooking in camp by daylight was no easy task, and darkness made it still more difficult. Our campfires were often of sagebrush which emitted only evanescent flames. Our lanterns dimly lighted with one small candle made only a glimmer in the darkness of the wilderness. My husband, too, had always been with me at night, but now had to take his turn as night watchman, and my little son and I would be left in our tent alone, while he was posted as sentinel on the outskirts of our encampment. Never before had I suffered with fear as I did while with that company. I could not rest or sleep while my husband was away from me, exposed to all the perils of the night and the treacherous foe. We might have been in the same danger before, but we were together.

My fears were not only of Indians. These people with whom we were traveling were the roughest, most uncouth and ignorant people that I had ever come in contact with. Perfectly lawless, fighting and quarreling among themselves, using language terrible to hear, they were the champion swearers of the world. They swore at their wives, at their horses, at

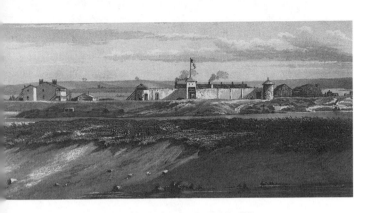

Fort Laramie on the Laramie River
as drawn by J. Goldsborough Bruff
Courtesy The Huntington Library

Fort Laramie
as drawn by Frederick Piercy
Courtesy Missouri Historical Society

311

each other, at the wind that blew, at the stones in the road. The air was constantly filled with their curses. The women of the company were suitable mates for the men. The whole company was made up of outlaws from Texas, Arkansas, and South-western Missouri. They imagined that they were so strong in number that they could whip any band of Indians, and it was their usual custom whenever the Indians approached our camp or sat by our camp-fires to tease and play different tricks upon them. On different occasions I was aware that the Indians looked on their manoeuvres with a resentful glare, and conversed with each other in low, muttered tones, and I trembled with fear for what they might do in retaliation. Many times I tried to expostulate with these men, but they laughed with scorn, saying they were not afraid of any band of Indians.

Very soon their bravado was put to the test. At the close of one day's long travel, we had barely set our camp for the night, when a lone, frightened pony express rider came galloping in haste into our camp, shouting to us that the Indians were near and would very soon attack us. While he was descending into a little canyon, they had suddenly come upon him from their ambush, pursued, and shot at him several times, and only because his horse was fresh and faster had he been able to escape them. Every minute we were expecting to hear the blood-curdling yells of the approaching foe. For the first few moments after the report reached us, the men who had hitherto boasted of their fearlessness were palsied with fright; however they soon rallied and made hasty preparations to stand and repulse the attack. It was a night I will not soon forget. Here, indeed, was a grave and perilous situation—overloaded wagons, tired horses and oxen, defenseless women and children. For what power was there in the hands of a few white men against a horde of Indians, bent on murder and robbery, and coming so suddenly on our faraway camp in the wilderness, where most of the numbers were defenseless women and children?

Our wagons had been arranged in the usual semi-circle enclosing the camp. Our animals were soon brought within and picketed as closely as possible. The men quickly put their weapons in order. The women held their children closely to their breasts not knowing how soon they would be ruthlessly torn from them and dashed to death or put to torture before their eyes. After hours of suspense, we began to hope that our fears were groundless, but this hope was soon dashed from our minds by the startling cry from another messenger that an attack from the opposite side was momentarily expected. Every ear was listening for the sound of the fleet feet of their ponies, every heart throbbing with anxious fear, but every lip was silent. At this hour, a fearful storm of rain and hail with continued thunder and lightning fell upon us. The sharp hail and the continued peals of thunder so frightened our restless stock that there was imminent danger of a stampede. The pelting rain flowed into our frail tents, wetting our pillows and blankets. At any other time, this would have been considered a great misfortune. Now we hardly noticed it while we sat through that terrible night, drenched to the skin, beaten upon by the gusts of wind and hail, deafened by the continuous peals of thunder, and every moment expecting the attack by the furtive foe. The darkness was so complete that we might have been surrounded by hundreds of the demons yet been none the wiser, and the uproar of the storm was so loud that hearing was as useless as sight. No one slept save the little children. The night which seemed interminably long passed at last and morning showed no enemy in sight. My husband and I uttered a prayer of thanksgiving. Absolutely, the fearful storm caused the attack to be abandoned.

In the course of a few hours we ventured on our way, hoping that we were not to be molested. Our number of nearly sixty men marched with loaded rifles on each side of the wagons to guard the women and children who were huddled closely within. The day was both long and anxious, and nightfall brought us little relief, for our next halt was among the charred remains of an express station which had been burnt by the savage foe. Half our men stood guard while the others slept with their guns at hand.

The now-frightened emigrants with whom we were traveling were more civil and subdued in their manner. This lasted for a few days, but as the fear of an immediate attack from the Indians wore away they resumed their usual tactics. They quarreled among themselves and were brutal and domineering to their wives, never caring for their comfort or well-being. The captain of the company was a tyrannical, ignorant man, who ruled with an iron hand. His every effort was to impress all that he was paramount and everyone must obey. It was he that regulated the length of the day's travel, selected the camp, formed the corral at night, appointed the guards and arbitrated all disputes. My hot Southern blood soon rebelled at his imperious and despotic way. Each day about an hour before camp time he rode with two or three of his henchmen for a mile or two ahead of the wagon train and selected our camping place for the night. His selections were frequently very unwise and uncomfortable. Sometimes his choice was a hillside, and our beds would slope too much for comfort, or a rocky spot by the road when a few rods either side would be smoother or less rugged. But whatever the discomforts, where he decided there we camped.

One night I felt it necessary to assert myself and renounce his petty authority. We had driven many miles that day over a winding, rough road and all were tired and hungry. When we came to the place where we were to pitch our tents, we found that it had been occupied the night before by emigrants who had preceded us, and, from all appearances, with a great number of stock. Within twenty rods of the place selected was a clear, grassy spot and just as near the water. A number of the women, although grumbling at the filth, prepared to make their lowly beds, while the men hurriedly raised the tents. My husband drove his team into the wagon stockade as usual. I said to him in an undertone, "You need not unhitch your oxen in this place. I will not camp here." He replied, "If we do not obey the rules of the company, we will have to leave it." "All right," I said, "the sooner the better it will suit me. I would rather trust myself to the mercy of the Indians than to travel another day with these ruffians and their ignorant captain. If you do not drive me to a cleaner place to camp and sleep tonight, I will take my blankets and go alone." He knew full well that I meant to do as I said. So without another word he turned his team and drove to the place I selected. The other women looked on my daring insubordination with wondering eyes, and, envious of my cleaner quarters, at last plucked up enough courage to follow my example, and with much profanity the camp was moved. That evening James and I held council together and we decided to withdraw from the company, feeling that we were safer and more comfortable traveling alone.

The next morning when the order was given to break camp and all were busy preparing to move onward except ourselves, we quietly remained in camp. Some of the more friendly women offered me their assistance, thinking I was not well. I thanked them kindly and assured them I was well, but felt tired and needed a longer rest, and that it was our intention to remain in camp until we were thoroughly rested. The men jeered at us and said by nightfall our scalps would hang at the belt of some wild Indian. We paid but little heed to their remarks. Finally perceiving that we were, indeed, going to stay behind, the captain gave the command and the big caravan drove on leaving us alone in the wilderness. We remained in camp two days, giving them an opportunity to get so far ahead that we might never overtake them or even see them again. Alone in the wilderness, we felt more secure and far happier than when traveling with this uncongenial band. Afterwards we heard repeated rumors that they had been attacked and almost annihilated.

From Laramie[1] for some distance we encountered no one save Indians. It was a barren and desolate region. Off our left hand were the Black Hills,[2] so called because they were covered with a dense growth of pine, cedar, and hemlock trees which gave them a dark and forbidding appearance. Farther to the south, at a distance of thirty miles or more arose Laramie Peak, towering up to a height said to be over six thousand feet. The milky streams in the

[1] Mrs. Porter's reference is to Fort Laramie, not the city of Laramie.
[2] These hills are not to be confused with the Black Hills of the Dakotas.

The Black Hills in Wyoming Territory
as drawn by J. Goldsborough Bruff
Courtesy The Huntington Library

Laramie Peak
as drawn by Frederick Piercy
Courtesy Missouri Historical Society

319

neighborhood of Laramie, running through the peculiar white clay soil, formed numerous buttes and bluffs, and by some strange alchemy of nature the most singular formations would crop out here and there, like ruined towers, castles, and battlements.

In a few days after leaving Laramie we came to the Sweetwater River, near which we traveled for a week or ten days and owing to its tortuous course we crossed it many times before leaving it near the South Pass. I must not forget to mention a famous landmark in the valley of this river and near our road, Independence Rock,[3] so named by a party of emigrants who made their camp there on a Fourth of July in the earlier emigration of 1849 and had held a grand patriotic celebration. Many of their names had been painted on the face of the huge rock, but time and long exposure to the elements had nearly obliterated them. This rock stood out on almost a level plain and was entirely detached from the mountains near it. In this fertile valley of the Sweetwater the grass was luxuriant, and our cattle regained the flesh and loss of strength that befell them on the rocky trails that lamed them so terribly. But soon again we struck another sixteen-mile desert and a mountain beyond, and after toiling up its long ascent and down into the little park on its further slope, we came upon a camp of weary Mormon emigrants.

[3]See the other story in this volume: Jesse Applegate, *Recollections of My Boyhood*, footnote 3, page 28.

These Mormon recruits were mostly Swedes and Norwegians and were accompanied by several Mormons who had been sent to Norway and Sweden for them, and who had induced them by alluring promises to take this long and perilous trip. There were young women with them using handcarts which they had trundled the long distance from the Missouri River.[4] They were a most unprepossessing lot, weatherbeaten and stolid. They were dressed in their native costume of stout woolen material. They wore heavy, striped yarn stockings that barely reached to the knee. Kerchiefs that had once been bright were carelessly knotted under their chins and formed their only head covering, but were no protection for their faces, which were nearly as brown as the Indians', in spite of their original fair complexions.

For several days we traveled along in sight of them and camped near them at night. My heart ached when I saw those poor girls take up their burdens every day, load up their handcarts, and push or pull them over those rugged mountains, stopping

[4]The Porters probably encountered one of the last handcart companies because the practice was abandoned in 1860. It was begun in 1856 because the Mormons lacked the funds to outfit wagon trains for all of their converts. Brigham Young, President of the Church, thought that the converts could walk from the Missouri Valley to Salt Lake City and push light carts that would contain their belongings as well as enough food for the trip. Three handcart brigades came through safely; two foundered with a loss of almost 200 lives.

*View from the Summit of Independence Rock
as drawn by J. Goldsborough Bruff*

Courtesy The Huntington Library

at intervals to rest themselves and wipe the per-
spiration from their dripping brows. Our conversation with them was necessarily very limited as they
spoke but little English. After a few days, we passed
them on the road and saw them no more.

One night somewhere between Laramie and the
Green River, we halted at the foot of a mountain
over which we had traveled laboriously all day. Early in the afternoon we discovered a spring of water
and fairly good grass for our cattle. While it was too
soon to make a camp on that long summer day, yet
our stock seemed weary and footsore, and we, ourselves, were willing to take the good thus provided
and go no farther. While we were pitching our tent
and making preparations for camp, a team of mules
and several men came in sight. They proved to be
French-Canadians, who like ourselves were bound
for California. On reaching our camp they told us
that the tribe of Indians roaming over that region
was hostile, and that we were incurring great danger
by remaining there alone. They insisted that we
join them and go on over the next mountain. But
we were weary as were our cattle. Their proposal
meant a long and heavy pull, certainly until midnight. We had encountered no troubles with the Indians so far, why should we fear now? We advised
them to tarry with us. But no, they were in a mad,
wild rush to push on and bidding us farewell, went
on their way.

Next morning after a refreshing and good night's

rest, we were up bright and early on the road. It took us several hours before we reached the summit of the next mountain with its remote view of the canyon below. After a while, we discovered what in the distance looked like the wagon of the Canadians, but as we came nearer we could discover no sign of life or movement in their camp. No mules were browsing in sight and not a man visible. When we came within hailing distance, no one greeted us. We found the wagon was rifled of everything. The ground bore traces of a struggle. The mules had evidently been stampeded and the men taken prisoners to the camp of the Indians to be tortured to death. We traced the tracks of the mules and ponies for some distance in an opposite direction to the one we were traveling; but as we had met no Indians we concluded that discretion was the better part of valor, and did not extend our search, feeling only too thankful that a merciful providence had been with us. Had we taken the advice of the men I am afraid we should never have lived to tell the tale.

After leaving the Sweetwater River, our road gradually led us to the beginning of the South Pass, which I imagined to be a narrow, difficult, winding gorge between towering mountains.[5] In this I was

[5]South Pass is part of the Wyoming Basin, a broad plateau in western Wyoming that is really an extension of the Great Plains. It can be said to divide the Northern and Southern Rocky Mountains. South Pass was first noted by Robert Stuart in 1812, an employee of John Jacob Astor, who was returning from Oregon.

Emigrants Attacked by Hostile Indians
from Ballou's Pictorial Drawing Room Companion

Courtesy Library of Congress

happily mistaken, and for a few days we traveled over a road as smooth and as hard as a well kept country thoroughfare. On reaching the summit of the South Pass, one could hardly believe that we were crossing the backbone of the Rocky Mountains. The gradual ascent was not laborious. And here we found the dividing line between the Atlantic and the Pacific, for as we traversed over several miles of rolling land, two low mounds, called Twin Buttes, marked the point where all the little streams and rivers flowed toward the Pacific. I could see but little difference in the taste of the waters, the alkali flavor still predominated. In the course of a few days in our gradual descent we struck a springy marsh of fifteen or twenty acres where the ground seemed to shake as we went over it, and in the center of this morass we found the so-called Pacific Springs.[6] The water was cold and clear, but so obnoxious to the taste that I could not drink it.

Not far from the Pacific Springs we struck the Oregon Trail where the road branched off farther to the north, while our route led us in a more southerly direction. We were now out of the South Pass, and camped one night on the treeless banks of the Little Sandy River. A band of Snake Indians were in our vicinity, and according to my usual custom I

[6]Pacific Springs is a bog about two miles from the Oregon Trail. Located on the Pacific side of the Continental Divide, it was frequented by travelers because it had potable water and because overlanders wanted to see water that would flow into the Pacific.

prepared for company. Strange to relate not one of them approached us. This alarmed us somewhat because we had been accustomed to have them drop in on all occasions, and in this seeming indifference we feared a sinister motive.

The fear of hostile Indians was not our only worry for once again our little hoard of money was running low. The numerous ferries over the Platte and its tributaries made heavy inroads into our slender purse. On one or two occasions it had been replenished by sales of flour and bacon to emigrants who had not laid in so large a store as we, but even with that help we were at our last extremity for money. Food we had in abundance, but only coin would pay our way over a formidable stream that must be crossed by ferry and was impossible to ford. My husband, worried beyond measure at our predicament, had fretted himself almost sick. I, probably owing to my nature of blissful ignorance, took a more optimistic view of the situation and urged him not to worry. We had been told that it would cost twenty dollars to cross the Green River by ferry. I fondly hoped that the amount had been exaggerated or that someway would be provided. My trust was not in vain for a few days before reaching that stream we were overtaken by a solitary horseman who rode by our wagonside until our noon halt. He asked my husband if he could share our noon meal with us, and said he would gladly pay for it.

He was a Frenchman by the name of Philip. We

never knew any other name for him. After dinner, he took my husband aside and explained why he was all alone in the heart of the continent. He had fallen out with the company with which he was traveling, and taking his guns and blankets, left them, relying for food solely on the wild game he could shoot. He begged my husband to board him for about a week or two until he arrived at his destination beyond the Green River. James felt some qualms about taking in a stranger and came to me for advice. At once, I replied, "Tell him we will take him for twenty dollars."

I have often thought since, if we had asked a hundred he would have just as gladly have paid it, as he seemed well provided with money. He proved to be a very kindly gentleman while with us for the few days before reaching his destination, and his twenty dollars carried us well along on our journey and tided us over a precarious time. For years afterwards when the hour looked darkest and both of us were discouraged I would say, "Don't worry, maybe Philip will turn up." The name was a synonym of good luck for us.

XI

Getting Along with the Red Men

IN DUE time we arrived at the Green River, which we had been told was a dangerous and difficult river to ford, and that to transport our livestock and wagon over its depths would take all our little hoard of money. Instead, we hailed it as an oasis in the desert for it furnished us with clear, sweet water to drink, and our thirsty stock reveled in it to their hearts' content. The Green River no longer held any terrors for us. The huge, flat-bottomed boat, drawn by ropes suspended across the deep stream and at a toll much less than we expected, safely landed us on the far side of the stream that had been such a great bugbear to us. Here we rested a few days. The river flowed through a narrow valley. The grass, though coarse, proved to be good feed for our cattle, and the rest put new courage and endurance into their weary frames. Here, too, were green trees on which to set our tired eyes. They were only willows and cottonwoods, yet we enjoyed a camp under their grateful shade.

A trading post had been established at this ferry for the few mountaineers who owned large herds of cattle. Other emigrants besides ourselves were camping here. Their broken-down teams forced them to trade their worn-out oxen for fresher ones on almost any terms. The mountain stockmen did a fast business with unfortunate emigrants, by taking woeful advantage of their necessity. My sympathy was strongly aroused by their distress. Two or three families had been delayed there for two weeks waiting for their cattle to get strong enough to resume their journey. With their own provisions getting short and the season growing late, they gravely feared that they would not complete their journey before the snow fell again on the mountains.

At this place, we became acquainted with an old trader who in his earlier life had been a man of considerable polish and intelligence, however owing to some unfortunate circumstances in his youth had drifted thus far over the continent in the early forties. Homeless, penniless, and an outcast, he managed in some way to establish himself here at the Green River, and by slow degrees had acquired several hundred head of cattle and a considerable band of horses. He also annexed several squaws for wives, and had any number of half-breed children, who swarmed around the filthy quarters that he called home. The rude huts they occupied were in the most squalid surroundings. For many years this had been his home, yet not the slightest effort had been made to improve his mode of living. With all that fertile land surrounding him there was neither garden nor orchard. Fresh fruits and vegetables were unknown to him and his half-breed family. He was said to be worth seventy-five or one hundred thousand dollars, yet he seemed to be perfectly satisfied with these most wretched conditions. Somewhere I had read that it would take only a few years for the white man to return to the aboriginal condition, and it certainly proved true in this man's case.

Most of the men who inhabited these trading posts had squaws for wives. It was quite the ordinary thing for the Indians to bring their most attractive and winsome daughters and offer them for sale to the white men. Those not quite so comely would bring thirty or forty dollars, while others more pleasing would bring sixty or seventy according to their charms. To my point of view they were the most repulsive-looking creatures. I could see neither beauty, grace, nor intelligence in their stolid appearance. Their manners and habits were disgusting and offensive. The women thus bought and sold were no truer to their masters than their more civilized sisters of the same caste in other countries, and were ever ready to decamp with any soldier or other man who offered sufficient lures by way of beads, blankets, or other gaudy paraphernalia.

After leaving the Green River, at many points we would come across the discarded belongings of the emigrants who preceded us. We were enabled to form an idea of the condition of their stock, whether horses or cattle, by the goods and chattels they were continually discarding in their endeavor to lighten the burden of their overworked and worn out teams. Once by the roadside, we came across a heavy, old-fashioned cookstove which some emigrant had hauled all those weary miles of mountain and desert, only to discard it at last. No doubt some poor, forlorn woman was now compelled to do her cooking by the primitive campfire, perhaps much against her will. I could imagine the heated arguments, when day after day that heavy stove had to be loaded and unloaded. No doubt the air was blue many times with the volley of emphatic and profane words hurled against that inoffensive but cumbersome article. A hand-hewn, heavy cradle nearby looked pathetic in its loneliness; and the tiny new-made grave that we had passed a few days previous told too truly the cause of its desertion. It was not unusual to see wagonboxes, log chains, and other heavy articles abandoned to lighten the loads. And the most amazing thing to me was that these things would remain there without attracting the notice of either Indians or herdsmen. They proved to have no value to these denizens of the wilderness.

The hills west of the Green River were thinly covered with straggling groves of pines and cedars. Grass was more abundant in the little valleys, and the streams of water had lost the milky look which was acquired from the clay-wash lying near the desert lands. We were still in the midst of sagebrush, even in these fertile valleys, but it was no longer universal and alone. The wild currant and other shrubs became more abundant. Occasionally, we came upon a little patch of land cultivated by some progressive Mormon. It was a matter of astonishment to us that the herdsmen of these fertile districts, with their cattle roaming over a thousand hills, had never experimented with cultivating the soil. They never knew the taste of cabbage or tomato. A potato was considered the greatest luxury, and was brought to the trading posts from miles away. As for cultivated fruit of any description, they knew it not. We found in the canyons a wild and sour gooseberry which proved to be fairly palatable, and at intervals near the streams grew a wild grass whose succulent roots gave out the flavor of the cucumber. We had watched the Indians eating this grass, and testing it ourselves, thought it very good, but it was rarely found. I had grown very tired of bacon day after day. The very smell of beans cooking nauseates me to this day. I have never overcome my distaste for rice in any form, and stewed prunes are still an abomination in my sight. Our diet was confined mainly to these articles. It was impossible to buy fresh vegetables on our route, and our canned fruit and vegetables had long given out. We had grown so weary of the sameness of our daily diet that an intense desire for something different grew upon us, and we looked forward anxiously to Fort Bridger where we hoped in a few days to find fresh meat and vegetables.[1]

[1]See Jesse Applegate, *Recollections of My Boyhood*, footnote 5, page 34.

From Laramie westward we were in the line of the celebrated Pony Express, which was established in April, 1860, to carry important mail more rapidly than was possible in the overland stage. Our daily excitement was in watching for its fearless riders as they flew by us on their swift ponies. It was nearly ten years in advance of the first overland telegraph, which could not be maintained until there were railroad tracks running parallel to it.[2] The Pony Express was an attempt to carry letters by private service from St. Joseph, Missouri, to Sacramento, California in ten days. This daring enterprise was an attempt to cover nearly two thousand miles of prairie, desert, and mountains by solitary riders from station to station. These stations were at intervals of about thirty miles. In a year's time the work had become more than human endurance could stand. The stations consisted of a rude hut for the keeper, enclosed in a high stockade where the relief ponies were corralled. Because we could always find water at these stations induced us to make extra efforts to camp near them at nightfall. Once it be-

[2]The Pony Express was established by the freight company of Russell, Majors and Waddell. Its purpose was to carry mail at high speed from the Missouri Valley to California. The company built 190 remount stations between St. Joseph, Missouri, and San Francisco. It acquired 500 horses and employed a corps of talented young riders. Service began on April 3, 1860. Unprofitable from the start, although it charged $10 per ounce, the Pony Express failed shortly after the completion of the transcontinental telegraph on October 24, 1861.

came our sad duty to bury the partially burned and
mutilated body of the man in charge of the station
to prevent the wolves and coyotes from devouring
his remains. The Indians had been there before us,
killed and scalped the keeper, took the ponies, and
left the stockade in flames. And we were obliged
to camp near the smoldering ruins.

One morning while we lingered near one of these
stations, a rider who looked like a mere boy came
flying into the post, the man whose place he filled
having been killed by the Indians. The pony had
made his way to the next station alone. This youth
had ridden hard through the darkness of the night
trying to cover both his own ground and that of the
man who had been shot. He quickly changed horses, took his package of letters, and was off again on
his perilous way. These brief stops at the stations
were all that broke the monotony of untold hardships and danger. While the riders were young,
sturdy, and robust men, one of the requirements
was that they must be of light weight, as the ponies
were not expected to carry more than one hundred
and fifty pounds. The superior endurance of those
ponies kept alive many a fearless man in his race
for life with roaming bands of Indians.

For some time after we had separated ourselves
from our unpleasant traveling companions, we traveled without adventure of any kind, and saw nothing of the Indians that were supposed to be on the
warpath. We flattered ourselves that we were too

near Fort Bridger to have any fears. One evening, however, as we drove into a little fertile valley, we came in sight of an encampment of the supposed foe, with a large band of ponies feeding on the rich grass. Their rude tepees were clustered near the stream within a mile of the road. Uncertain of the reception awaiting us, we made camp as usual. In a little while first one Indian and then another came around our fire, until I had an audience of several watching me prepare our evening meal. I was careful to bake an extra quantity of biscuit that night, for we were so completely at their mercy I thought it wise to conciliate them in everyway possible. I found it no easy task, as it required several skillets full before I had enough. James generously handed out his precious tobacco for them to smoke with him around our campfire.

Next morning we drove away from our camp, leaving a number of them who still hung around for the last cup of coffee. As we waved our farewells to them, we noticed one of them mount his pony and follow us, not closely, but keeping us well in sight. When we stopped for our noonday rest, he soon joined us, and, of course, we invited him to partake of our frugal luncheon, hoping that he would return to his band, but he continued to follow us until nightfall. When we prepared to camp, he did likewise. Staking out his pony with the long rope of braided leather which he carried, and approaching my box of cooking utensils, he took from it the large knife I used in cooking, and pointing to some coarse grass that grew near the water he proceeded to cut and gather an armful, which he placed under our wagon and prepared his bed for that night. While alarmed and anxious, we were powerless and made the best of our novel situation. I prepared a more bountiful meal when I found we were to entertain this most unwelcome guest. After eating a hearty meal, which he seemed to enjoy, he smoked a while with my husband. All this time there was no word of conversation, as neither he nor we could communicate except by signs. Finally, he rolled himself beneath the wagon, and we went to rest in our little tent, but slept fitfully with one eye open the balance of the night. This continued for three days and we concluded that he had adopted us and intended to remain with us for the balance of our pilgrimage. On the evening of the third day, after replenishing his inner man with a hearty supper, he arose, caught his pony which was feeding a short distance from the camp, and, pointing backward, tried to make us understand that he was going to return to his tribe. As soon as we divined that he was about to leave us, I tied up a loaf of bread, some bacon, a cup full of sugar, and gave it to him, and we saw him depart, wondering why he came and why he went.

Not for several days was the mystery explained. Meeting an old scout at a watering place where we stopped one night, we related the circumstance to him. He told us that the country through which we were going at that time was filled with Indians who were unfriendly to emigrants, and this Indian was sent with us to show that we were under their special care and not to be molested. If that were true, it went to prove that there was honor among these savage tribes of the wilderness. Our lonely and unprotected situation must have appealed to them, and our uniform kindness was rewarded in many ways perhaps when we knew it not. At any rate, we could truthfully say we never received any ill at their hands, and came through the various tribes without the loss of anything save one bright, new tin tea kettle that I had purchased in Denver. Its brightness proved too much of a temptation to an elderly squaw who came to visit us, and carefully seated herself beside it. It disappeared when she did under the folds of her soiled and tattered blanket.

Another circumstance I think is worth alluding to here. Once in passing a group of Indians, I noticed that one sat wrapped in his blanket the image of despair. The expression on his countenance showed that he was suffering great pain. My husband spoke to his squaw who was standing near and said to her, "Brave, heap sick." She shook her head but at the same time opened her mouth and pointed to her teeth, and then to the suffering brave. James approached the Indian and by signs coaxed him to open his mouth. He found the molar had a large cavity which was the cause of his suffering. I had brought with me several vials of toothache drops, for my little son had frequent attacks of toothache. Bringing forth one of the bottles containing the soothing drops and a piece of cotton, with the aid of a sharp splinter I inserted some of the remedy into the aching tooth. The effect was magical, and I was surprised to watch the change that came over the sufferer's expressive countenance. He raised his eyes that had been sternly fixed on the ground, rubbed his cheek slowly, then turned towards his squaw who was standing behind him watching the effect of the remedy the white squaw was employing, and in a low tone communicated to her that the pain was relieved. Then turning to the other Indians who were grouped around, he spoke in a louder voice. In a moment we were surrounded by them eager to see the little vial that contained the magical drops. It was critically examined and passed from one to another, and although we could not understand a word, yet their expressions of gratitude were perfectly intelligible. I left the bottle and the piece of raw cotton with the Indian sufferer for I was quite certain that the toothache would again return after we had departed.

Another time while waiting in camp over Sunday, I had been repairing some of my husband's red flannel shirts. One was too far worn to be of any further service, and I had relegated it to the ragbag. A number of Indian children stood around watching me at my work, and my sewing utensils seemed very curious to them. The idea came to me to fashion for them a rag doll and see what the effect would be on these stolid children of the wilderness. With a portion of white cloth taken from my workbag, and the remains of the discarded red shirt, I made a rag baby, marking the features of the doll with colored thread. My endeavors were closely watched by the curious children, and when I finished the doll, I handed it to the smallest girl. At first, the child did not seem to realize that she was to keep it. After each one of the children had examined it thoroughly, they gave it back to me. Finally, I made the little one understand that she was to keep it, and when one of the larger children attempted to take it from her, she uttered a weird cry and started off on a swift run with the rag baby hugged closely to her breast. In a little while two or three squaws came into our camp with the child and doll, and by signs asked for another. I soon discovered I would be very busy if I attempted to supply them with rag babies. But I made another for them, showing them how to do it, gave them the remains of the red flannel shirt and other pieces of cloth that I could spare, and sent them off rejoicing. This was my last effort, however, in trying either to instruct or amuse the Indians. Only on Sundays did we linger in camp long enough to have any extra time on our hands, and our inability to make ourselves understood made the effort tiresome.

XII

Salt Lake City

A<small>T LAST</small> we reached Fort Bridger, so named for a trader who first settled there. Later on it was used as an outpost and relief station for the great rush of Mormons to Salt Lake, and afterwards as a fort of the United States government. We were told that Fort Bridger was the terminus of the Great American Desert,[1] and we fondly hoped to get a supply of fresh vegetables within its borders. But the few potatoes were held at such a price that we could not afford to buy them, and they proved to be the only vegetable we found cultivated until we reached Salt Lake City.

As soon as we arrived at Fort Bridger, James went immediately to buy some fresh meat and vegetables, never dreaming for a moment that there would be any difficulty in getting them. On approaching the

[1]The name Great American Desert was given to the semi-arid region located between the 100th meridian and the Rocky Mountains. Early explorers Zebulon Montgomery Pike and Stephen H. Long both believed that it would become a barrier to national expansion because it would not sustain traditional agriculture. The lack of trees and tall grasses plus the high summer temperatures in the South and severe winters in the North contributed to this idea. Today, of course, with irrigation and highbred crops it is a highly productive agricultural region.

sutler of the fort he was informed that the government did not allow the sale of meat or other provisions to outside parties. No persuasion was to any
avail. James tried to explain that his wife was not
well and sorely needed fresh meat, but the man
turned a deaf ear to all his entreaties. Very much
disappointed James turned to go without it, when a
private soldier who overheard the conversation said,
"Stay, pilgrim, no sick woman shall go without a
bite of fresh meat while I'm around. We can't sell
any, but I can give her my ration and not go hungry
either." In this manner was the meat procured. In
return for the kind thoughtfulness of this soldier I
sent to him my beloved Ivanhoe.[2]

Most of our long trek between Denver and Salt
Lake, when not desert, was through and over the
interminable ranges of the Rocky Mountains. For
weary days on end we were continually ascending
and descending. We no sooner arrived at the top of
one rugged mountain when, as far as the eye could
reach, other ranges just as steep loomed up before
us, and it seemed an endless time before we struck
the long gradual slope or plain and arrived at the
summit of these grand old mountains through the
South Pass, and thence through Bridger and down
Echo Canyon,[3] where our shouts and songs rever-

---

[2]*Ivanhoe* was a romantic novel written by Sir Walter Scott
and published in 1820. The book was immensely popular
during the nineteenth century.

[3]Echo Canyon was used by migrating pioneers as early as
1846. Mormons started using it in 1847.

berated from the mountainsides. We followed its little stream until we reached the plain which we knew to be the center of Mormondom.[4] Ever since we had crossed the Green River, we had been told that we were now in the country of the Mormons, and we had been warned that if we desired their goodwill, we should be careful in the way we expressed ourselves about their peculiar institutions to the cattlemen or settler whom we might meet on the road. Especially we had been warned not to admit that we had emigrated from Missouri, as the people of that state had incurred the most bitter hatred of the Mormons. It was the Missourians who had ousted them from their first stronghold in Nauvoo, Illinois, and caused them to take the long perilous journey to this distant land, where they could not only preach but practice their religion without molestation. Fearful tales had been told us of how complete trains emigrating from Missouri were surrounded and captured by Mormons disguised as

[4]The Mormon Church, or the Church of Jesus Christ of Latter-day Saints, was founded by Joseph Smith in Seneca County, New York, on April 6, 1830. Based on the *Book of Mormon*, an ancient text, discovered and translated by Smith and by subsequent revelations, including one that sanctified polygamy, Church members were the subject of violent attacks. Mormons were driven out of Ohio, Missouri, and Illinois. The Church was seen by some as an anti-Christian cult, and its close-knit theocratically run and economically integrated communities were determined to be a threat to republican principles. Mormons fled to Utah where they hoped to find political autonomy and religious freedom.

Indians, the women and children kept in bondage, and the men put to death.[5]

It was now the close of a long, hot summer day during which we had been winding down through narrow ravines and over the abominable roads still used by all the heavy merchant wagons that bore goods and other provisions to the City of the Saints. Emerging from the hills we came out on the broad plateau that overlooked the valley of the Great Salt Lake. The city was still several miles from us, and although we had two or three hours of daylight before us, we had to curb our desire to enjoy the comforts and luxuries that we had hoped to find within its boundaries. It was not until almost noon of the following day that we descended—weary, dusty, and browned with over a thousand miles of jolting, fording, and camping—into the veritable city that so long had seemed a myth. To us poor emigrants it bore a most delightful aspect. It was regularly and handsomely laid out on a level plain. Little irrigating canals flowed on either side of the streets, whose

[5]These stories derived from the so-called Mountain Meadows Massacre, a tragic episode that took place in August 1857. There are different versions of what actually happened. One account holds that a group of Indians attacked a wagon train. When the attack failed, the Indians insisted that Mormons in the area help them or they would attack Mormon settlements. Mormon militia attacked the wagon train. More than 100 overlanders died. Another account argues that the Mormons invented the story about the Indians in the hope of escaping punishment after they attacked and pillaged the train.

clear, cold waters were led into the orchards and gardens surrounding every home. The houses of that time were generally small, one story buildings of adobe, and every householder had an acre of ground to cultivate around his home. The gardens offered an air of freshness and coolness that everyone could appreciate, but none more than the traveler who had just crossed the great desert. At that day, the City of Salt Lake boasted of only one business street on which were located the post office and principal stores.

Since leaving Denver, we had had no opportunity to get letters, and I did not allow any time to escape after reaching Salt Lake City before going to the post office. How eagerly I clasped the precious missives to my breast when they were in my possession. I was almost afraid to open them for fear that they might contain sorrowful news. Driving that thought from my mind I hastily read one after the other, and when I had been assured that all were well and happy as I had left them, then more at my leisure did I read again and again every word they contained. Letters from home! What a comforting sound to wanderers like ourselves, cut off from the past and beyond the pale of civilized life.

We camped for several days in the outskirts of the city, and enjoyed to our heart's content the lucious fruit and fresh vegetables that we were able to buy or trade from the Mormon women. These women thronged into our camp with everything in

the way of produce, which they were glad to exchange for any articles the emigrants desired to part
with. At that period when every pound of freight
had to be brought overland by wagons, the tariffs
were fabulously high, and if these Mormon women
could acquire anything by trading their fruits, vegetables, butter, and cheeses, they were that much
ahead. So here I parted with my comfortable feather
bed. Every Mormon who came into camp wanted to
buy it. At first, I steadily refused to part with it, but
finally I was offered an amount which in our press-
ing need for money I thought it unwise to refuse. So
great was the demand for feather beds and pillows
that I might have sold it for even a larger sum.
Through all the journey I had held on to my three
flat irons, but for some time I had stopped using
them, as the clothing we wore required only cleanliness. These flat irons I bartered with a woman for a
tub of fresh butter, which I hoped would last us
through to California. And I exchanged a much bat-
tered brass handled shovel and tongs for a pair of
cowhide shoes for myself, which in a few days grew
rough, red, and rusty, although they lasted until the
end of the journey. I was only too glad to trade
them many articles, which I could dispense with in
exchange for their fresh fruit and vegetables, butter,
eggs, and cheeses of which I laid in as large a supply as would keep for the rest of our trip.

While we camped in the outskirts of the city, we
found it necessary to buy hay for our stock. This

Salt Lake City about 1853
from a lithograph by Ackerman
Courtesy Missouri Historical Society

was brought to us every day by a Mormon woman, the hay tied into a huge bundle and carried on her back and shoulders. This required several trips before a sufficient quantity could be brought in this manner. A man came into camp one day to sell us some grain. While dickering with my husband over the price and quantity, he kept his eyes fastened on me as I stood preparing our dinner. Suddenly he came over and reached out his hand to shake hands with me. I gazed at him in amazement, and I suppose my countenance showed my surprise.

He said, "You do not know me?"

"No," I answered, "I do not."

"Well," he said, "I know you and you are the daughter of Robert Honeyman."

He then said that he had worked for my father when I was a little girl, and after telling me his own name, brought to my recollection the time, place, and circumstances. I could not deny to him that while we were not Missourians, yet we had emigrated from Missouri. I felt somewhat startled and annoyed to meet him in Salt Lake City. However, I assumed a smiling face and said, "O, yes, I now remember you well," and made him welcome to our humble camp. He informed me that he had embraced the Mormon faith, marrying a mother and two daughters, and invited us very cordially to visit him in his home. I replied that if his wives would care to see me, it would give me great pleasure to accept his invitation.

In the evening he returned bringing his wives to call upon me. They were plain, commonplace people on a par with most of the women I had seen there, except that they were Americans, while the majority of the women were foreigners. They insisted that we should dine with them the next day. To gratify my curiosity to see how a Mormon household was kept I accepted their invitation, and we enjoyed their hospitality exceedingly.

There was no reference to the difference in our opinions, and from all I observed, each wife was treated alike. The mother, who was also the third wife, entertained us, while the daughters, who were the first and second wives, prepared a very tasteful dinner. They seemed perfectly contented with the existing order of things. But many of the Mormon women with whom we conversed were dissatisfied and unhappy. They worked hard and looked worn and dejected, but I must say that I never saw a community wherein there was practiced so much thrift and industry.[6]

We lingered for several days in Salt Lake City

[6]Lavinia Porter was similar to most women who visited Salt Lake City. They reported that Mormon women were overworked drudges, victims of polygamy, and usually of lower class and/or foreign origin. Pioneer women had been exposed to a good deal of anti-Mormon literature, mostly novels by women, that depicted the lives of women within the Mormon community in lurid terms, and they no doubt played on the fears of women on the Overland Trail that they would be kidnapped and then forced into polygamous relationships.

and cleaned house so to speak. That is we unloaded and rearranged our stores, repacked our depleted boxes, aired and cleaned our bedding, which was impossible when we traveled each day, brushed out the accumulated sand and alkali dust, repaired the wagon which the constant wear over the bad roads made necessary, and had our faithful, old horse newly shod. We were very soon to find that we had overstocked ourselves with fresh fruit and vegetables. We hoped that they might last us a month, but had not counted on the hot sun across the Utah desert, which so wilted and shriveled them that they were no longer appetizing and we threw them away. The tub of fresh butter, which looked so hard and firm when stowed away in our wagon, was soon turned by the hot sun of the desert into liquid oil by day, though it hardened a little at night. For a while we used it even in its liquid state, but eventually it became so rancid that it, too, was left by the wayside.

XIII

Desert Travel

Leaving Salt Lake City, our road crossed the River Jordan. We did not get a view of the Great Salt Lake as it lay some twenty miles and a good day's travel beyond our direct route.[1] We left the green and fertile land around the near neighborhood of the city and again came on a desert as barren as the great Sahara. Here we encountered sixty miles of almost pure sand. Seas of water would not have produced verdure on its barren soil. The drought was intense and there was no cultivation or industry of any sort. The scanty vegetation was the everlasting sagebrush and greasewood which I am tired of mentioning. The mountains and plains seemed to divide the ground equally. The valleys were from ten to fifteen miles across, though in the clear air of Utah they seemed only half that distance. I remember clearly the beautiful sunsets. In this rainless climate the mountains in the full sunlight took on the hues of ruby and carnelian, and at sunset the twilight assumed tints of opal and amethyst. No artist,

[1]The Porters seemed to follow the route surveyed in 1859 by Captain J.H. Simpson that led south from Salt Lake to Tooele Valley and then westward. It was the route not only of the original Pony Express and Overland Stage but also of the Overland Telegraph.

however skillfully he might handle his brush, could do justice to the brilliant stretches of rare and roseate colorings of these indescribable sunrises and sunsets.

But the arid land produced little food for our stock. Here and there grew the bunch grass on which depended the life and sustenance of our cattle. Only at rare intervals would we reach a stream whose banks afforded forage for our stock, and rest and refreshment for weary and thirsty travelers. Springs were most infrequent and often we had to dig to a considerable depth in the shallow, dry bed of the streams for water, finding barely enough to partially slack the thirst of our cattle. And, oh, the suffering from the scorching, burning alkali dust. It filled the air, penetrated through everything, covered our bodies, found its dusty way into our food boxes, bedding, and clothing. All the water we drank was tainted with its soapy flavor. It choked up the pores of our skin, eating its way into the nostrils and lips. Our faces were continually cracked and sore from its action. Dreary and monotonous as this country seems now as you travel over it in a comfortable Pullman, it was indescribably more so in the days of the slow-moving ox team. It was over six hundred miles from Salt Lake to the base of the Sierras, but the roundabout way that sometimes we had to travel in order to find food and water for our stock made the distance much longer. The best time we could possibly make would not average over a hundred miles a week. At that period for miles over these inhospitable plains, there was not a habitation visible. Now on the line of the railways, thriving towns and villages abound, and the iron horse bellows forth his deep-throated song almost hourly. The thousands speeding over this unfriendly soil little realize the discomforts impeding our slow journey.

We occasionally met some peculiar characters while traveling across the plains and through the mountains of Utah and Nevada; men who had drifted over these tractless wilds, isolating themselves from the companionship of their kind, and becoming partial savages. The monotony of our journey was at various times dispelled by one of these men dropping into our camp, and we became infatuated in the strange stories of their wonderful adventures. It appeared that every hour in their roving lives had its dangers and hairbreadth escapes. Some were fur trappers and scouts, others stockmen and herdsmen. Apparently several had no other desire than to live close to nature and remote from civilization. We encouraged them to tell us about the remarkable episodes in their venturesome lives, and it seemed to give them as much pleasure to relate as it did us to sit alternately thrilling or trembling at the wonderful stories. None of the many tales we had read of western adventure could so have moved us, not even the famous Fenimore Cooper, over whose stories we had burned the midnight oil. Two of these frontiersmen met us on the road one day. They had been alone in the wilderness for weeks, hunting and prospecting. They turned back and went on with us for the balance of the day. We were informed that one of these men was the greatest Indian exterminator on the frontier. His whole family had been massacred by the Indians and his greatest pleasure was in shooting Indians whenever opportunity came along.

We looked forward to Saturday night in camp as a welcome rest and relaxation. Six days' travel was enough for man and beast. We needed the quiet and repose of Sunday. It was not always a complete rest for me, for there was the usual laundering and baking. Still it was a change from the continual moving on. It also gave us the opportunity to indulge in two extra hours of sleep in the morning which proved a blessing to me. Early rising was my *bête noire*. The extra time gave me a chance to cook a better Sunday morning breakfast. A yearning filled our souls, or rather our stomachs, for a broiled chicken, fried oysters, or an omelette. Hot rolls we had always for breakfast, but Sunday morning's flapjacks were our greatest treat. These were made from the sour milk I had carefully saved a day or two. Our milk supply was gradually failing as our little cow could no longer give us a sufficient quantity on the dry and scanty grazing. In place of butter the ever-ready bacon gravy thickened with flour and milk was used. We had both become adept in tossing the flapjacks up into the air, turning them over and back into the frying pan, and these had to satisfy us in lieu of all the good things that we had in our imagination. We were delighted if we had decent water to make our coffee palatable. Travelers on these desert wastes found minimal provision for sensitive stomachs. Fortunately our outdoor life and exercise found us with appetites whetted for bacon and beans.

By this time my condition became apparent to the most casual observer. Frequently, the squaws approached me and patting me on the bosom would say, "By and by papoose." The urgent need for some new maternity gowns appealed to me everyday. But where was I to procure them hundreds of miles from any dry goods emporium? Necessity, that stern mother of invention, came to my aid. Before starting on our journey, I had made, to protect it from the dust of travel, a stout covering of blue plaid gingham for my feather bed. This outer covering I had removed when I sold the bed in Salt Lake. Ripping open the plain, straight seams, I cut and fashioned, without guide or pattern, a comfortable and serviceable, if not a stylish, garment, making it by hand at odd moments in camp or as I rode along on my way. From a big, flowered dressing gown that my husband had discarded as being too effeminate to be worn on the plains, changing its lines from its too masculine contour, I made another suitable and befitting dress, although the coloring was almost too bright and gay for that style of garment.

Time hung heavily on our hands as we plodded along over the barren stretches of Utah. We became almost as lifeless as the country over which we were traveling. Even by day there was an all-pervading silence. No chirp of bird, no hum of insect. Far ahead of us a white line marked our road. It seemed to ever beckon us on over more arid stretches of desert sand and sagebrush. This part of our journey was one perpetual search for water, and when we were fortunate enough to find it, we did nothing but condemn and criticize it all night, grumbling at its quality and lack of quantity. Yet we left it in the morning with fear that we might not again find any so good. The nights became unbearable with the unutterable stillness. This unbroken silence seemed to overpower us with its subdued indifference. It struck a chill to our hearts, and we sought our lowly beds with dread and timidly slept under the distant and unfamiliar stars.

Just before reaching Fish Springs,[2] we passed one of the salt wells that were common to this part of the country. Its depth was unknown, but the water contained therein was so strongly impregnated with salt that it was like a strong brine. This well was six or eight feet in diameter, and all around it the vegetation was covered with a white incrustation. The suction of this strange well was so intense that it

[2]Fish Springs is located at the foot of the Great Salt Lake Desert. During the 1860s it was both a Pony Express and stage station.

would draw in anything used in attempting to explore its depths. A rude fence had been thrown around it to guard the unwary traveler.

Fish Springs was a large pool of water lying at the base of a low mountain. For three or four miles it sent out a large and copious stream, but the thirsty sands soon absorbed it. The water, while brackish, was said to abound in fish. We threw in our line and tried to coax a bite from the finny denizens, but the only bite we got was from the swarming mosquitoes, immense in size and venomous as starved creatures. They stung our cattle to the verge of madness, and at early dawn we were glad to get beyond their onslaughts. A rude stage station was established at Fish Springs, and the lonesome keeper greeted us warmly. The sight of travelers to pass the night brought some variety into his isolated life, which had no companionship save the horses and his dogs and cats. We filled his heart with gratitude by leaving with him some of our tattered and torn literature. From the keeper we learned that the nearest water was over thirty miles away, and he urged us, if possible, to make the drive in one day.

The next morning, long before the sun was up, we were traveling through a dusty, sandy pass. The sky was overcast with heavy leaden clouds and the dry heat was intense. Peal after peal of thunder shook the air, but only a slight shower overtook us. However, we hailed it with delight for while there was more thunder than shower, we were gratified

for any moisture. This unusual rain served to cool
the air, and we hurried along with renewed zeal,
hoping to reach by nightfall the point already described to us as Pleasant Valley. Darkness overtook
us long before we reached its precious locality. We
knew, however, that it could not be far off by the
way our thirsty cattle snuffed the air, and by their
increased gait, which required no urging. A little
later we drove into the valley, where the pure and
sparkling water of Willow Springs[3] greeted us with
its refreshing coolness. How we reveled in its pure,
sweet depths. Our thirsty cattle drank again and
again, stopped to graze awhile, then returned to
dip their brown muzzles into its leaping waters. The
vegetation around Willow Springs was the most
luxurious we had seen since we left Salt Lake, and
as we had overdriven our stock, we stayed there for
two or three days.

We were told by the keeper of this station that
we were now across the Utah Desert, that is the
northeast corner of it, though it extended some two
or three hundred miles south of us. For a time after
departing Pleasant Valley, our road lay over the
mountains of Utah, which brought us some relief
from the everlasting sagebrush and sand of the desert. These mountains were fairly wooded. A few
cedars raised their gnarled and stunted bodies from

[3]Willow Springs, now known as Callao, lies between the
Great Salt Lake Desert and the 12,000 foot Deep Creek
Mountains. It was a Pony Express station.

the ground to a height of ten or fifteen feet. There
were also pine of equally scrubby character, but in
the canyons grew large balsam firs. My little son engaged himself in gathering large quantities of the
gum from these trees, the flavor and chewing qualities of which resembled that of the spruce gum.

Our route through these Utah mountains led us
over innumerable ranges. We seldom lacked for water there, but the way was devious and wild. One
afternoon, leaving the higher ranges behind us, we
struck a level plain, and saw ahead of us a drove of
five or six hundred cattle which their drivers were
urging along a low, marshy piece of ground over
which had been built a rough pole bridge. Such a
large number crossing at one time had torn the frail
structure to pieces. As the ground was too miry and
uncertain for us to attempt the crossing, we were
compelled to hold up for a day until James with
the help of the herdsman repaired the bridge over
which our timid oxen reluctantly trod. Our horse
for a time utterly refused to trust his precious bones
on the uncertain structure.

When we arrived at Ruby Valley, we were told
that we were in Nevada Territory. I looked in vain
for the precious stones that I supposed had given
name to the little station.[4] On reaching Diamond

[4]Ruby Valley earned its name when members of an exploring party found some red stones they mistakenly
thought were rubies. The valley is located southeast of Elko,
Nevada, on the eastside of the Humboldt National Forest.

Springs, I found them also lacking in the sparkling gems whose name they bore.

Finally, we arrived at the banks of the Humboldt River. I say banks, for most of the way along its course was little else but banks. I had heard tales of the Humboldt since I was a child. I had studied its devious wanderings through sandy deserts in my geography at school. Mythical stories had been repeated by different people we met on our journey, and yet I was wholly unprepared for the sight of that river which appeared such an insignificant stream. In many places there was scarcely enough water to dignify it by the name of a stream, although it was said to be three hundred miles long. In the fullest part that I saw, it was never larger than an ordinary brooklet. Its narrow bottom at intervals produced a coarse grass, but so strongly impregnated with alkali, that no man who had any regard for the life of his stock would allow them to eat it, if there was any alternative. In some places they had to eat or die and many of them did eat and die, as the numerous whitened bones that covered its banks and borders testified. James turned his stock away from it if possible, preferring to let them browse on the bullberry or the buffalo bush, which grew here and there among the willows. Or if it was imperative that they should feed on this coarse grass in lieu of something better, he would take his sickle and cut the grass for them, as by so doing the stock would not get at the roots, which contained much more of the alkali. Along its ugly, sandy borders no tree worthy of the name was seen. But there were innumerable droves of gadflies, mosquitoes, and gnats—countless and bloodthirsty. There was no comfort to be found either night or day along its borders. During the day the heat was intense, and the thick dust permeated the atmosphere. We thought we had driven over many barren lands, but our pathway that ran along the Humboldt discounted anything with which we had come in contact.

Our pilgrimage through these scorching deserts of Nevada was long to be remembered. Each morning as the blazing sun rose above the horizon, our tired and sunburned eyes looked in vain for some green spot in all that burning sand, and as we slowly and wearily plodded along its glowing surface, overcome with heat and consumed with thirst, we suffered almost beyond endurance. Unless one has traveled by our slow method, they can have only the slightest conception of these blistering, waterless wastes. Many emigrants whose stock was in no condition to stand this long, continued travel without water, found their stock dying and leaving them with no means of transportation. Often they were compelled to abandon their wagons, pack a few provisions on a single ox or mule, and toil on afoot. The bones of hundreds of cattle lay bleaching in the sun. Graves without number were dug by the wayside. It was pitiful and heartrending to see them in such numbers. Scarcely a day passed that we did

not observe the lowly burial place of some poor sufferer, who had at last succumbed to the hardships of
this long journey. These rude graves were sometimes covered with a pile of stones. Others bore a
headboard on which was rudely cut the name of
him who lay beneath. For them no weeping willow
sighed a grievous requiem nor enfolded their lowly
mounds with its tender, swaying branches. No mar-
ble shaft praised their deeds or told their fame. No
flowers rare and sweet rested on the unconsecrated
soil. But the horned toad and lizard glided beneath
the growth of scanty weeds. Those lying here were
lonely now, deserted by their loved ones whose
bleeding hearts had been forced to leave them at
rest beneath the bitter soil.

Fortunately at this late day the horrors of this region have been overcome. In numerous instances
wells have been dug and water led into the arid desert. Railroads have been built, and in this age of
fierce and furious competition men and money have
overcome many difficulties. And now a trip westward to the Pacific Coast in a comfortable car is
available to all, and considered to be an interesting and restful trip of a few days. Since our long
hazardous journey in 1860, I have traveled back and
forth a number of times over much of the route we
slowly toiled over so long ago. It has been a constant source of wonder to me how we were able to
endure it.

XIV

Friends Along the Way

WE HAD been in the Humboldt region only a
few days when one night we drove into a
camp of emigrants who had preceded us all the way
from Salt Lake. Their teams, which consisted of
mules and horses, kept a day or two ahead of us.
But owing to the sickness of a valuable horse, they
had been delayed on the road. The company consisted of a white-haired and rugged old patriarch
from the State of Michigan with his aged wife and
two daughters, girls near my own age. A son and a
nephew, together with three hired men who had
charge of the fine horses completed the company.

Their traveling outfit consisted of a substantial
carriage fitted up with every comfort and conve-
nience for the tedious journey, and drawn by four
large mules; two huge prairie schooners carrying
their camp equipage and tents; and another wagon
conveying grain and provisions for the family and
horses. The camp wagon held every comfort that
could be devised for a family tenting on the plains.
An immense cookstove was loaded and unloaded
everyday for it required a great amount of cooking
to feed so many. A dining table of rough boards,
strong hickory-bottomed chairs, and any number of

minor comforts that were unknown to us with only our single team to carry all our possessions.

The old gentleman, whose name was Brookfield, was a grand-looking specimen of a western farmer. He was stout, rather short, with snow-white hair and beard, and a ruddy countenance beaming with genial good nature, and still vigorous in spite of his advancing age. His wife was just the opposite, painfully angular, and inclined to be somewhat shrewish—a perfect paragon of neatness, and just as much a stickler for order and cleanliness on the plains as she doubtlessly was in her well-ordered home in Michigan. The daughters were comely girls of eighteen and twenty with long, beautiful, naturally curling hair that hung in ringlets to their waists, and which curled so tightly that no amount of pulling could straighten it. These curls were a source of great curiosity to the Indians. Their own hair hung so straight they were fascinated by the difference, and they always watched the girls most intently. Sometimes an Indian, more curious than the others, would venture to examine the curls. Drawing one out to its extreme length and releasing it, he would look so surprised to see it quickly renew its original curl. The girls became uneasy at the sensation their hair produced and wore their bonnets whenever the Indians invaded the camp.

The son of Mr. Brookfield was a capable and attractive young man much like the father. The nephew was the cook and also the wag of the party, witty and quick at repartee, and a great practical joker. His name was Bert Brookfield. He called the old lady Aunt Debby, and he truly was a thorn in Aunt Debby's side. For morning, noon, and night he was ever-racking his brain for some joke to play upon his nervous old aunt. To me it was an amusing sight to watch Bert, as he gaily donned his cook's cap and apron preparatory to cooking what he called "an elaborate course dinner." Old Aunt Debby hovered around to see that he washed his hands before mixing the bread. He now and then pretended to wipe his floured hands on the seat of his pants or his nose on the dish towel or carelessly used the corner of a horse blanket to wipe dust from a frying pan, much to the horror of his fastidious aunt, who continually scolded and fretted until the meal was served.

The meeting with this congenial company was a source of great pleasure to us, since departing Salt Lake I had not even seen a white woman. James and I had gradually grown silent and taciturn, and had unwittingly partaken of the gloom and somberness of the dreary landscape. We no longer gaily sang or joked as we kept step beside our slow cattle. We were tired and jaded to absolute silence and to passive endurance by the monotony of the desert. This lively company of young people near our own ages brought new life and interest to us two lonely travelers. They were all musical. The girls had well-trained voices and sang sweetly, while the young men played on different instruments that they had brought with them. For the few weeks that we traveled together, the time passed pleasantly and harmoniously. Our camp at night was a season of mirth and good-fellowship. And no matter how long and tiresome was the day's drive, or how many vicissitudes we encountered, we each managed at nightfall to furnish our quota of amusement.

One morning at breakfast we heard Aunt Debby berating Bert because the coffee was not up to the usual standard. He insisted that he had prepared the coffee as usual, only the alkali water gave it a disagreeable flavor. I had finished up my camp work and was spending a few moments in visiting them in their camp. Aunt Debby was looking after Bert, keeping up her usual careful scrutiny over his pots and pans to see they were properly cleansed. I observed Bert taking up the coffeepot, and from its cavernous depths draw out a long and loathsome worm which he then held up for Aunt Debby to see. With a cry of horror she made a dash for his curly head. He nimbly eluded her clutches, but did not escape her tongue-lashing. He informed me afterwards that he had dug two or three feet into the banks of the stream for that worm with which to electrify his squeamish aunt and had put it into the pot after the breakfast was over.

Another morning Bert arose from his slumbers, making a great hue and cry over the loss of one of his moccasins, and went limping around the camp with one bare and unshod foot. As I watched him beating up his huge pan of batter for the hot cakes that he cooked every morning, he turned and gave me a sly wink denoting mischief on his part. Our drive for the day was to be one of unusual length. Everyone was hurrying his or her work in order to get an early start before the sun grew so intolerably hot. Aunt Debby was busily engaged in helping Bert stow away his cooking utensils. Her tongue in the meanwhile was running over with his many derelictions, while he drolly parried her sharp thrusts at his lack of order and neatness. Picking up his half-emptied batterbowl, he looked into it for a moment with apparent surprise and consternation. Then drawing forth the huge moccasin that he claimed had either been lost or stolen, held it up before the horrified eyes of Aunt Debby, all dripping with the remnants of the batter. These and similar harmless jokes he was constantly playing on the irascible old lady.

The few weeks spent with this company were the most enjoyable part of our journey. While their mules and horses made faster time than our oxen, yet at the end of the day, by driving a little later, we managed to camp together. Owing to the lameness of their fine bay stallion, they, too, made shorter drives. But after the animal had almost entirely recovered, Mr. Brookfield was anxious to make up his lost time and get his fine stock into California as soon as possible. He decided to still follow the Humboldt to its sink, and from there to take the road to California, where his final destination was to be Marysville. We had learned that the route by way of Carson Valley led us through more fertile lands with better forage for our cattle, a very important matter to us, though it was a longer and more indirect route. Very reluctantly we parted company with these good people, promising each other at some future day we should meet in California. But alas for such promises for we never saw or heard of them again, although we wrote to them and made enquiries concerning them from people of Marysville. Whether they changed their minds, like we did, and never arrived at their intended destination, we knew not. To this day I have never forgotten their pleasant companionship on the desolate plains of Nevada.

As we turned our faces in the direction of the Carson River, a feeling of thankfulness took possession of our hearts. We were leaving the alkali soil of the Humboldt Desert behind us, and though the Carson River was absorbed by the same desert, yet a glance at even its worst features was enough to convince us that it watered a far more hopeful region. Large cottonwood trees dotted the banks; here and there were willows; and the wild rose in full bloom occasionally cropped out on its sandy banks. Still the prevalence of drought was everywhere visible, and long before we reached Carson City, we traveled over miles of land doomed to sterility. As we neared the town, there appeared to be a great rush of miners and prospectors headed for some new mines that had opened up in that vicinity. Some of these men were so enthusiastic over the prospect that they urged us to go no further, but to locate in the new mines. Our minds, however, were set for California and we would not be persuaded. This embryo town was so small and scattered that we hardly knew when we entered it. Yet it aspired to be the emporium of the new gold region.

The features of the country had notably changed. From the dry and thirsty land of the sagebrush we gradually drove into soft meadows, with numberless rivulets flowing down from the Sierras. Owing to the shallowness of their beds they became easy to control, and had been made to irrigate a large portion of the land. Small farms and gardens occasionally came in view, and for our stock we found the sweetest and most nutritious grass in abundance. The village of Genoa was a most picturesque little spot.[1] It stood on a bench between the mountains and the valley with rivulets flowing through and around it to give fertility to its soil and fructify its gardens and green fields. I was charmed with its quiet beauty and seclusion, the brightness of its innumerable streams, and the grandeur of the nearby mountains whose emerald verdure affected my mind with a vividness which only those who have passed

[1]Located six miles from Lake Tahoe, Genoa, originally Mormon Station, was founded in 1851. It is the oldest white settlement in Nevada.

long months on a shadeless desert can fully realize. From Carson to the pretty little village of Genoa was a drive of nearly twenty miles. After spending a night in those charming surroundings, we began the ascent into the Sierra Nevadas, the last mountain range we would have to climb before we viewed the land we had traveled so long and far to see.

There were still two weeks of mountain travel ahead of us, and we proceeded slowly owing in a great measure to my condition. The continual jolting of the wagon over the uneven roadway was exceedingly trying to me, so much so in fact that I finally gave up riding altogether, taking my slow way up the mountain on foot. Day after day for the next two weeks I trudged wearily and painfully through the red dust of the Sierras from Genoa, at the eastern base, to the foothills of California. I had always boasted of my pedestrian powers, but when I surveyed that road winding up and still up, my pride in being a great walker vanished, and like the old bishop who was so fond of worldly comfort, I said, "All is vanity except a carriage." I could no longer mount my horse, and only by slow degrees made my way on foot, stopping frequently to rest the weary muscles. Then upward again, every nerve as tense as steel and every faculty alert, I climbed with painful toil.

After departing Genoa, we wound around the curved border of a narrow roadway excavated on the mountainside, and only a little wider than the wagon's tracks. So frequent and sharp were these curves that the forward yoke of oxen would be out of sight as I followed the wagon. Looking down the precipice on which we were traveling I shuddered at the thought of what might happen if our sturdy cattle made a misstep on the narrow roadway that seemed to hang on the mountainside. My little son had been suffering for several days with a sprained ankle and was compelled to ride, so on his account I was extremely anxious as I watched the wagon lurch around the sharp and narrow curves.

The scenery along these winding roads was magnificent. The tall pines grew straight as arrows and clinging to their sturdy trunks were beautiful variegated yellow and green lichens. The smaller trees of these immense forests were here in richest profusion. Hemlocks, balsam, pines, and fir trees filled up the intervening spaces. The whole forest seemed gay with life and motion. Squirrels frolicked and scampered from tree to tree. The agile and graceful chipmunk darted hither and thither in the low hazel bushes, chattering noisily as he ran as if scolding us for disturbing him in his own domain, his bright eyes twinkling as they peered up at us from some leafy bough. The bluejay, with his towering crest and noisy discordant call, flew swiftly through the dark foliage of the evergreen trees. Here and there a dusty lupine lifted up its blue-tipped stem, all strangely beautiful when compared with the alkaline deserts over which we had so recently toiled.

This first day's climb into the Sierras was a novel experience to me. These mountains were so different in aspect from the bare, bald Rockies. Ever and anon a little spring by the roadside gave the thirsty climbers a chance to quench their thirst. As I plodded slowly up the mountainside, I had ample time to observe all the beauties of its ever changing scenery. Winding around some steep cliff new surprises would burst upon my vision, here a transient view of still more towering summits covered with snow, there a glimpse of a stream flowing between or at the base of some deep and dark ravine. These beautiful mountains which rose like castellated towers astonished me with the immensity of their huge pines attaining heights that seemed wonderful. The enormous cones were often a foot long and the rich, green foliage, like long needles, swayed with the passing breeze. Lying prone by the wayside and crossing each other at every imaginable angle were hundreds of these monarchs of the forest laid low by the woodman's axe. It seemed a sacrilege to gaze upon them in their prostrate grandeur. On every side were huge stumps at whose bases lay the fallen trunks of the once noble trees. Civilization made roadways a necessity, and these grand old trees were the victims in the march for improvement. The Rocky Mountains failed to compare with the Sierra range in both the variety and grandeur of this great forest growth.

Bewitched by the beauty of the surroundings I

hardly realized that I had grown weary and footsore until the setting sun began to cast its shadows over the pine-hung slopes of these mountain canyons. Looking down this slope far below us lay the tiny hamlet of Genoa that we had left so early in the morning, but still in sight although we had climbed steadily above it that long September day. Under a huge pine tree we placed our tent, cooked our supper, and prepared to sleep our first night in the vastness of the great Sierras, breathing that balmy air that was balsam-tinctured from fragrant pines. Through the opened door of our snug little tent, we watched the moon as it shone down upon us through the interlacing boughs. I was too weary to sleep, and traced the movements of the bright and radiant sphere until it passed beyond my vision. At last, I must have fallen asleep for I was awakened long before dawn by the most unearthly shrieks ringing through the forest and coming back again in plaintive echoes from the hills beyond. These fearful wails were caused by a death in a camp of Indians who were located in our near vicinity, but of whose presence we had been totally ignorant.

XV

Journey's End

WE IMAGINED when we had progressed so near
to our journey's end that we had bid a final
adieu to "Lo, the poor Indian." But we were yet to
see a more degraded specimen of the red man than
had been our privilege hitherto. Certainly the Indians we met in the Sierra Mountains were more degraded and more filthy than any tribe we had met
in our wanderings. These Indians migrated from
the valleys to the mountains in the fall to harvest
the pine nuts growing so plentifully in these forests,
and on which depended their food for the winter
months. We came upon them everywhere through
these mountains. The lazy braves mounted, leading
the way unhampered and free, were followed by
troops of obedient and slavish squaws on foot, lad-
en with huge baskets into which the harvest of nuts
was loaded.

These Indians were inferior in size and stature.
The largest brave rarely exceeded in height a little
over five feet. They were wholly unattractive and
repulsive with large mouths and flat, ugly noses.
Their hair, black as jet, cut straight over their low
foreheads, hung at the back and sides in long, straggling strands. The squaws wore their hair thickly

plastered with pitch, and a broad band of pitch was smeared across noses and cheeks. They were horribly filthy and covered with vermin, and their dirty offspring were strapped as usual to a board and carried on their backs. While this band of Indians was busy harvesting their annual crop of pine nuts, one of the young squaws was suddenly taken ill and died. She was the wife of the chief, and great was the commotion among them at her untimely death.

It was the custom among these Indians, when a death occurred in their tribe, for the superannuated squaws to become professional mourners. They would immediately proceed to stain their already tarred heads and faces with a more ample supply of pitch, and then burst forth into the most dismal wails indeed. The forest and mountains reverberated with their unearthly shrieks for the dead. This weeping and wailing was continued through the long hours of the first night and all the following day until near sunset.

It was our privilege to witness the strange funeral ceremonies over the body of this squaw which was carefully rolled in her soiled blanket. Then a huge pile of dried pine branches was erected on which was placed her lifeless body. Her nearest relatives grouped themselves about the funeral pyre, while the others stood around the outside of the circle. For an interval of ten moments or more, perfect silence reigned. The loud wailing of the aged squaws had ceased and just as the setting sun was about to

sink below the horizon, one of these ancient mourners, an old squaw whose head was literally covered
with tar, raised her arms heavenward and stared
long and steadily at the sun as it slowly sank from
sight. At intervals, she muttered some low incanta-
tion, her bronze countenance lit up with a strange
intensity. For a short space of time she stood in this
position. Then, suddenly after a bloodcurdling
shriek, she sprang forward and seizing a brand from
the campfire, lighted the funeral heap. The flames
shot high in the darkened forest. The aged squaws,
whose bent bodies rocked to and fro in rhythmic
time, renewed their plaintive wailing and all the
other Indians of both sexes joined in a pathetic cho-
rus, and chanted a funeral dirge sounding to our listening ears like, "Emaylaya, emaylaya." All swiftly
turned their faces toward the setting sun, then back
again upon the funeral pyre. It was a strange, weird
sight to us, that circle of bronzed Indians around
the burning corpse. While the song or chant was
being sung each one swayed mechanically to the
measure of the dirge, but their stolid countenances
hid any expression of grief or woe.

For several days before reaching the summit of
the Sierras I toiled slowly up and over the narrow
winding trails, stopping frequently to rest and catch
my breath; on and on and always higher and higher,
occasionally meeting the mule pack trains carrying
freight and merchandise from California over to the
desert of Nevada. These mules were burdened with

every variety of merchandise, furniture, flour, and freight of all kinds, which was securely fastened onto packsaddles. Around their necks was strung a string of bells which warned teamsters and pedestrians of their approach. These mules never gave the right-of-way to anyone. In many places the road was so narrow and the mountain so steep above and below us that it was necessary to squeeze myself as closely to the cliff as possible, hunting if I had time, some place that had been excavated a little deeper in the side of the cliff than usual, and standing there perfectly still until they passed me by. Their burdened sides pressed close against me as they crowded along. It was rather trying to the nerves to have from sixty to a hundred pack mules rushing past one with scarcely room for one's body.

As we continued to climb upward, I found that I could not keep up with the team and our slow-moving oxen would outwalk me. In the early part of our journey I could quite easily outwalk them, but not so now. My husband frequently halted the team to wait for me. Oh, how glad was I to catch sight of the waiting wagon in which I could lie down for a brief respite. At last, we reached the summit in the early days of October, and camped a day and rested in Strawberry Valley.[1] The atmosphere at this altitude began to grow shivery at nightfall. A keen, frosty air permeated everywhere. Our camp was in

[1]Strawberry Valley was a stage station on the road from Genoa to Placerville.

close proximity of a lumber, or rather, a shake settlement. Four or five young and vigorous men from the New England States had located a timber claim in the heart of these immense pine forests, and were busily employed in getting out lumber and making the shakes that were in demand for building purposes all down through the Sacramento Valley. With true California hospitality they visited our camp, and as the nights were cold, insisted on our sharing the comforts of their cabin for the night. James turned to me to see what I thought of the proposition and I could easily see that he wanted to accept the invitation and have a conversation with these hospitable mountaineers. I, too, longed to be under a roof and sit by a warm fireside. Needless to say we accepted. Before we reached their cabin, I heard strains of music from a favorite opera which I was surprised to hear in this mountain wilderness. When the door to the cabin was opened, we found a young man who played the violin with the skill of a virtuoso.

The bright light from within the cabin showed us a most cheerful interior. There was an immense room with a roughly boarded floor. The spaces between the logs of which the cabin was built were unchinked and let in volumes of fresh mountain air. Within a rough stone hearth large logs were burning. A square homemade pine table occupied the center of the room. It held a few books, interspersed with pipes and tobacco. At one side of this room was a rough couch covered with the skins of wild animals and quite comfortable. There was a rocking chair that one of the men had made, the seat and back formed of skins like the couch. This was immediately whirled in front of the fire for my benefit, and it was a great luxury to be seated once again in a real rocking chair, as for the last six months I had either sat upon the ground or on a humble soapbox with neither arms nor back for support. Indeed, the smallest suggestion of home or home comfort was very grateful. The rough walls of the cabin were decorated with the various trophies of the forest. Antlers, skins of wild animals, Indian bows and arrows, and guns of various kinds were stacked in the corners or hung on the rough walls. The huge fireplace took up nearly one side of this room. Around the other sides were bunks built into the walls which served for beds. The mattresses, made from flour sacks and filled with hay, were fairly comfortable when covered with their gray and blue blankets. The whole interior presented an inviting and homelike look to us belated emigrants, and for a mountain cabin occupied solely by men it was much cleaner and more neatly kept than would be expected.

Our little son greatly amused these men with his childish prattle, and continually questioned them about the various trophies decorating the walls of the cabin, demanding the history of each one and the manner of acquisition. His infantile opinions,

Cabin in the Sierra Nevadas
as drawn by J. Goldsborough Bruff
Courtesy The Huntington Library

given without the least reserve and with a serious-
ness beyond his years, caused many a covert smile
and frequently a hearty laugh from them. Such a
long time had elapsed since they had seen or conversed with a child that they pronounced it a great
treat, and he was handed around from one to another until the Sandman caused his weary eyelids to
hang most heavily, and he called loudly for bed.
One of the larger bunks was assigned to us for the
night. Then the men lit their pipes and stole forth
into the night, giving me ample time to undress and
get to bed. At early dawn, they made themselves
just as scarce until I completed my morning toilet.
A knock at the door was answered by my husband,
and there stood one of our hosts with a glistening
clean, tin washbasin partially filled with warm water
and a clean flour sack for a towel, politely apologiz-
ing because he could not do any better for us. The
hearty breakfast was prepared in the rough shed adjoining the cabin, and I greatly enjoyed a meal that
I had not cooked myself. The biscuits made from
sourdough and soda were most excellent.

While eating our breakfast, the men insisted that
we should tarry with them another day. They appeared to take an unusually kind interest in us and
complimented my husband on the pluck and energy he had exhibited in so successfully engineering
his way across the plains alone and unaided. We
were both inspired with hope and confidence by
hearing that such enterprise and courage as we had

shown was certain to succeed in a new country.
Touring James around part of their claim, they
showed him their primitive workshop and told him
of different sections of good timberland waiting for
someone to preempt and open up. They told him
also much of their own prospects and the already
successful business they had acquired. Finally, they
wound up the conference of the forenoon with an
offer to James to stay and go into the lumber business with them, asking for no money in the transac-
tion. Of course, we had our good three-yoke of
oxen which were very much needed in a logging
camp. As a further inducement for us to stay, they
offered to build another cabin near their own for us.
A family in their camp would add so much pleasure
and company to their isolated lives, particularly as
the long winter was approaching.

James felt almost persuaded. Here was a business
and a means of living opened to us who were strangers in a strange land with little or no capital except
that vested in our traveling outfit. I think were it
not for my approaching confinement he would have
consented to remain with them. He finally told
them that he would abide by my decision. I was
weary enough from my long journey to stay and
rest, and under other circumstances would have giv-
en the kind and opportune offer a grateful acquies-
cence. But I was quite young and inexperienced,
and dreaded going through my coming ordeal so
far from nurse or doctor. I have since learned that

pioneer women in a new country can do without the services of either one and fare just as well. We enjoyed our stay with these men and reluctantly bade them farewell, promising them if we found no location or business suited to our wants, that in the coming spring we would return to their location among the pines of the Sierras.

As we began the descent of the western slope, the wayside houses grew more frequent and we met numerous trains carrying freight over the mountains into Nevada. Occasionally, a fruit wagon appeared with pears, apples, and other fruit from the fertile Sacramento Valley. This was the first fruit we had seen since we had left Salt Lake. The huckster kindly consented to sell me two pears for fifty cents and I think the price made them more enjoyable.

While we were descending what was then known as the Hangtown Grade, we stopped to water our stock at a wayside inn. The proprietor noticing that we were emigrants came out to our wagon and said to my husband, "Stranger, have you got any sugar to spare in your outfit? We're cleaned out. The freighter who was to bring our groceries from Sacramento is way behind time. There's nary a pound of that sweet stuff in the house, and the womenfolks are all clamoring for it." Fortunately, we were able to oblige him with several pounds, and as it was near dinnertime, he insisted on our coming into dinner with them. I demurred at making my appearance at dinner, even in a country hotel, as my blue plaid, gingham gown was much soiled with the red dust of the road, and I had neither time nor opportunity to make a fresh toilet. But all my excuses were overruled, and we were ushered into the rough dining room. I found the other guests were as unkempt looking as myself, so while enjoying the luxury of a meal with fresh meat well cooked, and plenty of vegetables with good mountain butter and cream, I forgot I was not dressed for dinner. Never was any repast more thoroughly enjoyed. The potatoes were soggy and the saleratus biscuit golden-hued. But oh! such a change from bacon and beans.

As we continued down the western slope of the Sierras, we found besides the towering pines other trees with a strange yet beautiful foliage. There was a large variety of oaks and the picturesque madroña with its bright and shining leaves, whose peculiar bark interested Robert, my little son, who discovered when he cut a branch that the red bark peeled off smooth and clean. The handsome manzanita with its brown berries furnished food to birds and bears and to the roving Indian as well. On the downgrades, as we more rapidly approached the foothills, we felt that, at last, our feet were planted on the soil of California, the far-famed land of gold, where we believed we could pick up the precious metal by the wayside.

How we searched the dust and rocks as we passed along for traces of the golden ore. We observed ditches running here and there filled with yellow water which in our ignorance we imagined was colored by the particles of gold running through them. Along the ravines and near the brooks were men prospecting and washing the dirt and gravel in a queer arrangement called a rocker, in the hopes of finding what they called "pay dirt." Many of the watercourses had been deeply and widely cut for miles, bringing the water to miners in their different locations. Little cabins which served to shelter the busy miners dotted the hills which were honeycombed and tunneled in every direction in the eagerness to find the precious metal. We were greatly interested and enthused as we lingered and talked with some of the more fortunate miners who had struck a rich find of pay dirt in the surface diggings. But the beauty of the surrounding country was much disfigured with all manner of ungainly heaps and ridges. Prospecting perhaps was necessary but it did not tend to beautify the face of nature. Beautiful little natural springs abounded, bright and clear as crystal; but each rill leading from them was turned to liquid mud by some devastating prospector. California in yielding up her wealth of gold surrendered much of her charm and beauty.

Near a branch of the American River we saw our first Chinamen.[2] These strange looking men were

[2] The first Chinese came to California as contract laborers to work in the gold fields. By 1852 there were about 20,000 Chinese laborers in California. Poorly paid, they worked in labor groups in mines that were deemed economically unproductive by white miners.

then a source of wonder to us with their queer habits, style of dress, and their long braided queues hanging down their backs or else tightly wound around their shaven heads, that were covered with a most peculiar hat looking like inverted washbowls made of straw. In groups of five or six they were digging the dry gravel and washing it with a sort of flume and wheel arrangement that brought the water down into the rocker. Several times we stopped to listen to the curious intonation of their voices. Once we made enquiries of a group of these strange men about the road we should follow, as we had arrived at a point where it forked in two different directions. But they stupidly looked at us and said, "No sabby."

Getting no information from the Chinamen, fate took us in hand and decided our direction. We took the road that appeared to be the most traveled, and thought we were on our way to Placerville, expecting by nightfall to camp within its outskirts. The sun was getting low and still no town in sight. A prospector carrying his pick and shovel and a bundle of blankets met us in the road. From him we learned that we were miles off our road to Placerville, but on the direct route to the town of Folsom. It had been our intention to drive to Sacramento via Placerville as we had been directed and make that city the terminus of our long pilgrimage. We felt chagrined that we were so far off the road. But the prospector, who seemed to be well-informed about

Chinese Coolies in the Gold Fields
Courtesy The Huntington Library

the area, advised us we were closer to Sacramento than if we had taken the road to Placerville.

Next day at noon we drew near a thrifty-looking farmhouse, and finding no place for our stock to graze because the land was fenced in, we drove up to the barnyard gate and sought permission of the rancher to drive within his enclosure and asked him to sell us some hay to feed our stock. To this he readily consented, allowed us to make a fire in his barnyard to boil our coffee, and seemed very accommodating. All the time he was walking around our cattle and appeared to be very much interested in them. They, in spite of their long journey, were in excellent condition, looking sleek and well-kept. James was a careful and prudent driver. He was always solicitous for the welfare of his stock, and kept them curried and groomed until their hides shone like satin. The rancher looked them over and over again, pleased at their gentleness and docility. He examined our wagon also, and asked numberless questions in regard to our journey, the length of time we had been on our way, and to what place were we going. Finally, he ended his interrogatory conversation with an offer to buy our whole outfit for the sum of four hundred dollars. This offer coming upon us so suddenly caused us both to hesitate for a moment before replying. Noticing our hesitation, he added, "I will give you and your family a week's board in the bargain, and that will give you time to locate yourselves." This almost took our breath away, coming upon us in such an unlooked-for manner. We could not in reason refuse such a satisfactory offer. It was a much larger sum than we had even hoped to get although we had been told that horned cattle were very high at that time in California. Within less than an hour's notice, our trunks and personal belongings were removed and our wagon, oxen, horse, tent, and camp equipage were turned over to the rancher. Imagine my consternation when he insisted on our going at once to his house. I had no opportunity or time to make a change in my attire, and dressed as I was in my soiled and tattered gown, dusty and dirty from the strain of travel and camp; my husband clad in his worn and begrimed red flannel shirt, his rough corduroys stuffed in his rougher boots; my little son in his worn outing garb, we presented anything but a prepossessing appearance. I dreaded woefully to face the wife who knew nothing of the strangers her husband was ushering thus unceremoniously into her well-ordered household. We met with a more civil reception than I expected, although she looked somewhat askance at our worn garb. We were at once shown into a very plain but clean bedroom adjoining the kitchen. My trunks were brought in and I unpacked some clean, fresh garments and after the luxury of a good bath and having removed the red dust of the road, we gladly donned the garb of civilized society, and looked and felt fit to be once more within the pale of civilization.

When the bell rang calling us out to supper, I was pleased to note the change in the demeanor of our hostess, who gazed upon us with ill-concealed surprise. Such is the power of good clothes, for the unkempt and soiled emigrants had blossomed out into really good-looking people. My husband, although browned by six months' exposure to the sun and wind, was wonderfully improved when shaved and dressed in a "biled" shirt and collar and well fitting clothes. I felt proud of him when I compared him with the somewhat slovenly rancher. As for myself, I had worn my shaker sunbonnet so closely and was always so vain of my white hands, never allowing myself to go ungloved save when cooking, that I bore no evidence of the emigrant when I discarded my emigrant garb. My fair-haired little son, Robert, looked exceedingly picturesque in his natty suit of blue. I could easily perceive that we were making a new and more favorable impression.

Our bedroom for the night was in such close proximity to the kitchen that I could overhear every word that was spoken there. The next morning I was awakened by a conversation between our hostess and the hired man who had come in with his pail of milk. "Has the boss been buying any emigrant cattle lately?" he asked. "Yes," she replied, "He bought out an emigrant family yesterday, and they are to stay a week with us." "Well," replied the man, "there are two dead oxen and one cow laying in the corral."

Nothing was said to us at breakfast about any dead animals. But after breakfast was over James went out to the corral to see for himself, and there lay stretched out dead and cold our beautiful, black Jill and Buck, our favorite lead oxen, and our gentle little cow. Each of them had apparently been well and sound the day before. Feeding that last day in the open foothills, they had eaten of the poison parsnip which grew there so profusely. At the time of the sale, they had shown no signs of illness, either to us or to the rancher. James insisted on returning some of the money that had been paid to him, but the man would not take it. He insisted that it was his loss under the circumstances of the trade.

Our hostess, the next morning, gave us a large airy room upstairs. During the day, the elderly lady, mother of the rancher, said to me, "We have a piano in the parlor that we brought around the Horn with us but no one here can play upon it. Perhaps you play?" I replied that before we left the States I had been considered quite a musician, but had had no practice for the last six months. At once, I was ushered into the unused parlor and the piano unlocked and divested of its rubber covering, and I reveled once more in the touch of the familiar keys, playing over and over my long neglected music. I soon had an audience from all the household, including the hired man and the Chinaman. My effort seemed to captivate them all, not that it was excellent, but because they were hungry for music. After discovering that I had this accomplishment, nothing was too good for us. Each vied with the other to make our stay delightful and begged of us to remain until the end of the month. But James was anxious to get into a business, and I was ready to get settled before my fast approaching confinement.

At the end of the week, we left the home of these good people, to whom we became very much attached. We quickly found in the neighboring town of Folsom, and about six miles from our new-found friends, a little cottage of two rooms, exceedingly small and primitive, yet roomy enough for our needs and no larger than we cared to furnish under the circumstances. We had not fully decided where we would locate permanently, and only provided ourselves with the bare necessities that we must have for comfort.

At last, we were settled down for a rest from our long and perilous journey. How I enjoyed the quiet of this humble little home, the cessation from the continual moving on—my morning's peaceful sleep without having to arise at the first peep of day and get ready to travel onward. And here, after an interval of two short weeks, the stork put in his appearance and our babe came to us, the mother of the grandsons for whom I pen these lines.

My dear husband was worried beyond all measure for fear that the long and tiresome journey would prove disastrous for me, but I came bravely through the trying ordeal.

Now I have ended the narrative of my six-month journey overland to California. Many things have been omitted owing to forgetfulness or lack of skill in selecting what to many would have been more interesting. Some things have been included which, perhaps, it would have been wiser to omit. I have tried to relate all faithfully as I remember it. While striving with my refractory memories, I realized that they were sometimes unsatisfactory to myself and probably would be to others, and, while I have forgotten much of the less interesting parts of the journey, yet, in the main I have kept close to the most striking incidents of our long trip. As we congratulated ourselves that all was well that ended well, we could happily say with California's own poet, Joaquin Miller, in his *Pioneer*:

> *"That rest, sweet rest is reckoned best,*
> *For we were worn as worn with years,*
> *Two thousand miles of thirst, and tears,*
> *Two thousand miles of bated breath,*
> *Two thousand miles of dust and death."*

Index

INDEX

Aberdeen, Lord, xxxv
American Fur Company, lviii, 31
American Revolution, 3
American River, 393
Anglo-American Treaty of Joint Occupation, xxx
Applegate, Charles, 4, 7, 79, 106, 136, 139, 171
Applegate, Cynthia, 92, 96
Applegate, Daniel, 3
Applegate, Edward, 4, 96, 100, 102
Applegate, Elisha, 4, 15, 19, 96, 100-01, 171, 181
Applegate, James, 16
Applegate, Jesse, 3-4, 7, 9, 24, 79, 96, 132, 135, 166, 171
Applegate, Jesse Applegate, xxvii, xxix, lx, 3, 7-9
Applegate, Lindsay, 3-4, 7, 79, 96, 135, 139, 181
Applegate, Melinda, 107, 153
Applegate Trail, 7
Applegate, Warren, 4, 15-16, 96, 100-02
Arapahoe, 274, 282
Argonauts, xxxviii, xl-xlii, xlvii-xlviii, l, lix, lxii-lxiii
Ash Hollow, 26
Astor, John Jacob, 326

Baker, Andy, 55-56
Baker, Charlotte Dunning, 187
Ballentine, George, xxxv
Beale, George, 68-69, 71

Bear River, 46, 60
Beaver Creek, 268
Bethel Institute, 9
Big Blue River, 27, 212-14
Big Sandy River, 214
Bijou, Colorado, 269
Black Hills, 112, 318
Blackfoot Indians, 34
Blue Mountains, 63, 72
Boise River, 64
Book of Mormon, 346
Bridger, James (Jim), 34
Brookfield, 370
Brooks, Juanita, xlii
Buffalo, 32, 227-31
Buffalo chips, 41, 256
Burnett, Peter, 24, 105
Burns, Robert, 262
Byron, Lord, 262

Cache-la-Poudre River, 285, 288
California, xxxv, xxxvii, xli, 8
California State Bank, 187
California Trail, xxxvii, lviii
Callao, see Willow Springs
Camp Drum, lviii
Capital Savings Bank, 187
Carson City, 374
Carson Valley, 374
Cascades, 109-10
Caw Indian, 24-26
Caw River, 24
Cayuse (Kiuse) Indians, 73, 80, 168-69
Central City, 280, 307

Champoeg, 119, 123
Charleston, 186
Cherokee Trail, 283, 288, 307
Cherry Creek, 274, 277
Cheyenne Indians, lvii, 25, 232
Cheyenne Pass, 296
Chief Halo, 176, 179-81
Chief John, 181-82
Chimney Rock, 38, 41, 112
Chinese, 393-94
Chinook language, 124, 164
Chugwater, 303
Civil War, li-lii, lxii
Clear Creek, 300
Coast Range, 142-44
Columbia River, xxxiv, li, 4,
    7-8, 77, 79-80, 88, 168
Cooper, James Fenimore, 90,
    359
Council Bluffs, xxxviii, lviii

Dalles, lviii, 105, 107
Dana, Richard Henry, xli
Day with the Cow Column, 4, 24
Days of '49, 153
Denver, 220, 234, 237, 263,
    268, 271, 273-83, 290, 306
DeSmet, Father Pierre Jean, 28
Devil's Backbone, 60-61, 107,
    112
Devil's Gullet, see Dalles
Doke, William, 96, 99-100,
    168
Drownings, 8, 96-100

East, John, 25, 72
Eaton, John, xxxii
Echo Canyon, 346
Edinburgh Review, xxxiv
Eldorado, xlvii

Elko, 365
Empire on the Pacific, xxxv

Faragher, John Mack, xlvi, 185
Fish Springs, 362-63
Fitzpatrick, Thomas, lv
Floyd, John, xxx-xxxi, xli
Folsom, 187, 394, 401
Fort Boise, 63-64
Fort Bridger, 34, 337, 340,
    345-46
Fort Hall, xxxvi, xliii, 51
Fort Kearny, lviii-lix, 221-22
Fort Laramie, xlvii, lviii-lix,
    31, 34, 289, 307, 309, 318,
    325, 338
Fort Nez Perce, 77
Fort Vancouver, xxxiii, xxxv,
    111-12, 123
Fort Walla Walla, xxxv, 77, 80,
    88, 126, 135
Fort William, 31
Fourth of July, 289-90
Fremont, John Charles, 46-49
Fremont Springs, 264, 267
Frontiersmen in Blue, 11

Gannt, John, xliii
Genoa, 375-76
Gervais, 120
Goetzmann, William H., xxxv
Graebner, Norman, xxxv
Grand Island, lviii
Grand River, 24
Grant, Richard, 51
Gray, W. H., xxxvi
Great Plains, 194
Great Register, 28
Great Salt Lake, lviii, 357
Great Salt Lake Valley, xxxviii

Green River, 46, 112, 325, 330, 333–34, 336, 347
Gregory, John, 280

Hangtown Grade, 391
Hannibal, 186, 198
Harmony Mission, 24
Honeyman, Robert, 353
Honeyman, Robert D., 186
Honeyman, Sam, 198, 207–08, 210, 213, 237, 269, 281
Hudson's Bay Company, xxx, xxxii–xxxiii, xxxv–xxxvi, 51, 63, 74, 77, 88, 111, 115, 154, 166, 168
Humboldt National Forest, 365
Humboldt River, xlix, liv, 166, 366

Independence *Expositor*, xxxviii
Independence, Missouri, xxxvii, xliii, xlix, lviii, lx
Independence Rock, 28, 31, 321
Indian cemetery, 67, 107–08
Indians, xxxix, li–lvii, 20, 25, 44, 61–63, 124, 240–41, 245–52, 291–94, 299–300, 340–44, 381–83
"Injun Fizic," 12–14
Ivanhoe, 346

Jackson, David, xxxii

Kalapooyas Indians, 127, 134, 160
Kanesville, Iowa, see Council Bluffs
Kearny, Stephen W., lvii

Kelley, Hall Jackson, xxxi–xxxii, xxxv, xli
Klackamas River, 118
Klamath Indians, 9

La Creole, 146
Lake Tahoe, 375
Last of the Mohicans, 90
Launders, Amanda, 186
Law for the Elephant, xlii, xlv
Lee, Daniel, xxxvi
Lee, Jason, xxxvi, xli
Lewis and Clark, xxxi, xxxiii, 93
Lindsay, Rachel, 3, 16, 19, 33, 69–70
Linn Lewis F., xxxiii
Little Blue River, 27, 214
Little Sandy River, 329
Lone Pine, 38
Long, Stephen, xxxiii, 345

Manchester *Guardian*, xxxiv
Manifest Destiny, xxxiv
Mason City, 207
McClellan, Alexander (Uncle Mack), 27–28, 79, 96, 100, 102
McKinlay, Archibald, 80, 85, 88, 95
McLaughlin, John, xxxiii, 115–16, 119
Medicine Men, 145, 172–76
Miller, Joaquin, 402
Mimaluse Island, 107–08
Mississippi River, 198
Missouri River, lviii, 201, 253, 263
Molalla Indians, 128–29

Mormons, xxxviii, xlix, 322, 337, 346-50, 353-54
Mount Hood, 94
Mountain Meadow Massacre, 348
Mountain men, 45
Myres, Sandra L., xlvi, 185

Nauvoo, 347
Nesmith, J. W., 21
New York *Tribune*, xlvi
Nez Perce Indians, 80
North Platte River, xxxviii, 32, 295
North West Company, 51, 77

Oakland *Tribune*, 187
Ogden, Peter S., 74
On the Mormon Frontier, xlii
O'Neil, James, 149
Oregon, xxxvii, xli, 4, 7-8, 20, 45
Oregon City (Tum Chuk), 109, 118-19
Oregon Fever, xxxii, xxxvii, 109
Oregon Territory, xxxv, 166
Oregon Trail, xxxvi-xxxvii, 329
Osage Indian, 20
Osage River Valley, 3-4, 11, 24
Overland Trail, xxix, 354
Oxen, xlii, 194-96, 397

Pacific Springs, 329
Paiute Indians, l
Parker, William, 96, 102
Pawnee Indians, lvii, 25-26, 248, 295
Perkins, H. K. W., 105
Perkins Mission, 105

Philadelphia *National Gazette*, xxxii
Pike, Zebulon, xxxiii, 345
Pike's Peak, 196, 198, 206-07, 214, 271
"Pike's Peak or Bust," 220
Pike's Peakers, 234
Pilcher, Joshua, xxxii
Pioneer, 402
Placerville, 394
Plains Across, xxxii, xxxiv, lv
Platte Purchase, 3
Platte Rivers, 32, 240, 259, 264
Polk, James K., xxxiv-xxxv
Pontneuf River, xxxvi
Pony Express, lx, 338, 357, 362, 364
Porter, James, 185, 193, 198, 205, 208, 225, 233, 259-60, 269, 278, 296, 302, 317, 330, 340, 346, 365, 385, 389-91, 397, 399, 401
Porter, Lavinia Honeyman, xxvii-xxix, xlii, xlv, liv, lx, lxii, 185-86
Porter, Robert, 197, 205, 209, 225, 269, 377, 386, 392, 399
Portland, 118
Prairie dogs, 42

Recollections of My Boyhood, 3
Reid, John P., xlii, xlv
Republican River, 221
Rocky Mountain Fur Company, 28, 51
Rocky Mountains, xxxii-xxxiv, 63-64, 189, 194, 196, 202, 221, 268-69, 271, 286, 288, 304, 329, 346

Rogue River, 166–67, 169
Rogue River War, 9, 181
Rose Tree, 27
Ruby Valley, 365
Russell, Majors, and Waddell,
  lx, 338

Sacramento, lx, 187, 338, 391
Sacramento Valley, 385, 391
St. Joseph *Gazette*, xxxviii
St. Joseph, Missouri, xxxvii,
  xliii, xlix, lviii, 198, 201,
  263, 338
St. Louis, 3
St. Louis *Beacon*, xxxii
Salem, 9, 120, 132
Salmon Falls, 59
Salt Lake City, xxxix, xlix,
  lix–lx, 283, 322, 345,
  348–49, 353–54, 358
Schaffer, Joseph, 9
Scott, Walter, 346
Shakespeare, William, 262
Shepard, Cyrus, xxxvi
Shortes, Robert, 109
Shoshone Indians, 51, 60
Sierra Nevada, xlix–l, 376–79,
  381
Simpson, J. H., 357
Sioux Indians, lvii, 34, 185,
  241–42, 248
Siskiyou Mountains, 166
Smith, Andrew, 125
Smith, Jedediah, xxxii
Smith, Joseph, 347
Snake Indians, 51, 60, 329
Snake River, xxxvi, 56, 59–60,
  107, 112
Socrates, 13
Soda Springs, 46

South Pass, lvii, 321, 326,
  329, 346
South Platte River, 32, 267–68
Sovey's Island, 117
Spaulding, Henry, xxxvi
Steamboat Spring, 50
Strawberry Valley, 384
Sublette, Milton, xxxv
Sublette, William, xxxii
Sutter, John, 169
Sutter's Mill, xxxvii
Sweetwater River, 28, 45, 112,
  321, 326

Taylor, Bayard, xlvi–xlvii
Times of London, xxxiv
Tooele Valley, 357
Tule Lake, 166
Tum Chuk, see Oregon City
"turnarounds," xliv
Two Years Before the Mast, xli

Umatilla River, 73
Umpqua, 166–167, 171, 179
Union Pacific Railway, 222
Unruh, John D., xxxii, lv
Ute Indians, 274, 277
Utley, Robert, lv

Vancouver Island, xxxv
Vasquez, Louis, 34
Vigilance Committee, 278, 280

Walaiipu, xxxvi
Walla Walla River, 79
Ware, Joseph E., xlvi
Washington, George, 3
Washington *National
  Intelligencer*, xxxii–xxxiii
Waskopum Indians, 108, 111

Watson, Virginia, 9
Westering Women and the Frontier Experience, xlvi, 185
Whiskey, 235-36
White, Elijah, 119, 148
Whitman, Marcus, xxxvi, 74
Whitman Massacre, xxxvi, 168
Whitman Mission, xxxvi, 74, 77
Whitman, Narcissa, xxxvi, 74
Willamette Valley, xxxi, 7, 77, 116-17, 120, 124, 131, 148, 165-167, 169
Willow Springs, 364

Wind River Mountains, 44
Women and Men on the Overland Trail, xlvi, 185
Wyeth, Nathaniel, xxxv-xxxvi, 51, 63

Yampa, 83
Yangoler Chief: The Kommema and his Religion, 9
Yellowstone Park, 44
Yoncalla Indians, 9, 172
York, 93
Young, Brigham, 322

List of The Lakeside Classics

The Lakeside Classics

Number	Title	Year
1.	The Autobiography of Benjamin Franklin . . .	1903
2.	Inaugural Addresses of the Presidents of the United States from Washington to Lincoln . .	1904
3.	Inaugural Addresses of the Presidents of the United States from A. Johnson to T. Roosevelt	1905
4.	Fruits of Solitude by William Penn	1906
5.	Memorable American Speeches I. The Colonial Period	1907
6.	Memorable American Speeches II. Democracy and Nationality	1908
7.	Memorable American Speeches III. Slavery	1909
8.	Memorable American Speeches IV. Secession, War, Reconstruction	1910
9.	The Autobiography of Gurdon Saltonstall Hubbard	1911
10.	Reminiscences of Early Chicago	1912
11.	Reminiscences of Chicago During the Forties and Fifties	1913
12.	Reminiscences of Chicago During the Civil War .	1914
13.	Reminiscences of Chicago During the Great Fire	1915
14.	Life of Black Hawk	1916
15.	The Indian Captivity of O. M. Spencer	1917
16.	Pictures of Illinois One Hundred Years Ago . .	1918
17.	A Woman's Story of Pioneer Illinois by Christiana Holmes Tillson	1919
18.	The Conquest of the Illinois by George Rogers Clark	1920
19.	Alexander Henry's Travels and Adventures in the Years 1760-1776	1921

413

Number	Title	Year
20.	John Long's Voyages and Travels in the Years 1768-1788	1922
21.	Adventures of the First Settlers on the Oregon or Columbia River by Alexander Ross	1923
22.	The Fur Hunters of the Far West by Alexander Ross	1924
23.	The Southwestern Expedition of Zebulon M. Pike	1925
24.	Commerce of the Prairies by Josiah Gregg	1926
25.	Death Valley in '49 by William L. Manly	1927
26.	Bidwell's Echoes of the Past—Steele's In Camp and Cabin	1928
27.	Kendall's Texan Santa Fe Expedition	1929
28.	Pattie's Personal Narrative	1930
29.	Alexander Mackenzie's Voyage to the Pacific Ocean in 1793	1931
30.	Wau-Bun, The "Early Day" in the North-West by Mrs. John H. Kinzie	1932
31.	Forty Years a Fur Trader by Charles Larpenteur	1933
32.	Narrative of the Adventures of Zenas Leonard	1934
33.	Kit Carson's Autobiography	1935
34.	A True Picture of Emigration by Rebecca Burlend	1936
35.	The Bark Covered House by William Nowlin	1937
36.	The Border and the Buffalo by John R. Cook	1938
37.	Vanished Arizona by Martha Summerhayes	1939
38.	War on the Detroit by Thomas Verchères de Boucherville and James Foster	1940
39.	Army Life in Dakota by De Trobriand	1941
40.	The Early Day of Rock Island and Davenport by J. W. Spencer and J. M. D. Burrows	1942
41.	Six Years with the Texas Rangers by James B. Gillett	1943

Number	Title	Year
42.	Growing Up with Southern Illinois by Daniel Harmon Brush	1944
43.	A History of Illinois, I, by Gov. Thomas Ford	1945
44.	A History of Illinois, II, by Gov. Thomas Ford	1946
45.	The Western Country in the 17th Century by Lamothe Cadillac and Pierre Liette	1947
46.	Across the Plains in Forty-nine by Reuben Cole Shaw	1948
47.	Pictures of Gold Rush California	1949
48.	Absaraka, Home of the Crows by Mrs. Margaret I. Carrington	1950
49.	The Truth about Geronimo by Britton Davis	1951
50.	My Life on the Plains by General George A. Custer	1952
51.	Three Years Among the Indians and Mexicans by General Thomas James	1953
52.	A Voyage to the Northwest Coast of America by Gabriel Franchère	1954
53.	War-Path and Bivouac by John F. Finerty	1955
54.	Milford's Memoir by Louis Leclerc de Milford	1956
55.	Uncle Dick Wootton by Howard Louis Conard	1957
56.	The Siege of Detroit in 1763	1958
57.	Among the Indians by Henry A. Boller	1959
58.	Hardtack and Coffee by John D. Billings	1960
59.	Outlines from the Outpost by John Esten Cooke	1961
60.	Colorado Volunteers in New Mexico, 1862 by Ovando J. Hollister	1962
61.	Private Smith's Journal	1963
62.	Two Views of Gettysburg by Sir A. J. L. Fremantle and Frank Haskell	1964
63.	Dakota War Whoop by Harriet E. Bishop McConkey	1965

Number	Title	Year
64.	Honolulu by Laura Fish Judd	1966
65.	Three Years in the Klondike by Jeremiah Lynch	1967
66.	Two Years' Residence on the English Prairie of Illinois by John Woods	1968
67.	John D. Young and the Colorado Gold Rush	1969
68.	My Experiences in the West by John S. Collins	1970
69.	Narratives of Colonial America, 1704-1765	1971
70.	Pioneers by Noah Harris Letts and Thomas Allen Banning, 1825-1865	1972
71.	Excursion Through America by Nicolaus Mohr	1973
72.	A Frenchman in Lincoln's America, Volume I, by Ernest Duvergier de Hauranne	1974
73.	A Frenchman in Lincoln's America, Volume II, by Ernest Duvergier de Hauranne	1975
74.	Narratives of the American Revolution	1976
75.	Advocates and Adversaries by Robert R. Rose	1977
76.	Hell among the Yearlings by Edmund Randolph	1978
77.	A Frontier Doctor by Henry F. Hoyt	1979
78.	Mrs. Hill's Journal – Civil War Reminiscences by Sarah Jane Full Hill	1980
79.	Skyward by Rear Admiral Richard E. Byrd	1981
80.	Helldorado by William M. Breakenridge	1982
81.	Mark Twain's West	1983
82.	Frontier Fighter by George W. Coe	1984
83.	Buckskin and Blanket Days by Thomas Henry Tibbles	1985
84.	Autobiography of an English Soldier in the United States Army by George Ballentine	1986
85.	Life of Tom Horn	1987
86.	Children of Ol' Man River by Billy Bryant	1988
87.	Westward Journeys by Jesse A. Applegate and Lavinia Honeyman Porter	1989